THE MASS OF THE WESTERN RITES

Cum Superiorum Licentia

Nihil Obstat:
  JOANNES GRAY,
   Censor Librorum.

Imprimatur:
  ✠ ANDREAS JOSEPH, O.S.B.,
   Archiep. S. Andr. et Ed.

Edimburgi,
  die 4 Aprilis 1934.

THE MASS OF THE WESTERN RITES

BY THE RIGHT REVEREND
DOM FERNAND CABROL
ABBOT OF FARNBOROUGH

TRANSLATED BY
C. M. ANTONY

SANDS & CO.
15 KING STREET, COVENT GARDEN
LONDON
1934

Made in Great Britain

PREFACE

THEOLOGIANS, historians, and liturgiologists are to-day in agreement in recognising that the Mass is the most important function of all Christian worship ; and that the greater part of the other rites are in close relation with the Eucharist.

This affirmation rests upon the most serious study of Christianity, in antiquity as well as in the Middle Ages ; and the various works regarding the Mass, which have been multiplied in recent years, have merely confirmed this truth. More and more have the faithful, in their turn, become convinced of it ; while even those who are without the Faith are beginning to interest themselves in the Mass, and to endeavour to know more of its history and to understand its meaning.

These facts explain the number of books which have recently appeared on this subject. A glance at the Bibliography printed at the end of this Preface will suffice to give an idea of their extent, and may serve as a guide to those who wish to study the question more deeply. This consideration might have dissuaded us from adding to all these works (some of which are excellent) another book on the Mass. But we may first remark that the *Bibliothèque catholique des sciences religieuses*[1] had, from the beginning, comprehended in its plan a volume on the Latin Mass as one of the elements of its synthesis.

Further, it may be noticed that the larger number of the books whose titles we quote are chiefly, and some-

---

[1] *La Messe en Occident*, of which the present volume is a translation, was published (1932) in the above series.

times entirely, occupied with the Roman Mass, while our own plan comprises a study of the Latin, or Mass of the Western Rites ; that is, of the Mass as celebrated in Africa, Gaul, Spain, Great Britain, and Northern Italy, and in the other Latin countries in the Middle Ages, as well as in Rome.

Now this comparison of the different Latin rites is most suggestive. Better than all other considerations it reveals first the relationship of these rites, and the fundamental unity of all the liturgies under their different forms. Then, as we shall see, it throws light on the rites of the Roman Mass which, consequently on the suppression of some of their number, can only be understood by comparison with more complete rites. It must be added that the Mass is so rich in material that each may study it from his own point of view, and, while receiving much benefit from the latest works on the same subject, may present his own under a new aspect. Thus, following Mgr. Duchesne's book, Mgr. Batiffol thought it worth while to give us his *Leçons sur la Messe* ; and assuredly no one will consider that these *Lessons* are a repetition of the work of his illustrious predecessor, or of any of the other books already published upon this subject.

To those who may recognise in our own study views already exposed by one or other of the authors quoted, we may remark that many articles in our *Dictionnaire d'archéologie chrétienne et de liturgie* (*anamnèse, anaphore, canon,* etc.) had taken chronological precedence of the greater part of these books, so that in drawing inspiration from them we have but made use of the *jus postliminii*.

This, then, is the line we shall follow in this new study of the Mass ; and, while conforming with chronology, it seems to us at the same time to be the most logical. We shall first examine the Mass in the first three centuries, during which a certain liturgical unity reigned, and while the different Christian provinces of the West had not each created its own special liturgy. We shall then explain (Ch. II) how and why, from the fourth to the seventh century, those liturgical characteristics which distinguish the various Latin families became definite. According to these principles we shall attempt to establish the classification of these liturgical families and their genealogy.

In the following chapters we shall rapidly sketch the general characteristics of the Mass in Africa, Gaul, Spain, Milan, and Great Britain. It goes without saying that the Roman liturgy having become our own, as well as that of the West (with rare exceptions), and also that of the East, the Far East, and the New World—in short, of most Christian countries—it demands detailed study, as well as a close following of its historical development from the fifth to the twentieth century.

We have, according to the usual method, placed in an *Excursus* certain questions which would have delayed the progress of the work, since they can be studied separately. Such are: the chants of the Mass, the liturgical gestures, the meaning of the word *Missa*, the ancient books now united in the existing Missal, the different kinds of Masses, etc. We hope that those who are willing to follow us on these lines will arrive at certain conclusions, and, if they are not specialists (for whom this book is not written), that their ideas as to the great Christian Sacrifice will be clearer and more precise.

The Mass as it is to-day, presents itself under a somewhat complicated form to the non-Catholic, and even to a large number of the faithful. The ceremonies, readings, chants, and formulas follow each other without much apparent method or logic. It is a rather composite mosaic, and it must be confessed that it does seem rather incoherent. Rites, indeed, have been added to rites; others have been rather unfortunately suppressed, and where this is the case, gaps, or what have been styled "gaping holes," appear.

But the historical and comparative method applied in this book explains the greater part of these anomalies, making it fairly easy to reconstitute the synthesis of the Mass, to grasp the guide-line, and, once in possession of the general idea which has presided at all these developments, to understand the whole better when light is thus thrown on the details.

The Mass thus studied throughout its different epochs reveals a magnificent theological and historical thesis. We have not been able to insist on this point as strongly as we could have wished, because in the first place these volumes are not intended to be books of spiritual edification, nor, strictly speaking, of apologetics. But it seems to us that here facts speak for themselves, telling us why the Mass has from its very origin taken its place as the true centre of the liturgy; how it has drawn everything to itself; how at one moment it was almost the whole liturgy, in the sense that, primitively, all Christian rites gravitated round it.

At the same time Sacrifice and Sacrament, the One Christian Sacrifice and, if one may say so, the most Divine of the Sacraments, it sums up and sanctifies all the elements which have made of sacrifice the centre of the greater part of all religions; first, by the idea that man owes to God homage for the gifts he has received from Him and that he recognises His dominion over all creation; then, by the idea that he must expiate his faults in order to render God favourable to him; lastly, by a certain desire to unite himself to God by participation in that sacrifice. Thus the Mass raises the idea of sacrifice to its highest expression, whilst purifying it from all the false notions which had obscured it in pagan religions.

For the Christian, too, it is the best means by which to unite himself with his brethren in communion with Christ. Prayer in common, the Kiss of Peace, above all the participation in the same Banquet of the Body and Blood of Our Lord are so many expressive, living symbols of Christian unity, of Catholicity, of charity.

For the Christian, again, the Mass is an efficacious help along the road of the spiritual life. One of his essential duties, common to all men, is to praise God in His works, to offer Him our thanks, to present our requests to Him : in a word, to pray. Now the Mass is the centre of the whole Divine Office ; we even believe it would be possible to show that at one time the first part of the Mass was the most eloquent and, indeed, the only mode of expression of this official prayer.

The Mass, then, sums up the greatest mysteries of our Faith. The faithful Catholic is present at the Last Supper, at the Passion and Death of Our Lord upon the Cross ; he realises what Christ has willed by the institution of this Divine Sacrament and by the accomplishment of His Sacrifice on Calvary. He is invited to share in that Banquet which was the Last Supper, when Our Lord gives Himself in Holy Communion ; and, being present at the bloody Sacrifice of Calvary, he sees what Christ has suffered for the sins of the whole of humanity as well as those of His own disciples.

Theologians and all mystical writers have dwelt upon these different aspects of the Mass, and when once the claims of erudition and of history are satisfied it will be easier and more profitable to go direct to these authors, for so far from being an obstacle, the exact knowledge of facts is, on the contrary, of the greatest assistance to true piety.

BIBLIOGRAPHY

LE BRUN (Pierre), *Explication littérale, historique et dogmatique des prières et des cérémonies de la Messe*, remains the most complete and learned work on the Mass. It has been many times republished, and has not lost its value. (First edition, 4 vols., Paris, 1726.) The first volume contains the *Explication de la Messe romaine*, the second and third, *Étude des diverses liturgies orientales et occidentales*, the fourth, dissertations on different subjects, notably on the *Silence des prières de la Messe*.

The work of Mgr. DUCHESNE, *Origines du culte chrétien*, which is in reality an *Étude sur la liturgie latine avant Charlemagne* (fourth edition, 1908), is an admirable synthesis of the Latin liturgies which has on more than one point shown the subject in a new light, though several syntheses, even in the opinion of the writer, are subject to revision.

Mgr. BATIFFOL, in his *Leçons sur la Messe* (Paris, 1919), has laid down on this subject the latest pronouncements of criticism. In the *Eucharistie (La Présence réelle et la transsubstantiation* (fifth edition, revised, Paris, 1913) he had already studied the history of Eucharistic dogma from its origins to the Council of Ephesus.

ADRIAN FORTESCUE, in *The Mass, a study of the Roman liturgy* (London, 1912), had approached the same subject a few years earlier ; his book treats specially of the history of the Roman Rite. See also his article *Mass* in the *Catholic Encyclopædia*.

JOH. BRINKTRINE, the latest comer, *Die Heilige Messe* (Paderborn, 1931), has also treated the subject specially as a historian and liturgiologist.

M. GIHR, *Le Saint Sacrifice de la Messe* (2 vols., Paris, 1901), a theological, ascetical, and liturgical *summa* upon the Mass, containing a great quantity of information.

AD. FRANZ, *Die Messe im Deutschen Mittelalter* (1 vol., 8vo, Freiburg-im-Breisgau, 1902).

Cardinal SCHUSTER, *Liber Sacramentorum, Notes historiques et liturgiques sur le Missel romain*, translated from the Italian (6 vols., Brussels, 1925-1930).

BIBLIOGRAPHY

Dom J. DE PUNIET, *La Liturgie de la Messe* (Avignon, 1928).

P. MARANGET, *La Messe romaine* (Brussels, 1925).

Dom E. VANDEUR, *La Sainte Messe* (Maredsous, 1928, *seq.*).

The articles *Eucharistie* and *Messe* in the *Dictionnaire de Théologie catholique*, and in DACL (which, once for all, may be said to stand for *Dictionnaire d'Archéologie chrétienne et de Liturgie*), and the same articles in U. CHEVALIER, *Topo-bibliographie*, for the Bibliography ; there is also a Bibliography in FORTESCUE, *op. cit.*, p. 541 *seq.* In our own pamphlet on THE MASS there is a chapter on the literature of this subject. See also in DACL the articles *anamnèse, anaphore, Communion, canon, Eucharistie, élévation*, and others mentioned in the course of our work.

Ch. ROHAULT DE FLEURY has written a fine monumental work in his *La Messe*, consisting chiefly of archæological studies (4to, Paris, 1883–1889). The most valuable information is to be found here upon the furnishing of churches, the ornaments and sacred vessels, and upon all those things connected with the service of the Mass.

AUTHOR'S NOTE.—The works of Duchesne, Batiffol, Gihr, Schuster, and De Puniet mentioned above have been translated into English.

CONTENTS

xii

CHAPTER I

THE MASS, FROM THE FIRST TO THE FOURTH CENTURIES. LITURGICAL UNITY

The Eucharistic Synaxis.—The aliturgical (non-liturgical, or without the Eucharist) Synaxis.—The days and hours of the Synaxis.—The Eucharistic Prayer.

IT must be laid down from the beginning of this chapter that during this first period the Mass has what we may call a universal character. No regional distinctions appear ; and our own divisions into Oriental and Occidental, or Greek and Latin liturgies, had no reality in those days.

It was not until the fourth century that the geographical and political division between the East and West was truly established. Thus during the first three centuries it may be said that there were no liturgical families, but only one single Christian liturgy, where, in a certain sense, unity reigned.

The word " unity," however, must not be taken too literally. It is true that so far there was no division into liturgical families, but there was great variety of usages and rites. The law was " great liberty," and it may be said that there is more difference between the liturgy of the *Didache*, that of Hippolytus, and that of Serapion than there was, later, between the liturgies of Byzantium, of Rome, and the Mozarabic and Gallican liturgies. The differences are rather those between church and church ; the old churches of Jerusalem, Antioch, Alexandria, Rome, and Carthage were great liturgical centres.

But the differences existing between the different churches did not prevent peace and unity from reigning amongst them. In the second century Polycratus, Bishop of Ephesus, tells us that Pope Anicetus invited St. Polycarp to celebrate the Mass. And a little later Firmilianus, Bishop of Cæsarea in Cappadocia, the correspondent of St. Cyprian, remarks in his turn that the varieties of ritual then existing (in the middle of the third century) made not the least difference to unity.[1]

What was the Mass during this first period ? How was it celebrated ? What were its principal elements, and, if evolution has taken place, what were its different stages ? To answer these questions the best method seems to us to study the following points :

1. *The Eucharistic Synaxis.*
2. *The aliturgical Synaxis (separated from the Eucharist).*
3. *The days and hours of the Synaxis.*
4. *The Eucharistic Prayer.*

1. THE EUCHARISTIC SYNAXIS.—The word "synaxis" comes from συνάξις, gathering together ; συνάξειν, to meet or gather together. It was early employed in the language of Christians to designate an assembly, and especially an assembly to hear Mass.

The Church was born in Jewish surroundings. It is a fact that the first Christians, Apostles or disciples, were Jews by birth, or proselytes, on the day of Pentecost, the true Birthday of the Church. So it was during the years that followed, until the day when, by the preaching of St. Paul, the Gentiles entered the Church, of which very soon they became a majority. This is of the highest importance, all the more because there was never any

[1] The text of Polycratus, *P. Gr.*, T. XX, col. 508 ; that of Firmilianus, edn. Hartel, T. III, p. 810 *seq.*

brutal rupture between the Church and the Mosaic religion. The Church indeed always condemned the Marcionites and all those who, with them, proscribed the ancient law and those who had come out from it.

Most preciously did the Church guard the Pentateuch and all the inspired books of the Jews. This means that She preserved faith in the God of the Old Testament ; that She kept the Decalogue—that is, the laws of universal morality and all the Old Testament theology. But at the same time She was no Judaiser. She separated Herself from the synagogue and declared Herself against it, as a distinct society which had its own organisation, institutions, and laws. Just as She condemned the Marcionites, so She expelled the Judaisers from Her company, as those who desired jealously to retain circumcision and the other Jewish practices.

It was the same thing as regards the liturgy. When the Church was born the Temple was still standing, with its sacrifices, its highly complicated ceremonies, its priesthood. It is true that the Apostles still went to pray at the Temple, but here one most important fact must be noted. The first of the faithful formed a band apart. The Jews saw in them a sect desirous of separating itself from Judaism, against which they fought furiously, and tried to suppress as a disloyal and dangerous body. And this separation was more keenly accentuated day by day. We can, of course, see how natural it was that many of the new Christians should still remain attached to the ancient form of worship. These were the *Judaisers*. We find them mentioned in the Acts. St. Paul in his Epistles fights against them ; raising his voice against those who wished to circumcise all new converts, to force them to observe the new moons, the Jewish feasts, etc.

3

All that had to cease. He claims the right of liberty for these new converts. It is not the Law and its observances which will save them ; it is the Faith in Jesus Christ, obedience to His precepts, docility to His teaching. Naturally, between these two parties there were innumerable shades of difference, but as time went on these shades gradually effaced themselves. These practices of the Law were only shadows ; figures reflected in the new worship, but which in the end must give way to it, *et antiquum documentum novo cedat ritui*.

Moreover, in a few years (A.D. 70) a most important event would give the final blow to the Jewish worship and its sacrifices. The Temple was destroyed by the Roman armies, and the inhabitants of Jerusalem were dispersed.

A new form of worship was instituted for the Christians in those private meetings, which are many times mentioned in the Acts. (Acts ii. 42, 46. Cf. Acts xx. 7, *seq.*) Prayer was offered, and the Breaking of Bread took place. This Breaking of Bread was the Mass.

In what, exactly, did it consist ? The converts met to celebrate anew that Banquet, the Last Supper, which took place in the Cenacle on the night preceding the death of Our Lord. This is stated in texts of the first importance, for it is upon their witness that the whole tradition of the Mass is based. There is first the witness of the three synoptic Gospels, St. Matthew, St. Mark, and St. Luke, whose accounts may be summed up as follows :

On the first day of the *Azymes*, which is Thursday, the Apostles, at the request of Our Lord Himself, prepared a room where He might celebrate the Pasch with His disciples. It was the Jewish custom, and Our Lord had assuredly not failed to observe it throughout the preceding years. But this time the banquet was to have a

4

supreme importance, for He knew that this meal was the last He should take with His Apostles.

Now, *cœnantibus eis*, as St. Matthew says, during the meal, and no doubt towards the end, Our Lord took bread, blessed it, brake, and gave it to His disciples, saying : " Take, eat, this is My Body." Then, taking the chalice (the cup containing wine mingled with water), He offered it to them, saying : " This is My Blood of the New Testament " (the New Covenant) " which is shed for many for the remission of sins." Then, *hymno dicto*, the prayer being said, they went out to the Mount of Olives. There Our Lord entered into His Agony, and the soldiers, led by Judas, came to seize Him (St. Matt. xxvi. 13–15).

We know what followed, and the story of that night whose details the Evangelists have given us ; the scenes of the Crucifixion and Death on Good Friday. The same account which we have just quoted from St. Matthew is found with little variation in St. Mark and St. Luke.[1]

As for St. John, faithful to his system, he does not repeat what the three synoptic Gospels have related ; but contents himself with completing them as occasion arises. Thus he gives us details omitted by them as to the Last Supper, and the discourse of Our Lord during and after the meal. His seventeenth chapter contains what is called the *Sacerdotal Prayer of Christ*, which may be considered as the Divine commentary on the Eucharist. In his sixth chapter, on the occasion of the multiplication of the loaves, he had set forth teaching of incomparable precision upon the Eucharist. " Except you

---

[1] St. Mark xiv.; St. Luke xxii. These texts have been studied and commented on with great learning by P. d'Alès, in one volume of this series, *L'Eucharistie*, p. 15 *seq*. ; we are thus dispensed from dwelling more fully upon them here.

eat the flesh of the Son of Man, and drink His blood, you shall not have life in you " (vi. 54).

Lastly, St. Paul is a fifth witness, and not the least. He, in his Epistle to the Corinthians (1 Cor. xi. 23–29), gives us a detailed account, the most ancient in our possession, of the way in which the early Christians celebrated the Eucharist. These different texts having been explained elsewhere, I content myself with noting certain principal points upon which almost every one is agreed.[1] It is a question of a repast which was the Paschal meal. At its close Our Lord took bread and wine, and in virtue of His Blessing and of His words, they were changed into His Body and Blood. We use the theological term *transubstantiated* to mark that of the bread and wine nothing is left but the species or appearances, the substance having given place to the Body and Blood of Christ.

It is a new covenant in the Blood of Christ shed to wash away the sins of the world, and to redeem us ; thus it is a sacrifice in intimate union with that of the Cross, which was to take place the next day ; a sacrifice, and at the same time a sacramental meal.

Upon this point, as upon many others, the synoptic Gospels do not enter into great detail ; they merely sum up and abbreviate. One thing, however, is certain : the capital importance of this act in the Life of Our Lord. This can be deduced even from the record of the synoptics, though they relate these Divine events with a disconcerting simplicity which in reality is Divine. The other Sacraments are not mentioned in the Gospels, or only mentioned in a few words. But here each synoptic, one after the other, carefully relates the same history, which, as has been said, St. John completes. The room where the feast is to be held has been chosen, prepared

[1] Cf. d'Alès, *L'Eucharistie*, p. 15 *seq.*

6

by Christ Himself. This meal is to be the last in His Life ; it is like the last meal of one condemned to death ; for the solemnity of death hovers over this brotherly love-feast. It is probably also the Paschal supper, which Our Lord was accustomed solemnly to celebrate with His disciples. His attitude, his very words, all have now a deeper meaning than ever before. He speaks of bread and wine becoming His Body and Blood, and of offering them as food to His Apostles.

It is the New Covenant, which is to replace the Old Covenant concluded between God and His people in the time of Moses ; the New Testament which takes the place of the Old. A new order of things is beginning, of which we may say with the poet : *novus ab integro sæclorum nascitur ordo.*

Now St. Paul's text proves that the Christians obeyed Christ's precept ; they renewed their celebration of that last banquet in memory of Him, *hoc facite in Meam commemorationem.* But they introduced a new element into it. According to St. Paul the Eucharist was accomplished at the close of another repast, which was the *agape.* This circumstance has complicated the history of the origin of the Eucharist, but I think the difficulty may be shortly summed up.

The *agape* was a repast celebrated by the Christians, and, as the word indicates, it was a feast of love, or charity. The details given by St. Paul make it easy to understand the possible abuses which might arise from it. The Jews, and even the pagans, had feasts of the same kind. Is the *agape* derived from either of these, or is it specifically Christian ? My own opinion is that this question is of little importance. But what we must note is that, according to St. Paul and other witnesses, it was at that time united to the Eucharist. Very soon—probably at the beginning of the second century—the two were separated on account of abuses, and towards the fourth century the *agape* was declining. It must not be confounded with those repasts sometimes celebrated by the Christians on the tombs of the martyrs, or in cemeteries, though these also had a liturgical character.

After the text of St. Paul, which throws great light on the question of the Eucharist, I will quote the *Didache*. The *Didache*, or " Doctrine of the Apostles," is a document discovered in 1883, which is extremely interesting but also most obscure, and about which opinions still vary. We may, I suppose, believe that it was written at the beginning of the second century. It was recognised almost generally as a description of the Eucharist from the moment of its discovery. In recent years many scholars—and those by no means the least important— have come to the conclusion that it describes the *agape*, and not the Eucharist. Others again, with, in my own opinion, greater reason, say that part applies to the *agape*, the rest to the Eucharist (Maclean, Thibaut). Here is the translation of the part which will interest us :

" *As to the Eucharist, give thanks thus.*
First, for the chalice :
We thank Thee, O our Father,
For the holy vine of David Thy servant,
Which Thou hast made us know through Jesus Thy
   Servant.
Glory be to Thee throughout all ages !
Then for the broken bread :
We give Thee thanks, O our Father,
For life and knowledge,
Which Thou hast made us know through Jesus Thy
   Servant.
Glory be to Thee throughout all ages !

8

THE MASS

*As this broken bread, formerly scattered over the mountains,
    has been gathered together to form a single whole,*

*So may Thy Church be assembled from the ends of the
    earth in Thy Kingdom,*

*For to Thee is all power and glory by Jesus Christ through-
    out all ages !*

*Let no one eat or drink of your Eucharist if he be not
    baptized in the Name of the Lord, for it was of this
    that the Lord said : ' Give not that which is holy unto
    the dogs.'*

After you are filled, give thanks thus :

We thank Thee, O Holy Father !

For Thy Holy Name

That Thou hast caused to dwell in our hearts,

For knowledge, faith, and the immortality

Which Thou hast revealed through Jesus Thy Servant.

Glory be to Thee throughout all ages !

It is Thou, Omnipotent Master,

*Who hast created the universe for the honour of Thy
    Name,*

*Who hast given food and drink to man, that he may enjoy
    them and render thanks to Thee ;*

*But Thou hast given us a spiritual food and drink, and
    eternal life by Thy Servant.*

*Above all, we give thanks to Thee because Thou art
    powerful.*

Glory be to Thee throughout all ages !

*Remember, O Lord, to deliver Thy Church from all
    evil,*

*And to make it perfect in Thy love. Assemble it from the
    four winds, that Holy Church,*

In Thy Kingdom which Thou hast prepared for it,

For Thine is all power and glory throughout all ages !

Come, Grace, let the world pass !

Hosanna to the God of David !

THE MASS OF THE WESTERN RITES

Let him that is holy, come !
Let him that is not, do penance !
Maran-Atha (The Lord comes).   Amen.
But as to the prophets, let them give thanks as they will."[1]

Besides the *Didache* there are numerous passages
containing allusions to the Eucharist in the writers at
the close of the first and of the second century.
St. Clement of Rome has a prayer which is considered
Eucharistic ; we shall come back to it presently.
St. Ignatius gives it the names of εὐχαριστία and of
breaking ἕνα ἄρτον κλῶντες. He insists that this should
be accomplished by the Bishop, and that it is a sign of
unity.[2] He uses the word θυσιαστήριον to design the
place of sacrifice, which clearly points out that, to him,
the Eucharist was also Sacrifice. It would also seem
that with him the *agape* is still united to the Eucharist
(Srawley, *loc. cit.*, p. 31).

The testimony of St. Justin in the middle of the
second century must be specially noted, since it is an
actual description of the Christian assembly :

" *As for us, after having washed him who believes and
has joined himself to us (Justin has just described Christian
Baptism), we lead him to that place where are assembled
those we call our brothers. With fervour we offer prayers
for ourselves, for the* enlightened[3] *(him who has just received the light of Baptism), for all the rest, wherever they
may be, in order to obtain with the knowledge of the Truth,*

[1] Trans. (into French), A. Laurent, in the Hemmer and Lejay
collection, *Textes et documents*. A commentary will be found in
Mgr. Batiffol, *L'Eucharistie*, p. 62 *seq.* The studies of Armitage
Robinson and Connolly place the *Didache* after the epistle of
ps. Barnabas.

[2] The different texts of St. Ignatius-Philad. 4, Smyrn. 6 & 8,
Eph. 20.

[3] On the use he makes of this word, cf. J. H. Srawley, *The
Early History of the Liturgy*, p. 32.

the grace to practise virtue, to keep the commandments, and thus to merit eternal salvation.

" When the prayers are ended we give each other the Kiss of Peace. Then to him who presides over the assembly of brothers are brought bread and a cup of water and wine mingled. He takes them, and praises and glorifies the Father of the universe in the Name of the Son and of the Holy Spirit ; then he makes a long thanksgiving for all the benefits we have received from Him. When he has finished his prayers and the thanksgiving, all the people present exclaim : Amen ! Amen is a Hebrew word meaning ' So be it.' When he who presides has made the thanksgiving, and when all the people have answered, the ministers whom we call deacons distribute to all those present the consecrated bread, the consecrated wine and water, and they carry them to those who are absent. We call this food the EUCHARIST, and no one can have part in it unless he believe in the Truth of our Doctrine ; unless he have received the bath for the remission of sins and regeneration ; and unless he live according to the precepts of Christ. For we take not that Food as common bread and common drink. Just as by virtue of the Word of God, Jesus Christ our Saviour took flesh and blood for our salvation, thus the Food consecrated by the prayer formed of the very words of Christ, that Food which nourishes by assimilation our own body and blood, is the Flesh and Blood of Jesus incarnate. Such is our Doctrine. The Apostles, in their memoirs which are called Gospels, relate that Jesus Himself announced these things to them. He took bread and, having given thanks, said to them :

" ' Do this in memory of Me : This is My Body.' In the same manner He took the chalice, and having given thanks, He said to them : ' This is My Blood.' And to them alone He gave it. The evil spirits have imitated this institution in the mysteries of Mithra : bread and a cup of water are presented in the ceremonies of initiation, and *certain formulas are pronounced which you know, or which you may know.*"[1]

It is well to cite even the testimony of the apochryphal writings, some of which indeed are heretical, but which often give us priceless information as to the usages of the second and third centuries. A German author [2] has made a special study of all these texts on the Eucharist. For the heretics also celebrated the Eucharist after their manner ; they consecrated bread and wine ; they considered the rite as a sacrifice ; some forbade wine, declaring they would only consecrate water, whence their name of *Aquarians*.[3] Sometimes they give the text of the prayer they recited over the bread and wine, and which produced, they thought, its change into the Body and Blood of Christ.

At the beginning of the third century we have a text the very high value of which has long since been recognised, and which an English scholar has attributed to St. Hippolytus. This text is that of the Eucharistic *anaphora*, or of the Canon recited at Rome at the beginning of the third century. To this also we shall return later on. Nor must we forget the African writers of the third century, notably Tertullian and St. Cyprian, whose testimony we shall study in Chapter III.

Lastly, in the fourth century, we have the text of another *anaphora* recently discovered. It is that of Serapion, the friend of St. Athanasius, and Bishop of Thmuis in Egypt. This we shall deal with in Chapter IV.

2. THE ALITURGICAL SYNAXIS (WITHOUT THE EUCHARIST).—The liturgic or Eucharistic synaxis, as it is de-

---

[1] 1st Apol. LXV, LXVI, trans. Louis Pontigny, coll. Hemmer-Lejay.
[2] Struckmann, *Die Gegenwarth Christi in der hl. Eucharistie nach den Schriftl. Quellen der vornizän. Zeit*, p. 90 *seq.* Cf. Woolley, *Liturgy of Primitive Church*, pp. 53 *seq.* and 138.
[3] Cf. the article by Mgr. Batiffol, DACL, *Aquariens*.

scribed in these texts, is a gathering exclusively Christian, to which none but the faithful are admitted. The names usually given to it are *Eucharistia* or *Fractio Panis*, either equally appropriate, because this rite is, above all, a Eucharistic prayer of thanksgiving ; and the breaking of bread for distribution to the faithful is an essential act of it, an integral part.

But beyond this Eucharistic gathering there were others which may have been connected with the Eucharist, but which are distinct from it, and in fact are sometimes separated from it. Thus, in that room in which the Eucharistic mystery had already been accomplished, where the Church was to be born, we find the Apostles, after the Ascension, meeting together and persevering unanimously in prayer (Acts i. 14). Later on Peter and John, after having appeared before the synagogue, returned to their brethren and addressed that sublime prayer to God which is yet not a Eucharistic prayer (iv. 23 *seq.*). When Peter was put into prison by Herod the whole Church united in prayer for him (xii. 5, and further on, 12, *multi congregati et orantes*).

Pliny, at the beginning of the second century, in his famous text on the Christians, speaks of a first meeting which they held upon a fixed day, *statuto die*, probably Sunday ; it took place before the dawn, and they sang hymns to Christ as God. In the evening of the same day they met together again for a meal in common, in which some have seen the *agape*, but which was far more probably the Eucharist. Many other allusions to these aliturgical synaxes will be found in Clement of Rome, Ignatius, etc.[1]

St. Justin also speaks, in the text already quoted, of a meeting at which were read the Holy Scriptures and the

[1] Ign., Eph. 5, 13 ; Magn. 7 ; Smyrn. 6. In our *Monumenta Ecclesiæ*, Dom Leclercq has gathered all the texts from the writers of the first three centuries which concern the Eucharist and these aliturgical synaxes.

memoirs of the Apostles, and at which certain prayers were recited. This meeting was followed by the Eucharistic service. Thus prayers, readings, chants, all served as prelude to the Eucharist. We have here, I believe, the first really precise example of what we call to-day the Pre-Mass, or Mass of the catechumens, as to which I will only say one word. Even in the existing liturgy we find traces of this aliturgical synax separated from the Eucharistic service, as, for example, in the office for Good Friday. It seems evident that this ceremony proceeds from that used in the synagogues on the Sabbath : the singing of psalms, reading the law and the prophets, homily—all this is just the material of the Mass of the catechumens. It also agrees with what was said at the beginning of this chapter. From the synagogue the Church freely borrowed those customs which would adapt themselves to her liturgy ; but she completed and made perfect such rites. Here, for example, the reading of the New Testament has been added to that of the Old, and we have the admirable whole of the Mass of the catechumens, which will often be mentioned in the course of this book.

The fact to be retained is this : there were, amongst the Christians of the first three centuries, beyond the Eucharistic synax, other gatherings which were aliturgical, and which must be distinguished from the Mass, although in many cases the aliturgical synax was followed by the Eucharist. In the same way the *agape*, a meal quite distinct from the Eucharist, at one time preceded its celebration. The two cases are analogous, and when once this distinction is clearly understood it becomes easier to interpret the ancient texts on the Eucharist ; it is because this analogy was not taken into account that so many writers on this subject have fallen into confusion and error.

The pagans were not excluded from these non-liturgical synaxes as they were from that of the Eucharist. Catechumens were admitted to them, and even heretics ; but when the Eucharistic service began all these people were sent out, *foris canes*, as was somewhat rudely said.

As to the vigils celebrated at the tombs of the martyrs, they were another form of synaxis which borrowed not only from the aliturgical gathering but from the *agape*, and from the liturgical synaxis itself. It was a local anniversary service which took place in the cemeteries, where psalms were chanted and the story of the passion of the martyr was read ; and which was often followed by the *agape* and by the Eucharist. It was sometimes called παννύχια, because it was celebrated at night, and was supposed to last from the previous evening until daylight next morning. We shall say no more about them here, as they do not exactly form part of our subject, but the ancient writers often speak of them ; abuses occasionally took place, and in the end they were suppressed.[1]

3. THE DAYS AND HOURS OF THE SYNAXIS.—Pliny tells us that the Christian synaxes (liturgical or aliturgical) were held before the dawn, and in the evening. Tertullian and St. Cyprian also speak of these early or nocturnal meetings, as well as the different canonical documents of the third century.[2] In order, on days of fasting, not to break the fast, the meeting was kept back until the hour of None, or even till Vespers. Because these gatherings were often held at night the pagans called the Christians a race of night-birds—*lucifugæ*.

From the Acts it would seem that the faithful assembled thus daily. Pliny speaks of a certain fixed day,

---

[1] Cf. the *opusculum* of M. Gastoué, *Les Vigiles* (Paris, 1908).
[2] Maclean, *op. cit.*, pp. 128, 129.

probably Sunday, which, of course, has been from the beginning the liturgical day *par excellence*. But from a very early date, especially in the West, Wednesday and Friday were days of meeting ; while in the East the day chosen was Saturday. Thus was constituted the Christian week, with its Sunday and its Station days, Wednesday and Friday. In one sense it might be said that the Christian week preceded the Christian, or liturgical, year. The latter, however, does in its germ certainly date from the primitive epoch. Easter and Pentecost are as ancient as Sunday itself ; and have contributed in no small degree to the importance of Sunday, since both Feasts were celebrated on that day. Now Easter and Pentecost early formed the sacred Fifty Days ; the two Feasts depended on each other chronologically and liturgically. There was a preparation for Easter, in which we see the beginnings of Lent.

The principle on which Easter was celebrated applied, from the fourth century, to the Birth of Christ ; thus we have the Feasts of Christmas and Epiphany. From this the entire liturgical year was derived. But from the beginning of this century Jerusalem was already ahead of all the other churches ; her liturgical year was complete ; she celebrated not only Easter and Pentecost, but also the Birth of Christ, the Presentation in the Temple, Lent with all its exercises, Holy Week. All these anniversaries were celebrated in the Holy Places. Thus, if we may so speak, a local liturgical year was created, soon to be imitated in many other churches, and first of all in that of Rome.[1]

The anniversaries of the martyrs were also solemnly celebrated, and gave birth to as many Feasts. The compilation of ecclesiastical calendars was in full flower

[1] Cf. our book, *Étude sur la Peregrinatio Silviæ, les églises de Jérusalem au IVe siècle* (Paris, 1895).

in the fourth century. But this subject leads us away from our own, and we must return to the Eucharist.

4. THE EUCHARISTIC PRAYER.—In the texts we have quoted from the three synoptic Gospels Our Lord pronounces no prayer for the institution of the Eucharist : none, at least, is given us. Neither does St. Paul make any allusion to such a prayer. There are not wanting those who have wished to supplement this silence ; and it has been said that such terms as *hymno dicto* (St. Matt. xxvi. 30) after the institution (see St. Mark xiv. 26) presuppose a prayer. It has been also said that, the institution of the Eucharist having taken place after the Paschal meal, Our Lord of necessity recited the prayers in use on that day, as well as the psalms called *Alleluiatic*. Bickell's whole thesis rests on this hypothesis ; he endeavours to discover traces of the Jewish Pasch in the ancient liturgies, especially in the *Apostolic Constitutions* ; and other scholars have followed him along this road. Quite recently Père Thibaut has undertaken the same task again, in a most interesting thesis. But as has been said, other interpreters contest all relation between the Jewish Pasch and the Last Supper of the Christians.

Some consider St. John xiv.-xvii. as a Eucharistic prayer, of which Probst finds vestiges in the ancient liturgies. This is possible ; but here we are upon hypothetical ground. With more likelihood we may see an anaphoric prayer, " a fragment of an evidently liturgical character " (Duchesne), in a text of the Epistle of Pope St. Clement. This we do not translate here, since it has so often been reproduced elsewhere.[1] After the text of the *Didache*, which has become classic, and which has been given above, it will be well to cite that of St. Hippolytus already alluded to, and which under its primitive

[1] Cf. particularly Mgr. Duchesne, *Origines du culte*, pp. 51, 52.

form is a prototype of all *anaphoræ* and Eucharistic prayers, which scarcely do more than develop and paraphrase its theme.

We render thanks to Thee, O God, through Thy well-beloved Son Jesus Christ, that in these last days Thou hast sent Him as Saviour and Redeemer and Angel (messenger) of Thy will, Who is Thine inseparable Word, by Whom Thou hast made all things, and in Whom Thou art well-pleased ; Thou hast sent Him from Heaven into the Virgin's womb, where He became Incarnate and manifested Himself as Thy Son, born of the Holy Ghost and of The Virgin ; then, accomplishing Thy Will and conquering a new and holy race, He stretched out His Hands in His Passion in order that He might deliver from suffering those who have believed in Thee ; and at the moment when He delivered Himself voluntarily to His Passion, in order to destroy Death, to break the devil's chains, to spurn hell under His Feet, to enlighten the just, to fix a term, to show forth the Resurrection, taking the bread and giving thanks, He said : Take, eat : This is My Body which shall be mangled for you. Likewise the cup, saying, This is My Blood which is shed for you : when you do this you do it in memory of Me. Remembering then His Death and Resurrection we offer Thee this bread and this chalice, thanking Thee because Thou hast deigned to permit us to appear before Thee and to serve Thee. And we pray Thee to send Thy Holy Spirit upon the oblation of the Holy Church, and uniting them as one, that Thou wilt give to all the Saints who participate (in the Sacrifice) to be filled with the Holy Ghost and fortified in the truth of the Faith, so that we may praise Thee and glorify Thee by Thy Child Jesus Christ, by Whom to Thee is glory and honour, to the Father, Son, and Holy Ghost, in Your holy Church, now and for all ages. Amen.[1]

[1] Trans. (into French) from the attempt to restore the Greek text made by Dom Cagin, *Eucharistia*, pp. 294–296.

We have also spoken above of the text of that *anaphora* made by an Egyptian Bishop of the fourth century. In a sort of euchology intended for the Bishop, Serapion has composed prayers for the blessing of oil and water, for Baptism, for Ordinations, for the sick and for the dead. A whole series of prayers is recited before the *anaphora* (*n.* xix.-xxx.) in that part which we have called the Pre-Mass. The Mass of the faithful is composed of the *Prayer of the faithful*, of the *anaphora* properly so called, which follows the ancient theme of the Prefaces : the mercy of God in creation, in the Incarnation, the recital of the institution of the Eucharist, the *anamnesis* and *epiclesis*, the final doxology of the *anaphora*, and the blessing over the people.[1]

To give an idea of the Mass at this epoch we may perhaps mention a text which was drawn up in the fourth century, though most of its leading features are more ancient, and to which certain liturgiologists have given a rather exaggerated importance, as they consider that it represents the Apostolic *anaphora* better than any other. Yet it has not the same value as the *anaphora* of Hippolytus, though it uses his text. The liturgical design of the Mass is as follows : readings from the Old and New Testaments, preaching ; then, prayer for the catechumens, penitents, and those in other categories ; the *oratio fidelium*, the Kiss of Peace, the ablution of the hands, the Offertory, Preface, *Sanctus*, the prayer of institution, the *Anamnesis*, *Epiclesis*, Memento, Communion, thanksgiving, and dismissal. Book VIII of the *Apostolic Constitutions* is especially interesting on account of the influence it exercised in the East, and even in the

---

[1] I have analysed this text in the article *Messe* of the *Dictionnaire de Théologie Catholique*. The French translation will be found in Mgr. Batiffol's *L'Eucharistie, loc. cit.*

West, and at Rome.[1] This is a fresh argument in favour of that liturgical unity in the first centuries ; Hippolytus, Serapion, the *Apostolic Constitutions*, and even Clement of Rome and the *Didache* all exploit a theme which presents numerous analogies.[2]

We find one custom, which is that of the celebrated church of Antioch, retraced in the *Apostolic Constitutions*. In another church which rivals that of Antioch in antiquity and fame—that of Alexandria—we have the Canon of Balizeh, which appears to go back to a period less remote, and which shows a different custom. But here, as with the different Eucharistic prayers which we have given, we have a text with a universal tendency, in spite of certain regional characteristics.[3]

We must now gather a few conclusions from all these texts. The first is this :

From the very beginning of the Church there existed an essential rite, distinct from that of the synagogue ; a rite which, from the first moment, seems to take the lead amongst all others, of which in a manner it is the centre. It consists of the reproduction and reconstruction of Our Lord's last repast, of the Last Supper in the Cenacle.

This rite is found everywhere. We have quoted the texts of Clement of Rome, of Ignatius of Antioch, of Justin, etc. But we could have multiplied our witnesses. A Christian traveller of the third century, Abercius, who had journeyed through the East as well as the West, tells us in a famous inscription :

[1] Drew, and after him Fortescue (notably in the article *Mass* in the *Catholic Encyclopædia*), have attempted to bring out the resemblances between the Roman Mass and that of the *Apostolic Constitutions*.

[2] We have analysed this text from the *A. C.* in our article *Messe*, quoted above. Cf. col. 1355.

[3] We have analysed this in DACL, art. *Canon*, col. 1847 *seq.* In Chapter III we shall cite the text of the Canon in the book *De Sacramentis*, which brings us to the end of the fourth century.

" My name is Abercius : I am the disciple of a Holy Shepherd Who feeds His flocks of sheep on mountains and on plains ; Who has eyes so large that their glance reaches everywhere. He it is Who has taught me the faithful Scriptures. He it is Who sent me to Rome. . . . I have also seen the plain of Syria and all its towns— Nisibis on the borders of the Euphrates. Everywhere I went I found brethren. Paul was my companion. Faith led me everywhere ; everywhere it served as my food, a fish from the spring, very great and pure, caught by a Holy Virgin ; continuously she gave it to eat to her friends ; she also has a delicious wine, which she gives with the bread."[1]

This rite, considered as a banquet and a sacrifice, has banished all the other sacrifices. Although the Church borrowed so largely from the Jewish liturgy, she left them their sacrifices. Those who attempt to discover analogies between the rites of paganism and those of the Christians cannot deny that the peaceful and unbloody Sacrifice of the altar has put an end to all sacrifices of blood. That river of blood which flowed through all pagan temples has been stopped by the Sacrifice of the Lamb.

This rite was accomplished with bread and wine. (Certain eccentrics are pointed out, such as the *Aquarians* or *Hydroparastes*, who, already prohibitionists, forbade all wine, even at Mass.) Those who partook of it wished to renew the scene in the Cenacle in relation to the Sacrifice of the Cross ; and were persuaded that under the species of bread and wine they received the Body and Blood of Christ.

The rite, as has been remarked, presents numerous variants when it is studied according to the testimony of different Churches, and great liberty of interpretation

[1] On *Abercius* and his inscription, cf. DACL, under this heading.

and improvisation still reigns ; but the general and essential features are the same. What is called the Eucharist, the fraction, the *anaphora*, the eulogy, the synaxis, is always and for all the same rite as that which we call the Mass.

Through the different witnesses quoted we can find a starting-point in the third or fourth century, whether it be the *anaphora* of Hippolytus or of Serapion, or the Canon of *De Sacramentis* ; and thus we are able to retrace our steps through century after century till we come to the time of the Apostles, and to Christ Himself. Thus we may say that an unbroken chain binds our Mass to that of the Apostles, to the Last Supper. It is the proof of the Apostolic origin of our Mass.

From that time—that is, from the first three centuries —we see, both as regards the Mass and Baptism, a tendency to develop the very simple original rite. To the kind of liturgic synaxis described, for example, in St. Paul's meeting at Troas, where, after the Apostle's sermon those present " broke bread " before separating, the heads of the Church under whose control the liturgy was constituted, added sometimes one ceremony, sometimes another.

The union of the aliturgical synaxis to the Mass is, already, a considerable fact ; it is a prelude which in our own day has the same extent as the rite of Sacrifice, or of the Mass properly so called. Hippolytus gives us an *anaphora* which is a model of precision and concision. It is a brief, weighty sermon in a single breath ; for the whole *anaphora* proceeds without a break from the Preface to the conclusion, which is the *Amen* of the faithful. The Fraction follows ; the Communion, thanksgiving, and dismissal.

The centuries to come had a tendency to add fresh rites to this. The *Liber Pontificalis*, on which, however, we cannot always rely in these matters, gives us in this case an exact idea of the facts. Such a Pope added the *Sanctus* to the Preface ; another added the *Agnus Dei* ; another, a sentence to the Canon ; yet a fourth has added another sentence. Then there would be a prayer for the offering of the bread ; another for the censing ; a third for the Communion. Until the day when Leo XIII ordained a series of prayers for the Church, the Gospel of St. John was the conclusion of the Mass. There have been those who said that all these trees prevent us from seeing the forest ; and it must assuredly be admitted that those who are for the first time present at High Mass must find themselves rather at a loss.

But those who have studied the liturgy and its history will readily find the great lines of the primitive Mass in the Mass of the twentieth century.

BIBLIOGRAPHY

Dom CABROL and Dom LECLERCQ, *Monumenta Ecclesiæ Liturgica* (Vol. I), *Reliquiæ Liturgicæ vetustissimæ* (Paris, 1900–1902)—(all the texts of the writers of the first three centuries on the Mass and Liturgy).

F. PROBST, *Liturgie der drei ersten Jahr.* (Tübingen, 1870) ; *Liturgie der vierten Jahr.* (Münster, 1897) ; *Die abendländische Messe vom 5 bis zum 8 Jahr.* (Münster, 1896).

G. RAUSCHEN, *Florilegium patristicum*, Fasc. VII. *Monumenta eucharistica* (Bonn, 1909).

Dom CAGIN, *Eucharistia. L'Anaphore apostolique ou canon primitif* (Paris, 1912).

R. H. CONNOLLY, *The So-called Egyptian Church Order*, in *Texts and Studies* (Vol. VIII, 1916).

R. MAXWELL WOOLLEY, *The Liturgy of the Primitive Church* (Cambridge, 1910).

A. JOHN MACLEAN, *Recent Discoveries* (London, 1915).

F. E. WARREN, *The Liturgy and Ritual of the ante-Nicean Church* (London, 1912).

J. H. SRAWLEY, *The Early History of the Liturgy* (Cambridge, 1912).

CHAPTER II

THE MASS IN THE FOURTH AND FIFTH CENTURIES, AND ITS DIVISION INTO LITURGICAL FAMILIES

Divisions into liturgical families.—Analogies between the Oriental and Latin Liturgies.—Divergencies between the different Western Liturgies.

THE proposition developed in the previous chapter that in the three first centuries, and even until the end of the fourth, hardly any distinction can be made between the liturgies of different countries, may be taken for granted. But from this moment certain customs which made it possible easily to distinguish between the liturgies of these different lands were established ; on one hand between East and West ; on the other, between the different provinces of these two great halves of the Roman Empire. As Mgr. Duchesne has justly remarked, the liturgical provinces fall into line with the great ecclesiastical provinces—in the East, Antioch and Jerusalem, closely united from their origin, as contrasted with Alexandria; in the West, Rome, round which were grouped Italy, Africa, Gaul, Spain, and, very soon, England and Germany.

If we apply that principle, the first division necessary is that between East and West.

The day on which Constantine in 325 founded Constantinople, and transported to the city of Byzantium the seat of empire with all its functionaries, that division was accentuated. Habits, standards of cultivation, social, political, and even religious tendencies present changed characteristics. Each of the two parts of the

Empire had its own language ; Greek for the East, Latin for the West ; and this difference made itself felt in the liturgy. The Roman liturgy had been Greek until towards the middle of the third century ; but the place of Greek was taken by Latin, and the traces of the older language were gradually effaced. The *Kyrie Eleison* and other similar words still to be found in this liturgy are not, as was formerly wrongly believed, relics of the primitive language, but expressions of universal usage, like *Eucharist, acolyte, exorcist*, etc., or else, terms which have been introduced in later years.

Greek and, for some parts of the East, Syriac, were henceforth the languages of the liturgies born in those countries. The liturgy of Rome was in Latin, as that of Africa then was, and as those of Gaul, Spain, and Milan soon would be. Few can refuse to see in this difference of language, without mentioning political, administrative, or social differences, the establishment of a profound separation between East and West on the one hand, and, on the other, a certain relationship between the provinces of the West.

Thus, in our opinion, the first division to establish between the various liturgies is that between East and West.

In the East, as already noted, another division existed. The two churches of Antioch and Jerusalem, neighbours, and closely allied as they were, had a liturgy which spread over a part of the East, in Syria, Asia Minor (Cappadocia, Pontus, Bithynia, and Cæsarea), and later to Constantinople, Mesopotamia, and Persia. It is represented by the liturgy of the *Apostolic Constitutions* (fourth century), the Greek liturgy of St. James (sixth century, and perhaps earlier), the Nestorian liturgies of Mesopotamia and Persia (liturgy of Addeus and Maris), the Byzantine, or liturgy of Constantinople (St. Basil and St. John Chrysostom), and the Armenian liturgy.

The church of Alexandria followed a use which differed in several ways from the preceding, as may be established by the *anaphora* of Serapion, and by that of Balizeh, of which we have given a summary in the previous chapter. In this chapter, too, may also be seen the plan and sequence of the prayers in the *Apostolic Constitutions* and in other liturgies of this class.

In the Latin West various liturgical divergencies took shape at Rome, in Africa, Milan, Gaul, Spain, and the Celtic countries. These correspond with that rupture of political unity which was the consequence of the barbarian invasions of the fifth century ; of the breaking up of the Roman Empire in 476, and of the separatist tendencies which were the result of these events.

We arrive, then, at the following division :

ORIENT (EASTERN LITURGIES)	OCCIDENT (LATIN LITURGIES)
Antioch-Jerusalem (Syrian type) Alexandria (Egyptian type)	Rome Africa Milan Gaul Spain Celtic countries

To this division we will return in Chapter V. ; but it may be said at once that as far as the West is concerned, some part of it is based on mere conjecture, and that liturgiologists are by no means all agreed upon particular points. There is, however, a distinct tendency to gather all Latin liturgies into one and the same group.[1]

But henceforward it must be noted that liturgical unity is not broken by these divisions. The East and West had characteristics in common. The various Latin liturgies, including the Roman, borrowed largely from the Oriental, notably from that of Constantinople.

[1] Mgr. Duchesne connects the Gallican and Syrian, and the Roman and Alexandrine types of liturgy (fourth edition, p. 55).

Rome exercised considerable influence over all the Latin churches, and fresh analogies are continually visible between all these different liturgies, either as the result of borrowing, or of their original unity.

It must not be forgotten that travel and other relations between East and West were much more frequent than is sometimes imagined. There were many Greek or Eastern Popes of Rome during the first three centuries. At Milan, seven of the ten predecessors of St. Ambrose have Greek names. St. Ambrose himself by his literary training was more Greek than Latin. One striking example in the history of the liturgy is found in Etheria, who in the fourth century came from the heart of Spain to Jerusalem, and while there described with great precision all the Feasts of the year. She does not fail to note that such and such functions are not carried out in her own country in exactly the same manner as at Jerusalem ; while others are similar to those of her own liturgy. Upon her traces followed pilgrims in increasing numbers, eager to visit the Holy Places. Numerous Bishops were attracted to the East by the Councils, or else driven there by the fate of exile, like St. Hilarius. All of which goes to explain the liturgical exchanges. Mgr. Mercati has very truly remarked that connections were established between the Arians of East and West, and that this also contributed to the system of exchanges. It has, moreover, become possible to discern this reciprocal influence of East and West through the study of the most ancient calendars and creeds.

Thus there is nothing astonishing in the fact that Oriental elements can be discovered in the Latin liturgies. It is indeed our own opinion that the cause of the analogies between the two groups is to be found rather in the common origin of all liturgies, whether Eastern or Western, or in the exchanges just mentioned, than in the sudden transportation, by the act of a Bishop or some other personage, of an Eastern liturgy into a Western country.

Here, then, are some of the divergencies which can already be distinguished between the different Western liturgies. Gaul, Spain, and Upper Italy followed the Oriental Use (notably that of the Church of Constantinople) as regarded the place of the diptychs, the Kiss of Peace, and even the *epiclesis* ; while Rome stood apart, either because she had on these points changed her primitive custom, or else because she had had a special Use from the beginning. For the rest, such as the variability of the prayers of the *canon*, the use of the *Qui pridie* for the Consecration, the importance given to the story of the institution of the Mass, the tendency to compose sacramentaries and other liturgical books, all the Latin countries seem to follow the same current, and there is nothing to show that these books presented special characteristics, whether they were composed at Rome, Milan, Capua, in Gaul, or in Africa. Still, all such compositions reveal a liturgical progress which affects only the West, while the East appears to be unaffected by it.[1]

The liturgical vocabulary, the calendar, and certain institutions like Lent, and even the Ember Days, also offer characteristic analogies in the Western liturgies.

During this period (fourth-fifth centuries) two liturgies alone, that of Rome and that of Africa, are directly known to us through documents, or by the texts of the authors. As to all the others—those of Upper Italy, Gaul, Spain, and the Celtic countries—the sources from which we may study them are of a much later age than the fifth century, or even than the sixth. I do not say that there is nothing in them which makes for the earlier date, but such inductions are necessarily based on hypothesis.

[1] Cf. *Books of the Latin Liturgy* (Sands, 3s. 6d.).

From this moment the design and the framework of the Mass appear with sufficient clearness. In Chapter I we saw of what the first part is composed : the Pre-Mass, or *aliturgical* synaxis is a preparation, with psalms, readings, and a homily. We shall study it more in detail in the developments which it has gained in the sixth and seventh centuries. Its general characteristics have been outlined by St. Justin and other authors quoted in the preceding chapter.

The second part, the Mass properly so called, or Mass of the faithful, was to receive some additions, but henceforth we know that the catechumens and unbaptized were dismissed at this point. The faithful alone remained for the Offering, or Offertory ; they had brought the bread and wine which served for the Sacrifice, as well as other gifts which were also blessed at Mass. A special prayer for the Church, or *Prayer of the Faithful*, was now said, and the Kiss of Peace was its natural conclusion ; doubtless it was only in consequence of the suppression of this prayer, or from other circumstances, that in certain liturgies the Kiss of Peace has been placed immediately before the Communion, where its existence is not less justified.

The Eucharistic prayer, or *anaphora*, follows ; of this we have had specimens in the *anaphoræ* of Hippolytus, Serapion, Balizeh, and the *Apostolic Constitutions*. The chant of the *Sanctus* took its own place in the fifth century, and has divided the Eucharistic prayer into two portions. The story of the Institution is the centre of this prayer, which ends with the doxology and *Amen*. Then follow the Fraction and Communion. The latter, like the Offertory, involved the passing up of the people, which occupied some time, and from an early date (probably the fourth century) the singing of a chant was instituted at both these moments. Psalm xxxiii. was usually chosen for the Communion, chiefly on account of the verse, *Gustate et videte quoniam suavis est Dominus*, which is here so applicable. Afterwards a prayer of thanksgiving was made ; the Pontiff blessed the people for the last time and sent them home.

Such were the general lines of the Mass in the fourth-fifth centuries. In studying the Latin liturgies, especially that of Rome, we shall see how these principal parts are adorned with new rites and more numerous formulas. Other rites perhaps have been suppressed, but in the main, in the East as in the West, according to the different rites, the framework remains the same.

Nothing can be simpler, more logical, and, if we may say so, more rational than this rite which is faithful to primitive tradition. There are certain suppressions which break the general line, or additions which complicate the original design. Certain truths had to be insisted on, certain errors to be fought, new formulas had to be emphasised by the gestures of the priest, or favour shown to recent devotions.

After having studied the Latin, Gallican, Mozarabic, Celtic, Ambrosian, and Roman liturgies, we shall attempt, not to reconstitute the primitive Latin liturgy, since this would be but a premature effort, but to establish some of its general characteristics.

BIBLIOGRAPHY

On the classification of liturgies :

H. LIETZMANN, *Messe u. Herrenmahl* (Bonn, 1926), p. 262.
Mgr. DUCHESNE, *Origines du Culte chrétien*, p. 64 *seq.*
SALAVILLE, *Liturgia*, pp. 887 and 873.
FORTESCUE, *The Mass* (1914), a table of the liturgies, p. 76.
JANIN, *Les Églises orientales.*
Mgr. DUCHESNE, *Les Églises séparées*, 1 vol. (Paris, 1896).
BRINKTRINE, *Die Heilige Messe*, p. 19 *seq.*

CHAPTER III

THE MASS IN AFRICA

Origin of the African Liturgy.—The African Mass.

OF all the Latin liturgies the African is the only one of which no liturgical document, properly so called, remains to us. All its books have perished ; there are neither Sacramentaries nor Lectionaries ; no *Ordo* or *libellus* of any kind existing. Yet it is the most ancient of the Latin liturgies ; it might indeed be said to have been almost the only one known during the first three centuries, since, until the middle of the third century the Roman liturgy was said in Greek. This fact is of supreme importance.

Yet though this absence of all liturgical documents is to be deplored, we find, on the other hand, in African writers up to the fifth century a very large number of allusions to the liturgy, and even several formulas of prayer. In this latter item the African liturgy is the richest of all ; but it is none the less true that the lack of authentic liturgical documents makes any study of this rite more or less deceptive, and necessarily hypothetical. We will, however, do our best to supplement this want.

THE ORIGIN OF THE AFRICAN LITURGY.—The first question which arises is : what is the origin of this liturgy ? The greater number of liturgiologists will reply : Roman. We, however, may well wait for the close of this study before drawing the same conclusion ; the question touches that of the origin of the African

Church, and both must be resolved simultaneously. Was this Church founded by the Church of Rome ? If so, it would be difficult to put aside the contention that Rome, in founding the African Church, did also introduce her liturgy there, since it is hardly possible that Roman missionaries should not have brought their own liturgy with them, or that at a given moment the Africans should have changed it. In any case there is no text to be found in favour of such a conclusion. Unfortunately, the question of the origins of Christianity is here obscure, as it is in most other countries. Many historians hold to the Roman origin, it is true, and it may well be the most probable opinion ; but it cannot be proved by direct and decisive arguments. Relations between Africa, Alexandria, and the East were frequent, and it may be that the earliest missionaries came thence to Africa. Some have wished to support this theory, as we shall see, by certain analogies between the African and Alexandrine liturgies ; but neither would this be a very solid proof, for the resemblances between Africa and Rome from the liturgical standpoint are very much more striking.

Let us for the moment be content to state that the question of the origin of Christianity in Africa cannot enlighten us as to that of its liturgy. Keeping simply to the texts, we must remember, as was said at the beginning, that this liturgy is Latin. Although Greek was freely spoken in this province, and though Tertullian wrote some of his treatises in Greek, the African liturgy is Latin, and to prove this it would be enough to cite the formulas found in the writings of the same Tertullian, of St. Cyprian and other writers, or even in the inscriptions of Roman Africa.

THE AFRICAN MASS.—In Tertullian and St. Cyprian we find numerous allusions to the Eucharist and the

Mass. By these we know that the synaxis or meeting took place before the dawn ; that the Sacrifice, or actual Mass, was preceded by readings, prayers, chants, and by the dismissal of the catechumens. Tertullian blames the heretics who allow these last to be present at the Sacrifice. We also know that the bread and wine were consecrated by the words which Our Lord pronounced at the Last Supper. St. Cyprian sharply rebukes other heretics (Aquarians) who, by a misplaced scruple, left out the wine and declared that they offered the Sacrifice with bread and water ; reminding them that the water used at the Mass must be mixed with wine. These two writers also allude to the litanic prayers, to the dialogue which precedes the Preface, to the *Pater*, and to some other rites, such as the dismissal of the faithful at the end of Mass.

St. Augustine completes this information. We may accept his description given by Mgr. Batiffol (p. 100) of the Pre-Mass. The Bishop, he says, awaits in the *secretarium* (a place close to the Basilica) the moment of entrance. He enters solemnly, but St. Augustine does not speak of the chant which should accompany his entry, and which corresponds with the Roman Introit. He salutes the people, probably with the *Pax vobis*, but it does not appear that this greeting was followed by the prayer or collect customary at Rome. The readings, as in Spain, Gaul, and elsewhere, were three in number—the first taken from the Prophets (and called Prophecy, or prophetical reading), the second from the Acts of the Apostles or their Epistles (the Apostolic reading), while the third was from the Gospel. This was followed by the homily of the prelate, who commented on one or another of these lessons ; for usually the events of the day, anniversaries, or the Feast itself had determined both the course of reading and the Bishop's sermon.

Sometimes the text of the Old Testament or the New was read without choice or interruption ; this was the *lectio continua*, of which traces may be found in our existing missal (see, for example, the chants for Communion in Lent, the readings for Holy Week, or in Paschal Time, etc.).

In other passages St. Augustine speaks of only two lessons, the Epistle and the Gospel, but between the two a Psalm was sung (our Gradual), which the Saint considered as a lesson, and on which he sometimes commented. After the homily the catechumens were dismissed—*catechumeni discedite*, says St. Augustine. The Mass of the Faithful was thus composed :

> Prayer of the faithful ;
> Reading of the Diptychs ;
> Offertory, with chanting of a Psalm and a prayer over the offerings, which corresponds to our Secret, or the *Oratio post nomina* ;
> The *anaphora* or Eucharistic prayer, which is interrupted by the *Sanctus* ;
> The recital of the institution, which is the centre of the Mass ;
> *Epiclesis ;*
> Fraction (before the *Pater*, as at Rome until the seventh century) ;
> Kiss of Peace ;
> Benediction ;
> Communion, with the singing of a Psalm ;
> Thanksgiving ;
> Dismissal.

Let us consider some of these different points enumerated. The *Prayer of the Faithful, preces, precatio, deprecatio*, consists in the indication by the Bishop of the object of the prayer, of an invitation by the deacon, and of a final prayer by the Bishop. This devotion may be compared to the solemn prayers at Rome on Good Friday, which also contain the indication of the object for which the prayer is offered, *Oremus* ; the deacon's order, *Flectamus genua* (here, an instant of recollection or silent prayer) ; followed by *Levate*, and the prayer of the Bishop. The design is the same. We may also compare the *preces fidelium* of the Mozarabic rite, to which an allusion has been found in the works of St. Fructuosus, which at once takes us back to the third century. For Africa, St. Cyprian also makes an allusion to a prayer of this kind.[1]

The *Prayer of the Faithful* is described at length by St. Augustine, who tells us that it is the deacon who announces the prayer, but the Bishop who reads it. He exhorts the people to pray for infidels, for catechumens, and for the faithful.[2] In Africa, as at Rome, the faithful offered the bread and wine, and the Bishop asked God to accept them. While the offering was being made, a Psalm was sung (the offertory). In St. Augustine's day this custom was not ancient, for he was obliged to write a book (now lost) against a certain Hilarius, who condemned it.

The mixing of wine and water in the chalice is one of those universal traits which we have mentioned as a proof of the unity of the primitive liturgy. St. Cyprian explains this act by saying that the water is the symbol of all Christian people, thus mingled in the chalice with the Blood of Christ (*Ep.* lxiii.). St. Cyprian, too, is the

[1] Because of this *Prayer of the Faithful*, W. C. Bishop thinks that the relations between the Mozarabic liturgy and that of Africa were closer than those between Africa and the Roman liturgy.

[2] Mgr. Batiffol quotes these different texts (p. 141) ; they will also be found, and in greater number, in our article on the *Liturgie de l'Afrique, etc.* (DACL).

most ancient witness we possess as to the dialogue before the Preface, *Sursum corda, Habemus ad Dominum* (*De dom. orat.*, 31). St. Augustine, after him, explains the meaning of these words, and completes them, quoting the beginning : *Dignum et justum est.* This prayer, which we call the Preface, comes after the *Prayer of the Faithful*, and continues till the final *Amen*, at the close of the last doxology. It is during the course of this prayer that by the might of the Divine Word the bread is changed into the Body of Christ, and the wine into His Blood (*Sermo* CCXXVII).

After this prayer, which is that of the consecration of the elements, St. Augustine mentions the *Pater*.

In the article on *l'Afrique* (*Liturgie post-nicéenne de l'Afrique*) I have quoted other texts of St. Augustine, of Optatus, and of St. Fulgentius, which allude to the canon, especially to the *anamnesis*. The Kiss of Peace was given after the *Pater*, as at Rome. St. Augustine also frequently refers to the Communion, defining it in the terms : *accedere ad mensam, ad altare, nostis fideles ad quam mensam.* It was given under both kinds, and he seems to give even the formula for Communion : *accipite et edite Corpus Christi et potate Sanguinem Christi*, to which the faithful answered *Amen.* The Communion chant was Psalm xxxiii., as was the custom generally at this time. There seems to have been a blessing before the Communion, as there was in Gaul and Spain.

All these features are fairly general, and in themselves not sufficient to determine precisely to which class this liturgy belongs. However, Mgr. Duchesne and other liturgiologists with him declare without hesitation that, excepting for insignificant details, the African liturgy is identical with that of Rome. Le Blant has pointed out numerous analogies in the inscriptions of these two places.

I have also mentioned that the African resembles in a few points the Mozarabic liturgy. W. C. Bishop presses this point in the article cited, and Fr. Thibaut supports him. But let us remember that these resemblances may be explained by the relations between the two provinces, and also by the fact on which we have throughout insisted : the original unity of all liturgies.

BIBLIOGRAPHY

Cf. our article in DACL, *Afrique* (*Liturgie de l'Afrique ante-nicéenne* and *Liturgie de l'Afrique post-nicéenne,* and the Bibliography at the end of the article).

W. C. BISHOP, *The African Rite,* in the *Journal of Theological Studies,* Vol. XIII, 1912, pp. 250-277.

Dom W. ROETZER, *Der heil.-Augustinus Schriften als Liturgie-geschichtl. Quelle* (Munich, 1930).

Cf. also Dom H. LECLERCQ, *l'Afrique chrétienne,* 2 vols. (Paris, 1904).

P. MONCEAUX, *Hist. littéraire de l'Afrique chrétienne* (Paris, 1901).

CHAPTER IV

THE MASS AT ROME, FROM THE FIFTH TO THE SEVENTH CENTURIES

DOCUMENTS AND TEXTS.—THE ROMAN MASS : Station.—Litany.
—Introit.—Kissing of the Altar.—Collect.—Readings and
Chants (Gradual, Alleluia, Tract, Epistle).—Gospel.—THE
MASS OF THE FAITHFUL : Offertory.—Singing of the Offer-
tory.—Secret.—Preface.—Sanctus.—The Roman Canon.—
Fraction and Pater.—Immixtion.—Kiss of Peace.—Com-
munion.—The last Prayers and Dismissal.—Conclusions.

DOCUMENTS AND TEXTS

WE have, to enlighten us as to this period, several allusions in contemporary writers ; while certain liturgical
documents explain, with more or less exactitude, how
Mass was celebrated at Rome about the sixth and
seventh centuries. Other writers of the fifth, and even
of the fourth, century, such as Arnobius and the Jew
Isaac, allude to the text of the Roman canon. Pope
Innocent I (401–417) in a celebrated text forbids the
recitation of names (Memento of the living and the dead)
at the Offertory in the Roman canon (as was the Gallican
and Oriental custom, and also probably the most ancient
usage). The Popes Boniface I (418–422) and Celestine I
(422–432) attest that the Emperors also were prayed
for in this place.[1] Pope Vigilius, in a letter to Profuturus,

[1] The *Liber Pontificalis* says that this same Pope Celestine
instituted the Introit, and that before his time only St. Paul and
the Gospel were read at the Pre-Mass. But this text is derived
from an apochryphal letter (cf. Mgr. Batiffol, p. 105). The
Liber Pontificalis makes other allusions to modifications introduced into the Mass by the Popes. Of these we shall speak
further on.

38

says that at Rome the text of the canon only varies at Easter, Ascension-tide, Pentecost, and the Epiphany. He sends the Bishop that text of the canon which he believes to be of Apostolic origin. The authors of the eighth-ninth centuries, Bede, Agobard, Amalarius, also bear witness to the Roman canon.[1] In a celebrated work of the close of the fourth century, sometimes attributed to St. Ambrose, and which in any case is almost contemporary with him, which is inspired by his writings, and which belongs to a church of Upper Italy, the author quotes the prayer of Consecration, which, with a few variants, is the very text of our own canon. It is of such importance that it must be given here :

TEXT OF *DE SACRAMENTIS*	ROMAN CANON
	Te igitur . . . *Memento Domine . . .* *Communicantes . . .* *Hanc igitur oblationem . . .*
Fac nobis (inquit sacerdos), hanc oblationem ascriptam, ratam, rationabilem, acceptabilem, quod figura est corporis et sanguinis Jesu Christi.	*Quam oblationem tu Deus, in omnibus, quæsumus, benedictam, adscriptam, ratam, rationabilem, acceptabilemque facere digneris : ut nobis corpus et sanguis fiat dilectissimi Filii tui Domini nostri Jesu Christi.*
Qui pridie quam pateretur, in sanctis manibus suis accepit panem, respexit in cœlum ad te, sancte Pater omnipotens, æterne Deus, Gratias agens, benedixit, fregit, fractum que apostolis suis et discipulis suis tradidit dicens : accipite et edite ex hoc omnes : hoc est enim corpus meum, quod pro multis confringetur.	*Qui pridie quam pateretur, accepit panem in sanctas ac venerabiles manus suas : et elevatis oculis in cœlum, ad Te Deum Patrem suum omnipotentem, tibi gratias agens, benedixit, fregit, deditque discipulis suis dicens : accipite et manducate ex hoc omnes : hoc est enim corpus meum.*
Similiter etiam calicem postquam cœnatum est, pridie quam pateretur, accepit, respexit in	*Simili modo postquam cœnatum est, accipiens et hunc præclarum calicem in sanctas*

[1] I have given all these texts in DACL, article *Canon*, col. 1852 *seq.*

cælum ad te, sancte pater omnipotens, æterne Deus, gratias agens, benedixit, apostolis suis et discipulis suis tradidit, dicens : accipite et bibite ex hoc omnes : hic est enim sanguis meus.

ac venerabiles manus suas item tibi gratias agens, benedixit, deditque discipulis suis, dicens : accipite et bibite ex eo omnes : Hic est enim calix sanguinis mei, novi et æterni testamenti : mysterium fidei ; qui pro vobis et pro multis effundetur in remissionem peccatorum.

Hæc quotiescumque feceritis, in mei memoriam facietis.

Ergo memores gloriosissimæ ejus passionis et ab inferis resurrectionis, in cælum ascensionis, offerimus tibi hanc immaculatam hostiam, hunc panem sanctum et calicem vitæ æternæ ;

Unde et memores, Domine, nos servi tui, sed et plebs tua sancta, ejusdem Christi Filii tui Domini nostri, tam beatæ passionis necnon et ab inferis resurrectionis, sed et in cælos gloriosæ ascensionis : offerimus præclaræ majestati tuæ de tuis donis ac datis, hostiam puram, hostiam sanctam, hostiam immaculatam, Panem sanctum vitæ æternæ, et Calicem salutis perpetuæ.

et petimus et precamur, ut hanc oblationem suscipias in sublimi altari tuo per manus angelorum tuorum sicut suscipere dignatus es munera pueri tui justi Abel et sacrificium patriarchæ nostri Abrahæ et quod tibi obtulit summus sacerdos Melchisedech.

Supra quæ propitio ac sereno vultu respicere digneris : et accepta habere, sicuti accepta, habere dignatus es munera pueri tui justi Abel, et sacrificium patriarchæ nostri Abrahæ, et quod tibi obtulit summus sacerdos tuus Melchisedech sanctum sacrificium, immaculatam hostiam.

Supplices te rogamus, omnipotens Deus : jube hæc perferri per manus sancti Angeli tui in sublime altare tuum, in conspectu divinæ majestatis tuæ : etc.

There is no doubt that we have here two editions of the same text ; and as that of *De Sacramentis* is localised in Upper Italy and dated about the year 400, it is the most ancient witness we possess as to the principal parts of the Roman canon, which only appear in the Sacramentaries some time after the seventh century. The question as to whether the Roman canon is not older even than that of *De Sacramentis* is discussed by liturgiologists. Mgr. Batiffol is of this opinion, but we, on the contrary, think that the former bears traces of closer composition, of a more carefully guarded orthodoxy, and that consequently it is a text corrected from *De Sacramentis*. We shall see, in studying the list of names in the *Memento* of the living and that of the dead, that Mgr. Batiffol argues with good reason that he can date these fragments from the pontificate of Symmachus (498–514). We thus have the state of the Roman Mass, or at least of the chief parts of the canon, at the beginning of the fourth century.

A Sacramentary of a very special character, called *Leonine*, because it has sometimes been attributed to St. Leo, and which seems to have been composed in the fifth century, contains Prefaces some of which seem to refer to events which took place in the previous century. It gives us other valuable indications as to the Roman liturgy of that time. The references to churches, to cemeteries, to Roman Saints, and even to the *chronique scandaleuse* of the day, are numerous. The style of the prayers, the use of the *cursus* and of rhythm, the liturgical terminology—in short, everything in this precious document has a Roman character.[1]

Another Roman Sacramentary, the *Gelasian*—attributed to the Pope of that name, Gelasius I (492–496)—has been altered and retouched up to the eighth or ninth century; but, strictly speaking, its text is not authentic; and its principal elements only go back to the end of the fifth century. Like the *Leonine*, we may, by studying it,

---

[1] In the volume already quoted, *Books of the Latin Liturgy*, we give fuller information about the Leonine Sacramentary. Cf. p. 71. See also our article *Léonien* in DACL.

find in it many Roman characteristics. It is divided into three parts : the Masses of the Feasts of the liturgical year, from Christmas to Pentecost, the *Proper of the Time*, as we call it ; the Masses of Saints, from St. Felix (Feb. 14) to St. Thomas the Apostle (Dec. 21), or the *Proper of Saints* ; and the third part, containing Masses for Sundays, Votive Masses, and those for special circumstances. Whoever drew up this Sacramentary knew the *Leonine*, and has borrowed numerous formulas from it, though these are quite differently arranged ; the Roman style is even more evident than in the *Leonine* ; the liturgical year takes the first place in the *Gelasian*, and exercises a preponderating influence on the liturgy.[1]

A third Roman Sacramentary, the *Gregorian*, presents itself under conditions analogous with those of the *Gelasian*. In spite of the uncertainty we must feel on finding it retouched again and again up to the ninth century (especially in Gaul), we cannot doubt that we have here a document of Roman origin. The author has taken the *Gelasian Sacramentary* as the basis of his work, which he reshapes, curtails, sacrificing all that appears to him purely archaic, but utilising the other elements. The attribution to St. Gregory (590–604) of this Sacramentary (with the exception, of course, of all the changes and additions which it underwent from the seventh to the ninth centuries) has been eagerly contested ; but the most important liturgiologists are more and more inclined to accept the indications given by tradition on this point. In recent times an attempt has been made to recover the primitive *Gregorian Sacramentary*, and the discovery of a copy at Monte Cassino is of the greatest importance.[2]

[1] On the *Gelasian* see also *Books of the Latin Liturgy*, p. 77, and the article *Gélasien* in DACL.

[2] Cf. *Books of the Latin Liturgy*, p. 77, and the article *Grégorien* in DACL.

THE MASS AT ROME

At Rome again, during this period of the sixth-ninth centuries, when the liturgy became of such importance, liturgical books were composed which have not the same characteristics as the Sacramentaries, but which complete them. These books are the *Ordines Romani*. The Sacramentaries give us the text of the prayers to be recited, but usually without indications as to the nature of the ceremonies. The *Ordines*, on the other hand, take as their aim the description of the ceremonies themselves; those of the Mass, in particular, giving on this point the necessary information. Their composition is spread over a period of many centuries (seventh-fifteenth). These *Ordines*, some of which are of Roman origin, have, like the Sacramentaries, been retouched in Gaul, where the greatest liturgical activity was displayed from the eighth-eleventh centuries. But one of these *Ordines*, the first of the series, is exempt from any retouching; it goes back to the eighth century and perhaps beyond it, and has even been, with some probability, attributed to St. Gregory himself.[1] In any case, it is possible without scruple to describe the Roman Mass in the seventh century under St. Gregory on the information here contained.

Whatever doubts we may have as to their composition, all these documents do clearly show the interest taken by the Roman Church from the fifth-eighth centuries in the liturgy. No other Church can display a collection of documents of equal importance. Even now we have said nothing as to the composition of those music-books which are called *Gregorians*, as we prefer to treat that question in an Excursus (see p. 212).

---

[1] I have given some information on the *Ordines Romani* in *Books of the Latin Liturgy*. Since then M. l'Abbé M. Andrieu has published the first volume of an important work in which the principal *Ordines Romani* are described and published: *Les Ordines Romani du haut moyen âge*. I, *Les Manuscrits* (*Spic. sacr. Lovaniense*). (Louvain, 1931, 8vo, xxiv–632 pp.)

Another indication of the interest taken by the Popes in the organisation and direction of Christian worship can be found in the *Liber Pontificalis*. Some portions of its testimony have been quoted at the beginning of this chapter. But this document, which was not drawn up before the fifth century, professes to enlighten us upon the most ancient period of all, and to attribute to the earliest Popes certain acts concerning the liturgy, especially concerning the Mass.[1] All this information is by no means of equal value, and we may well ask what were the sources from which the author has drawn his information as to the first centuries. But from the fourth, and particularly from the fifth century onward, his testimony is of real value.

THE ROMAN MASS

It is by comparing all these documents, and by completing them by each other that certain contemporary liturgiologists have endeavoured to reconstruct the Roman Mass in the seventh century. Such are Edmund Bishop, Atchley, Dom Wilmart, Mgr. Duchesne, Mgr. Batiffol, and Dom Jean de Puniet, whose works are mentioned in the Bibliography ; all having arrived at nearly the same results. Their reconstruction can therefore be accepted with confidence.

It should be added that this Mass is really that celebrated at Rome by the Pope during the great solemnities ; but it is also that of the Bishop in his cathedral, and that of the simple priest in his church, the number of ministers and clerics and the splendour of the ceremonies being always excepted ; there is no essential rite peculiar to the Pope. We shall describe it here in some detail, for if modifications have been brought in later,

[1] Cf. Lejay, *Le Liber Pontificalis et la Messe Romaine, Revue d'Hist et de Litt. religieuse*, Vol. II, p. 182 (1897).

the Mass has remained substantially the same, and in the following chapters on the Roman Mass from the seventh-twentieth centuries, we need only note what has been added or omitted. But the very fact that this is the Mass of the Pope and of his court explains any changes, for such a ceremony, in the presence of many Bishops and of a numerous assembly, could hardly remain unaltered. The *Liber Pontificalis* mentions several of the reforms which were made in it, but not all, since St. Gregory alone, as we know by his correspondence, made many alterations, of which the principal are : the introduction of the singing of the *Kyrie*, changes in that of the *Alleluia*, the alteration of the place of the *Pater*, important modifications of the Gelasian text, and probably of the chant. We must not, then, be astonished if the Roman Mass has conformed far less to the primitive form than the Mozarabic, Gallican, or Ambrosian Masses, and more especially the Eastern liturgies.

The Popes possessed an authority which allowed them to change any part of the ceremonial, and they used it.

THE STATION.—The faithful, according to an invitation which was given at a preceding assembly, met in a church, whence they went in procession to another church, called the Church of the Station. The word *statio* is old Latin, which in military language means a watch or vigil. Hermas and Tertullian have given it the Christian sense of prayer and fasting ; thus Wednesday and Friday are called *Station Days*, because they were days of fasting, on which Mass was celebrated. The word also means the plenary assembly of a church, and St Cyprian uses it in this sense. Finally it became a liturgical term at Rome, in the sense given above : that of a gathering of the faithful for the Papal Mass.[1]

[1] On all this, cf. Batiffol, *Leçons sur la Messe*, pp. 30, 31.

45

In the Roman missal we still find certain days designated in this way : *Statio ad Sanctum Petrum, Statio ad Sanctum Paulum,* etc. This means that on that day Mass was said at St. Peter's (of the Vatican), or at St. Paul's (Without the Walls), or at any other church mentioned. Such churches are the most ancient in Rome ; the greater number existed in the time of St. Gregory (end of the sixth century), and many are very much older.[1] In all this we have the elements of a little course of topography and Roman archæology ; and scholars like Armellini, Grisar, Morin, Schuster, and others have carefully described these venerable churches. Every day during Lent, and some other days in the year, have under the heading of the Mass some indication of this kind. This list, according to Mgr. Duchesne, goes back to the seventh century, but Dom Morin considers it originated two centuries earlier. The greater number of these churches exist to-day ; but the Station which in St. Gregory's time was so solemn a ceremony is now little more than a memory.

Sometimes Mass was celebrated in the catacombs on the outskirts of Rome, and this was especially the case on the anniversary days of the death of a martyr, when it was probably said on the tomb in which his relics reposed. But after the year 410, when Rome was taken by Alaric, these cemeteries were exposed to the incursions of the barbarians, and it became the custom to transport the bodies of the martyrs to churches in the interior of Rome.

The church where the Station was to take place was a *Basilica,* a great building inspired by architectural tradition as this was understood in the third and fourth centuries, but modified since by the Church for Divine

[1] The procession of the Station is described in the Excursus, p. 227.

service. Many of the most ancient Roman churches, such as St. Clement, St. Sabina, St. Laurence-Without-the-Walls, have preserved this form. And even those which have been altered again and again, like St. Paul-Without-the-Walls, have been reconstructed on the same plan. It was that of a long building with a central nave, separated by columns from two lateral naves to right and left, with an altar at the end and in the axis of the principal nave ; and behind the altar, an apse. At the end of the apse was the *cathedra*, or Bishop's chair, and, all around it, stalls for the clergy ; this was the choir. The part surrounding the altar is the sanctuary, with an *ambone*, or pulpit, or sometimes two, one to right, the other to left.

To-day, as the altar usually has a retable and a taber-nacle, the priest when standing before it turns his back to the people ; so that when he greets them with *Dominus vobiscum* he is obliged to turn round. The Bishop would be hidden on his *cathedra* at the back of the apse, and could hardly follow the ceremonies, therefore his throne, as well as the stalls of the clergy, have been moved to places before the altar. But if we wish to understand the ancient positions, it will help us to remember that at that time the altar was a *table* (hence its name of *mensa*) of wood or stone, forming either a solid block or else raised on four feet, but in any case without a tabernacle ; so that the officiating priest would face towards the people, as he does to-day at *San Clemente*. In our own churches, of course, he officiates on the other side of the altar ; the Gospel side being the left and that of the Epistle the right. As we explain elsewhere,[1] another consideration has brought about these changes : the practice of turning in prayer towards the East, the region of that light which is the image of Christ, Who

[1] See Excursus, *Liturgical Gestures*, p. 220.

Himself came from the East. The question of the orientation of churches was an important one in Christian architecture from the fourth-twelfth centuries.

In the catacombs the tomb of a martyr could be used as an altar. When, lest their relics should be profaned, the bodies of the martyrs had been brought from the cemeteries in the Roman *campagna* into the churches of the city, they were usually placed beneath the altar. In any case, the altar was henceforth a sacred object. The word *mensa* (table) recalled the Last Supper of the Lord ; it was an image of Calvary where Christ was sacrificed for us ; frequently it was a martyr's tomb ; upon it was accomplished the tremendous Eucharistic Mystery, and thus it was dear to the devotion of the faithful. The liturgy ordains that the priest shall kiss it at the beginning and during the course of Mass ; that he shall cover it with a *Corporal*, the image of that winding-sheet in which Our Lord was buried ; that he shall surround it with honour. All this was not instituted in the same detail during the earliest centuries, but it is a legitimate development of Catholic piety whose growth in intensity throughout the ages which followed we are now about to contemplate.

At the time we are now considering (seventh century) there were neither crosses nor candles, neither tabernacle or retable ; nor were there any of these things till the ninth, or even the eleventh, century.[1] But the *ciborium*, a kind of dome, or daïs, usually supported by four columns, was in use from the fourth century onwards, and sometimes at Rome it was made of precious metal. The marbles, mosaics, chandeliers, and candelabras, the lamps hanging from the vaulted roof and other ornaments in use from the time of Constantine, show us that the Church has come out of the catacombs, and that

[1] Mgr. Batiffol gives examples, *Leçons sur la Messe*, pp. 54, 55.

to primitive austerity has succeeded the desire to surround Divine worship with splendour, upheld by the generosity of Christians.

Let us return to the church where the faithful assembled, and whence they started in procession, with the clergy and all those holding ecclesiastical office up to the Pope himself, for the church where the Station was to be held.

THE LITANY. *The Kyrie Eleison.*—During the march of the procession they sang a prayer which resembles neither the Collects nor Prefaces ; which is neither an Anthem, a Responsory, a Tract, nor a Psalm, like those to be found in the Mass. It is a *Supplication,* as the Greek etymology indicates. A cantor, or perhaps the priest himself, said an invocation, which all the people repeated, or to which they responded by an acclamation. The most ancient memorial of this which we possess is the litany, which is said before the Mass of Holy Saturday.

At an early date (fourth century) Rome adopted the principal invocation of the Eastern liturgy, the *Kyrie Eleison* (Lord, have mercy upon us). But Rome added the *Christe Eleison,* and thus we have that chant to the Trinity with which in future all litanies were to begin :

> *Kyrie Eleison* (*thrice*)—*The Father ;*
> *Christe Eleison* (*thrice*)—*The Son ;*
> *Kyrie Eleison* (*thrice*)—*The Holy Ghost.*

The *Kyrie Eleison* is thus borrowed from the Greek liturgy, but marked with the seal of Rome. When St. Gregory was reproached for having introduced it into the Roman liturgy he could not deny the fact that he had done so, but he pointed out that he had modified its form. Among the Greeks it was sung by all ; at Rome it was sung by clerics, the people repeating the words after them (or, according to the correct expression, *responding*). Furthermore, says the Pope, the

D

people confine themselves to these acclamations at the daily Masses, while at others (probably at the stational Masses) other words are added. What are these words ? Other invocations, probably, such as we see in those litanies preserved to us, like that of Holy Saturday.

Apart from the Mass the litany was frequently used in processions and in the canonical office, and St. Benedict remarks this in the sixth century.[1]

THE INTROIT (Lat. *introire*, enter) is really the commencement of the Mass. It is a chant sung while the Pontiff proceeded solemnly from the sacristy to the church. It was usually sung by cantors, and as was customary for all psalms from the fourth century onwards, closed with a doxology, *Gloria Patri et Filio et Spiritui Sancto*. Our *Introits* have preserved but one verse of the psalm and the doxology. Sometimes the words are chosen from other books of Scripture than the Psalter ; they are even occasionally taken from the Apocryphal books. The Roman liturgy, usually so severe, shows itself accommodating upon this point. The *Accipite jucunditatem* of the Tuesday after Pentecost is taken from IV book of Esdras (apocryphal), which has also furnished the *Introit* for the Mass of the Dead, *Requiem æternam dona eis Domine*. That *Introit* of many Feasts, *Gaudeamus in Domino*, is also extra-scriptural ; while the *Salve Sancta Parens* of Masses of Our Lady is taken from Sedulius, a poet of the fifth century.

We have already said (p. 38, note) what must be thought of the text which attributes the introduction of the *Introit* to Pope Celestine (422–432). But its presence is noted in the Gelasian Sacramentary and in *Ordo Romanus I*.

[1] The question of the *Kyrie Eleison* and of the *Litany* have a certain importance in the history of the liturgy ; cf. DACL, arts. *Kyrie Eleison* and *Litanie*.

From this Mgr. Batiffol concludes that it is a Roman creation of the sixth century—at least, under the form described. One of St. Gregory's successors, Hadrian (772–795) attributes the composition, or at least the arrangement, of the Roman Antiphonary to the former Pope ; and tells us at the same time that this book began with *Ad Te levavi*, the first words of the Advent *Introit*. The Gelasian books began with the Feast of Christmas : the celebrated lines are as follows :

> *Gregorius præsul, meritis et nomine dignus,*
> *Unde genus ducit summum conscendit honorem.*
> *Renovavit monumenta patrum priorum.*
> *Tunc composuit hunc libellum musicæ artis*
> *Scolæ cantorum anni circuli : Ad Te levavi.*[1]

Elsewhere (Excursus, ii. p. 212) we shall speak of the music composed for the *Introit*. It is enough to say here that it has not preserved the characteristics of a processional chant any more than it has the primitive form of a psalm.

THE KISSING OF THE ALTAR.—At the Pontifical ceremony on Good Friday the prelate with his ministers leaves his throne at the beginning of the office, goes to the altar, kisses it, and returns to his place. This is an act of the most remote antiquity ; a mark of devotion to that altar which is sacred ; and which when the church was consecrated was blessed with so great solemnity. Mgr. Batiffol rightly reminds us that this act is peculiarly Roman (*loc. cit.*, p. 117). It is repeated many times during Mass (cf. Excursus, *Liturgical Acts*, p. 232).

THE GLORIA IN EXCELSIS.—At certain Masses, after the *Kyrie*, the *Gloria in Excelsis* is sung. It has no relation to the *Kyrie*, and is not sung or said in the ancient

[1] Cf. article *Introit* in DACL.

Masses for Vigils, nor in those of Holy Week, nor of
Lent, nor of ferials, and in reality its proper place is not
in the Mass any more than in any other office. Indeed,
at the beginning, it was not, as it is to-day, consecrated
to the Mass alone.[1] It is a doxology in honour of the
Father and the Son. The Holy Spirit only comes in at
the end ; and this is perhaps an addition. It is thus
very probably anterior to the fourth century, for from
the time of the Arian disputes the doxology was almost
always trinitarian.[2] This is confirmed by its presence in
the *Apostolic Constitutions*. It was early adopted by
Rome, with many other Greek formulas ; but, to begin
with, only at the first of the three Christmas Masses,
where its place is admirably justified.

Pope Symmachus extended its use to every Sunday
and to the Feasts of the martyrs ; but only for episcopal
Masses ; it was said by priests only at Easter. Then,
little by little, as was the way with so many other chants
and ceremonies, the reserves were done away with, and
its use became much more frequent. It is almost unnecessary to say that it is an admirable prayer ; that it
is the expression of a very beautiful mysticism, and that
it is of great Christological importance. It has been the
subject of many works, to which we can only refer.[3]

THE COLLECT.—The Pontiff arrived at the church to
the singing of litanies if there was a Station, or to that
of the *Introit* when the procession came from the sacristy.
He greeted the people, as St. Augustine has told us,
with the *Pax vobis*, or *Dominus vobiscum*, to which they
responded *Et cum spiritu tuo* ; after which the celebrant

[1] Cf. the article *Gloria in Excelsis* in DACL.
[2] Cf. our article *La doxologie dans la prière chrétienne des
premiers siècles*, in *Mélanges, Grandmaison, Recherches de science
religieuse*, 1928, Vol. XVIII.
[3] The list of these will be found in DACL, art. *Gloria in Excelsis*.

said a prayer of a very special nature, called the Collect. The general term is *oratio*. There are three of these prayers in the Mass—the first that just mentioned ; the second the *oratio super oblata*, or Secret ; and, lastly, the *oratio ad complendum*, or Post-Communion. The Collect is the *oratio prima*. As it was said at the moment when the faithful were assembling for Mass, some have thought that this was the origin of its name, *oratio ad collectam*, prayer at the moment of meeting. Others have thought it was derived from the fact that the celebrant here collects and expresses the intentions of all those present. The term is not exclusively Roman ; in the Gallican liturgies we find prayers called *collectiones*.

We have a large number of such prayers in the Roman missal. Their character is easily recognised, especially that of the most ancient, which are really of Roman origin, and which are distinguished by the clearness of their style, and the elegance and symmetry of their composition. Such is the following, chosen haphazard :

Deus qui ineffabilibus mundum renovas
sacramentis : praesta, quaesumus, ut Ecclesia
tua et aeternis proficiat institutis,
et temporalibus non destituatur auxiliis.
Per Dominum. . . .

(Friday of the fourth week in Lent).

The old Roman books, such as the Leonine, Gelasian, and Gregorian Sacramentaries contain a great number of these prayers, which are of equal interest from the literary and theological standpoints.

The character of these prayers in the Roman liturgy has been much praised ; they are always short, precise, elegant, and of a scholarly rhythm. Those of the other Latin liturgies, such as the Gallican and Mozarabic, are, on the contrary, much longer and more diffuse, clearly betraying a time when the Latin tongue was scarcely spoken except by the barbarians, and was falling into decadence.

We see that there was at that period no question of the prayers now said at the foot of the altar (Psalm xlii., the *Confiteor* and the rest). It was only later that these were added to the Mass (cf. Chapter IX). Not only, however, have we preserved the use of the Collects, but the greater part of them are very ancient, dating from the seventh and even from the fifth century. Originally there was only one Collect ; now we have often a sequence of several—memorials of another Feast, prayers to the Holy Ghost, to Our Lady, or for other intentions.

THE READINGS AND THE CHANTS (GRADUAL, ALLELUIA, TRACT, EPISTLE).—The *Collect* is followed by a reading or lesson from Holy Scripture (Old or New Testament) called the *Epistle*, because it is often taken from the Epistles of St. Paul. It was read from the pulpit by one of the ministers, usually a Lector. To-day it is reserved for the sub-Deacon. It is usually contained in a special book called the *Epistolary*. The most ancient of those copies, which have come down to us under the title of *Lectionaries*, go back to the eighth century, or to an even earlier epoch, that of the seventh century. In some ancient copies of the Bible these lessons are marked. The study of the *Lectionaries* is most useful for the right understanding of the liturgy.[1]

We have seen that in Africa (fourth and fifth centuries) there were sometimes three lessons—one from the Old Testament (Prophecy), one from the Epistles or Acts of the Apostles (Apostolic reading), and finally the Gospel. On certain days like vigils or the Ember Days we have several Lessons in the Roman Mass ; on the vigil of

[1] See *Books of the Latin Liturgy*, p. 32 *seq.*

Pentecost there are six ; on that of Easter, twelve. But these are exceptional cases, and these vigils were really night offices, each with their own special characteristics.

The custom in the Mozarabic and Gallican liturgies is to have three lessons—the Prophecy, the Apostolic Lesson, and the Gospel. It is also, though not without exceptions, the Eastern custom.

Liturgiologists have asked whether, at a certain epoch —say, before the fifth century—the Roman Mass had not also its three Lessons, of which the first was omitted later on. In any case, the reading of the Old Testament during Lent has taken the place of the Apostolic Lesson. With the three Lessons we can better understand a certain gradation in the form of the Pre-Mass—Old Testament, New Testament (from the Apostolic part), and, lastly, the Gospel, which in solemn Masses is surrounded with great solemnities. It has also been pointed out that in the Roman Mass the *Alleluia* follows the *Gradual*. Two consecutive chants are not according to the ancient and normal custom, in which a reading should be followed by a chant or responsory. The psalmody or singing of a psalm alternates with the reading. This would be another indication of the presence of three Lessons—the *Gradual* after the *Prophecy*, the *Alleluia* after the *Epistle*.

As a matter of fact, the *Gradual* to-day follows the *Epistle*, as also, according to circumstances, does the *Alleluia* or the *Tract*. The *Prose*, when there is one, follows the *Alleluia*, on which it originally depended.

The *Gradual* was thus styled at Rome because it was sung from the pulpit on the altar steps, *Gradus*. Its generic name is *Psalmus responsorius*, as St. Augustine tells us. This particular way of singing a psalm in responses differs from the Anthem. It was executed by a cantor, the choir answering with a refrain or *Response* taken from the same psalm. Our own *Gradual* has kept these general characteristics ; it is sung by a cantor, or a *schola*, the choir taking up part of the verse ; but the rest of the psalm has been suppressed. The *Gradual* is one of the chief elements of the Pre-Mass ; we have seen the importance attached to it by St. Augustine, who sometimes commented on it in his homilies, and regarded it as one of the Lessons. At Rome until the time of St. Gregory it was, like the Gospel, sung by a Deacon. St. Gregory, however, doubtless found some inconvenience attached to this practice, and withdrew this privilege from the Deacons. But the *Gradual* kept its place of honour among the chants of the Mass, while the singing of the Anthems *Introit, Offertory*, and *Communion*, which are, chronologically, later than the *Gradual*, was carried out by the *schola*, or by the people themselves, since these chants were instituted to occupy the faithful during the course of a procession.[1]

The *Alleluia* is a chant of a special character. Of Hebraic origin, like *Amen* and *Hosanna*, it was adopted by the Christians, and is found in the Apocalypse. It is frequently used, like the *Sanctus* and other acclamations ; but not at first in the Mass. The word means *Glory to God*, and often occurs in the Psalms, some of which are called *alleluiatic* for this reason. The time and occasion of its introduction into the Mass are not very well known. But the custom existed from the days of St. Augustine, who speaks of the *Jubilus*, a kind of prolonged *melopeia* on the last " *a* " of *Alleluia* ; but he does not say whether it was followed by a psalm, as it is to-day. It was chiefly sung on Easter Day and in Paschal time.

Sozomenus tells us that it was only sung at Rome on that day, but is his information accurate ? The real custom was to sing it during the whole of Paschal time.

[1] Cf. Excursus, *The Gregorian Chant*, p. 218.

And St. Gregory, again inspired by the Greek custom, extended its use beyond Paschal time, probably to every Sunday and Feast day of the year. Doubtless through its analogy with the *Gradual* a verse of Scripture was sung after it, but this verse is not always taken from the Psalter.

The *Alleluia* is omitted on vigils, on certain ferials, at the Office of the Dead, and from Septuagesima till Holy Saturday. In some countries in the Middle Ages this suppression of the *Alleluia* was marked by a ceremony called the *Burial of the Alleluia*, held on the Saturday before Septuagesima. It is needless to say that this ceremony was not observed in Rome, nor any others which appeared contrary to the austerity of the liturgy. Tropes, Proses, and the Mysteries which were derived from them did not originate in Rome. It was by no means at an early date, and even then, as it would seem, almost against her will, that she adopted four of the most beautiful of the Proses : *Victimæ pascali laudes, Veni Sancte Spiritus, Dies Iræ, Lauda Sion,* and much later, the *Stabat.*

But at the time of which we speak (fifth-seventh centuries) there was no question of these compositions. We shall speak of them in Chapter IX, and shall then see how they were attached to the *Jubilus* of the *Alleluia*. To-day, when the *Alleluia* is omitted, its place is taken by a much more ancient chant, the *Tract.*

The *Tract* (*Tractus*) is also rather obscure in its origin. What is certain is that the manner of its singing (it has no refrain nor is it repeated, hence its derivation from *tractim,* meaning *with a single stroke*) is of the highest antiquity. St. Benedict refers to it in his Rule, but in connection with the Office, in which it was probably used before its introduction into the Mass. In the Roman antiphonary it has preserved its original character better than the other chants; it is almost always a psalm, or at least several verses of a psalm, and even the tone to which it is sung recalls more faithfully its psalmodic origin.

THE GOSPEL.—The reading of the Gospel is the end of the Mass of the catechumens; in a certain sense it is its crown and fulfilment. This gradation observed between the reading of the Prophecy, that of the Epistle, and finally of the Gospel, is more marked, as we have noted, in certain other liturgies than in the actual Roman Mass; but, on the other hand, Rome has always surrounded the singing of the Gospel with great solemnities. The function was reserved for the Deacon, who was accompanied to the pulpit by acolytes bearing candles and incense, and the book was kissed by the celebrant. All that was the custom in St. Gregory's time; and this Roman practice is the same as that of the church of Jerusalem in the fourth century, as Etheria tells us. St. Benedict too, at the end of the fifth century, in the office for vigils (matins) for Sundays and Feast days, which he has so carefully composed, seems to have been inspired by the same principles and to follow the same lines as those of the Pre-Mass, with its singing of psalms, readings from the Old and New Testaments accompanied by responses, the *Te Deum*, and lastly the solemn reading of the Gospel. Those Gospels to be read at Mass at that time, as also to-day, were usually contained in a special book called the *Evangeliarium*. The richness of its binding, the perfection of the penmanship, and the beauty of the illumination of some of these books is a further proof of the devotion of Christians to the Gospel. As to this the *Ordo Romanus I*, which we are analysing here, tells us that the *Evangeliarium* used at the Papal Mass was enriched with jewels; and that in order that

these jewels should not be stolen it was enclosed in a
casket sealed with the seal of the *Vestararius*, and only
opened at the moment of the reading of the Gospel.

Another Roman custom of the eighth-twelfth centuries was that the Deacon reading the Gospel should
turn to the south, and not to the north, as he does to-day.

The *Credo* was neither read nor sung in the Roman
Mass until much later (see p. 129).

The dismissal of the catechumens and others outside
the fold customary in the fifth century, and which was
maintained much longer in some other liturgies, was
suppressed at Rome, probably in the sixth century.
The diaconal prayer at this juncture was also suppressed,
and the Mass of the catechumens closed with the reading
of the Gospel. But the Gallican, Mozarabic, and Celtic
liturgies have preserved this diaconal prayer which
formerly had its place in the Roman Mass (cf. p. 60).

THE MASS OF THE FAITHFUL

OFFERTORY.—It is still the custom for the celebrant
to turn towards the people after the Gospel and to say :
Dominus vobiscum, Oremus. This salutation is generally
followed by a prayer. Here, after this solemn announcement, the priest reads the Offertory and carries out
certain functions, but no prayer follows. Something
has evidently been suppressed here, and the anomaly
has naturally intrigued the liturgiologists. Mgr. Duchesne
thinks that the *Prayer of the Faithful* used to be in this
place, and this hypothesis has secured widespread ap-
proval. It is certainly specious, for that prayer had its
own place, and that an important one, in most of the
ancient liturgies. After the departure of the catechumens
and others outside the fold, who were not allowed to
assist at Mass, the faithful were invited to pray for

several intentions : the Church, The Pope, Bishops and other ministers, the Emperor, the sick, travellers, etc. This prayer is no longer found in the Roman Mass, but during Holy Week (since it is there that we must always seek the traces of the most ancient customs) we have in Good Friday's morning office certain solemn prayers which are nothing less than the *Prayer of the Faithful*, and which may be considered as one of the jewels of the Roman liturgy. Was it a prayer of this kind which was announced by the *Dominus vobiscum* and *Oremus* mentioned above ? It would certainly be possible, but another conjecture has been made, and this appears to be better founded. We may first remark that the *Prayer of the Faithful* has not entirely disappeared. The *Te igitur* recalls it, and sums up its principal features. Lastly, the Ambrosian, so near a neighbour of the Roman liturgy, has at this very place an *Oratio super sindonem* ; this linen cloth is the *Corporal*, which at this moment is placed upon the altar. The Roman Mass has the same ceremony, but of the prayer has only retained the *Dominus vobiscum* and *Oremus*. The Gelasian Sacramentary has also preserved traces of this prayer.[1]

At the Roman Mass, after the Deacon had spread the Corporal presented by the acolyte upon the altar, the Pope descended from his throne, and went to receive the offerings, those of the men first, the order of precedence being sedulously observed, according to Roman tradition. It may perhaps be said here that St. Benedict, who was very faithful to the Roman spirit and often draws his inspiration from the Roman liturgy of his day (sixth century), has a whole chapter, *De ordine congregationis*, in which he too insists on the order of precedence for the Kiss of Peace, the Communion, and for the whole choir office. After the men's offering came

---

[1] Ci. Bishop and Wilmart, *Le génie du rit romain*, p. 45.

that of the women, who occupied the other side of the nave, the congregation at that time being divided in two parts.

The offering was made in the following way : each person offered a small flagon of wine and a loaf ; the wine was emptied into a great chalice, and the bread placed in a white cloth held by two acolytes. It goes without saying that as yet there was no question of un-leavened bread ; that offered here is the usual leavened bread. This distinction between leavened and un-leavened did not then exist ; it was only much later, and especially about the eleventh century, that a quarrel, which in our own opinion was unnecessary, arose between the Eastern and Western churches on this subject.[1]

The most important thing to notice is that the offering as we have just described it is a Roman custom, also followed in Africa and at Milan. In the Gallican, Moz-arabic, and Greek liturgies the preparation of the offering was made before Mass.

After the offering had been made the Pope returned to his throne and washed his hands in preparation for the Sacrifice ; after which he went to the altar, where the oblations had been placed, the bread on one side, the chalice into which the wine had been poured on the other. Mgr. Batiffol aptly recalls a fresco at Ravenna, and also the famous chalice of Gourdon (sixth century), preserved in the Cabinet of Medals. A reproduction of the latter is given in DACL, at the word *calice*.

THE OFFERTORY CHANT.—All the time that this was going on—doubtless rather a long time—the *schola* had

[1] Naturally both sides have tried to support their contention by means of ancient texts and customs, and the number of theses written for and against unleavened bread is considerable. Cf. DACL, *Azymes*, and another article on the same subject in the *Dict. de théol. catholique*.

sung the *Offertory* psalm ; and when the Pope arrived at the altar he made a signal for the singing to stop, whether the psalm were finished or not. This *Offertory* chant, as well as those of *Introit* and *Communion*, had not, we repeat, the importance of the *Gradual*, which formed a whole apart ; the former might be interrupted or abridged without difficulty. If the *Introit* is a Roman creation of the sixth century, as Mgr. Batiffol declares, the *Offertory* and *Communion* chants are older, and were probably first instituted in the church of Carthage. We may remember that St. Augustine was obliged to write a book to defend this custom of chanting a psalm during the Oblation and the Communion.[1]

THE SECRET.—What, first of all, does this word mean ? More than any other it has given rise to discussions. Is it a substantive or an adjective ? Very naturally it has been compared with analogous terms like *Missa* for *Missio*, *Oblata* for *Oblatio*. Thus, it is asked, is not *Secreta* for *Secretio* ? Bossuet, who was the first to risk this interpretation, did so with circumspection ; the *Secretio*, or *separation*, meaning the separation of the oblations. Others have taken it to be an adjective qualifying the word *Oratio* understood ; thus it would mean a secret prayer, or one said in a low voice. Each interpretation presents serious difficulties. In our own opinion, and that of others, *Secreta* is a substantive synonymous with *Mysteria*. Thus we sometimes find the expression *Oratio super Secreta* ; and again, the whole canon is called *Secreta*, the *Mysteries*.[2]

At the epoch of which we are speaking this was the

[1] Cf. Batiffol, *op. cit.*, p. 151 *seq.*, and Excursus on *Chants of the Mass*, at the end of this volume, p. 212.

[2] On this great controversy of the *Secret des Mystères*, revived by the last vol. of the Abbé Bremond (Vol. IX), see Excursus, *The Chants of the Mass*.

only prayer made over the oblations, *super oblata*. The Offertory prayers in the present Missal, *Suscipe sancte Pater* and the rest (cf. p. 174), are of more recent introduction, and probably of Gallican origin. There was then no question of censing the *oblata* at Rome. Doubtless at the *Introit* and the *Gospel* a golden censer was carried (*thymiamaterium aureum*), but this was merely a vase of perfume which was not used for censing ; it was not the *thuribulum*. This custom is of Gallican origin, and was not introduced at Rome until after the eleventh century.[1]

The *Secret*, the only *Offertory* prayer, had thus at that time a special importance ; and its formulas should be carefully studied in our Missal. In its composition, and it may be said in its functions, it corresponds to the *Collect* and the *Post-communion*. Each of the three, as the principal prayers of the Roman Mass, has its own *rôle*, but all three correspond ; they are fashioned in the same mould and follow the same laws of composition and rhythm. Attention has often been called to the sobriety, simplicity, firmness, and elegance of the purely Roman style, which has so well preserved the chief qualities of the best classical manner. These characteristics will be noted all the more clearly if we compare these prayers with the corresponding composition of the other Latin liturgies, of which some examples are quoted in Chapters VI and VII. But what is especially remarkable is less the literary quality than the depth and certainty of the teaching given us in these Roman prayers. Here, above all, appear the mastery and the superiority of the liturgy of that Church which is Mother and Mistress. To speak only of the *Secrets*, we find that more than one

[1] On the whole of this question cf. also Mgr. Batiffol, who shows the difference between these two terms very well (*loc. cit.*, p. 155) ; cf. also DACL, *Encens*.

affirms the faith of the Roman Church in Transubstantiation ; and Bossuet has made good use of this fact against the Protestants in his explanations of the prayers of the Mass.

THE PREFACE.—The adoption of the *Sanctus* as well as other circumstances have led the Roman and the other Churches, both Greek and Latin, to divide into several parts that Eucharistic prayer which, in the second and third centuries, forms a single uninterrupted whole up to the final doxology (before the *Pater*) (cf. p. 67).

The first part of this Eucharistic prayer has become what is called at Rome the *Preface, Præfatio* (a word in use at Rome from the sixth century, and already mentioned at the Council of Carthage in 407). It was a general term, meaning rather a prayer or blessing than an introduction, in the sense the word is used to-day. There are *Prefaces* for the blessing of fonts and of the holy oils, and for ordinations. The *Exultet* at the blessing of the Paschal Candle is also a *Preface*.

That it was an improvised prayer the great number of its formulas would prove. Many of these date back to the fourth century. The Leonine Sacramentary contains a rich collection of *Prefaces*, many of which bear the stamp of their time and allude to contemporary events (fourth-fifth centuries). The Gelasian has also a large number, but the Sacramentary of St. Gregory accepted only eleven, to which were added later (eleventh century) the *Preface* of Our Lady, and in our own day that of the Dead, one for St. Joseph, one for Christ the King, and another for the Sacred Heart.

All these *Prefaces* present the same general characteristics ; they begin with the same protocol ; they are addressed to God the Father Almighty through Jesus Christ Our Lord. On this point the *Preface* is not distinguished from the *Collects* and other Roman prayers. But it has greater scope; it refers to the Feast which is being celebrated, or even to contemporary events (as in the Leonine), or to the blessing about to take place (baptismal fonts, ordinations, Paschal Candle, etc.). At Mass the *Preface* always closes with a formula leading to the *Sanctus*.

The Roman *Preface* is composed with the same care and according to those same rules of the *Cursus* as are the *Collects* and other prayers. These *Prefaces* are usually as remarkable for their workmanship as for their theological teaching, as, for example, that for the Holy Trinity and that for Christmas. If our present aim were to comment on the prayers of the Mass, it would be necessary to pause here for some time to underline the importance of the *Prefaces* of our Missal, of the *Communicantes* which on certain days accompany them, and to compare them with the *Illationes* or *Contestationes* of other Latin liturgies, notably with those of the Mozarabic rite, which are sometimes actual theological treatises or biographies of Martyrs and Saints.

THE SANCTUS.—The *Sanctus*, like the *Gloria in Excelsis*, the *Te decet laus* and other chants, goes back to the most ancient Christian antiquity. It is in reality taken from the Old Testament, from Isaias. It must have been in use at other times than in the Mass, as we see by a quotation from Tertullian, and by the Acts of SS. Perpetua and Felicitas. Its introduction into the actual Eucharistic prayer towards the fifth century, or even before it, has somewhat modified the form of the latter by dividing it into several parts. It exists in two forms: in the Eastern Church the *Sanctus* is usually read as it exists in the text of Isaias. Rome, however, added to these words the second part: *Benedictus qui venit in nomine*

Domini, the words sung by the multitude at Jerusalem to welcome the Messiah on Palm Sunday. The other Latin liturgies have followed Rome in this custom, and this again is a point on which all these liturgies betray their unity.

THE ROMAN CANON.—The word *Canon, Canon Missæ* in our Missal, is the title of all the prayers which follow the *Sanctus*. No other indication is furnished in the Missal to show where the *Canon* ends, and it would seem to continue till the Last Gospel inclusively. But according to a text of St. Gregory which we shall quote in connection with the *Pater*, and also in accordance with other witnesses, the *Canon* really ends with the solemn doxology which precedes the *Pater*, or at the *Fraction*. The word χανών signifies *rule*; the meaning here is that this is an official prayer, one established by an invariable rule.

Pope Vigilius indeed, in 538, in a text already quoted, remarks that at Rome, contrary to what prevailed elsewhere, this prayer never varies except on certain Feast days, such as Christmas, Epiphany, etc.

The word *Canon* is Roman. In the East the corresponding prayer is called the *Anaphora*, from ἀναφερῶ, I offer. In the Gelasian Sacramentary the word *Actio* is applied to this part of the Mass. It is the supreme *action*, and *agere, agenda* are taken in the same sense. We even have in our existing *Canon* the terms *Infra actionem*, during the action, which recall the ancient word *actio*.[1]

To-day it comprehends the following prayers :

Te igitur ;
Memento of the Living ;
Hanc igitur ;
Quam oblationem ;

---

[1] Cf. our article *Actio* in DACL.

THE MASS AT ROME

Qui pridie ;
Unde et memores ;
Supra quæ ;
Supplices Te ;
Memento of the Dead ;
Nobis quoque ;
Per quem ;
Pater, with prelude and embolism.

This very division of the *Canon* into a dozen prayers, which often are not correlated would in itself be enough to reveal a fragmentary state by no means primitive. Indeed we shall see that, whatever be the antiquity of such and such a formula, the Roman *Canon* as a whole goes back but to a date about the year 400.

The *Canon* corresponds with the most ancient of the Eucharistic prayers as this is described by St. Justin in the second century or at the beginning of the third by St. Hippolytus. It is a prayer with a single inspiration, beginning with the *Dominus vobiscum* or *Sursum corda* of the *Preface*, continuing with the recital of the Institution, and ending after a doxology with the *Amen* of the faithful. These are the true limits of the *Canon* ; they are at least the most ancient.

Great is the temptation both for archæologists and liturgiologists to try whether it be not possible to re-constitute the Roman *Canon* in its primitive form, and to give it a more logical, more homogeneous sequence. To this many have yielded, and in our article *Canon* (DACL) we have mentioned the chief attempts which have been made in this direction. They will also be found in Fortescue's book ; and, since his time, other hypotheses have been presented for consideration.

It is discouraging that each critic has a different system, and that none, we may say, has arrived at a really definite result. We may safely disregard such study, and take the Roman *Canon* just as it is ; remarking that its actual form is assuredly not primitive, and what we may call the joins are clearly shown by certain signs which will be pointed out in the consideration of each of these prayers.

Nevertheless, whatever be the variety of the sources whence its compiler has drawn it up, the composition as a whole betrays itself as the work of a single hand. That *scholasticus* of whom St. Gregory speaks with some disdain has certain methods in his style which Brinktrine, I think, was the first to point out. First of all, the use of two parallel terms :

> *rogamus ac petimus,*
> *accepta habeas et benedicas*
> *catholicæ et apostolicæ fidei*
> *sanctas ac venerabiles*
> *respicere et accepta habere*
> *sanctum sacrificium immaculatam hostiam*
> *partem aliquam et societatem*
> *de tuis donis ac datis*
> *famulorum famularum que tuarum,*
> *quorum tibi fides cognita est et nota devotio,*
> *pro quibus tibi offerimus vel qui tibi offererunt :*

(this last passage, it is true, is no doubt an addition)

> *servitutis nostræ . . . et cunctæ familiæ tuæ,*
> *rationabilem acceptabilemque*
> *omnis honor et gloria*
> *non æstimator meriti sed veniæ largitor.*

A tendency to triplicate the terms :

> *hæc dona, hæc munera, hæc sancta sacrificia,*
> *hostiam puram, hostiam sanctam, hostiam immaculatam.*

The sacrifice of the three Patriarchs—Abel, Abraham, Melchisedech :

> *per ipsum, cum ipso, in ipso,*
> *passionis, resurrectionis, ascensionis.*

The accumulation of five terms :

> *benedictam, adscriptam, ratam, rationabilem, accepta-*
> *bilem,*
> *creas, sanctificas, vivificas, benedicis, præstas.*

Other similar remarks could be made on the characteristics of this style. But these are sufficient to prove that we have to do with a writer who loves prose that is rhythmical, measured, symmetrical, and occasionally rhymed.[1]

Another question arises with respect to the *Canon* : Has it an *epiclesis*, and, if so, what is its place ? The *epiclesis* (ἐπικλέω, I call) is a prayer of invocation to the Holy Ghost to sanctify the gifts offered. Its place is generally among the prayers which follow the Consecration ; and some of these formulas indeed declare it is to the virtue of the Holy Ghost and not to the words of the Institution that the miracle of Transubstantiation is due. Many liturgiologists say with Edmund Bishop that there is no *epiclesis* in the Roman Mass. Others, like certain Anglican divines, count it a crime of the Roman Church to have cut it out. Others again recognise the Roman *epiclesis* in such and such a prayer before or after the Consecration. Let us say there is no *epiclesis* in the Roman Mass in the ordinary sense of the word ; but that this does not mean there has never been one.[2]

Te igitur.—In our Missal this is the first prayer of the *Canon* ; it does not close with a doxology like all Roman

---

[1] Brinktrine, *Die Heilige Messe*, p. 198, has done little more than indicate this aspect of the *Canon*, but a philologist might draw most interesting comparisons from it.

[2] Cf. our article *Epiclèse* in DACL.

prayers, and seems, if one may say so, sharply interrupted by the *Memento* of the Living. Yet it is an
admirable prayer, on all the terms of which it would be
easy to comment. But we can only refer to the writers
quoted in the Bibliography, whose aim is to explain all
the prayers of the Mass. By a simple comparison with
the *Prayer of the Faithful* we can see that it is inspired
with the most beautiful traditions of Christian antiquity.
The mention of the Pope first of all is not due merely to
the fact that this prayer was originally compiled at
Rome and for Rome ; it was an established use in most
churches to pray for the Pope, and also for the Bishops
with whom they were in communion.

Memento of the Living.—This is composed of the
Memento proper and of the *Communicantes*, which ends
with a doxology. The very place of the *Memento* in the
Canon forbade the mention here of those for whom the
Mass was being offered, which in other liturgies is made
in an audible voice. In those chapters devoted to these
liturgies we shall see the importance given to the reading
of the Diptychs (Chapters VI and VII ; see also our
article *Diptyques* in DACL).

The *Communicantes*, beginning as it does with a participle, is a phrase without a verb which it has been vainly
tried to explain. This would incline us to adopt the
opinion of those who consider that it should be attached
to the *Te igitur*, from which it must once have been
separated, or to another prayer. In any case the list of
names given in it is very interesting. First of all Saint
Mary the Virgin with her titles, *semper virginis, genetricis
Dei*, which takes us back to the time of discussions on
the perpetual virginity or the Divine maternity of Our
Lady (end of fourth century and Council of Ephesus,
431). Next comes a list of the Apostles, which puts
St. Paul beside St. Peter, and which may be compared

with the other lists of Apostles found in the New Testament, which differ in many points from the Roman list. (DACL, *Apôtres*.)

Following the twelve Apostles come twelve Roman martyrs, specially honoured in that city ; five Popes ; St. Cyprian placed close to St. Cornelius, his presence indicating that the old quarrels between him and that Pope are forgotten. Then St. Laurence, the great Roman martyr ; St. Chrysogonus, more obscure, but whose name is well known at Rome and whose Basilica is mentioned in the sixth century ; John and Paul, whose Basilica on the Cœlian is celebrated ; and, lastly, Cosmas and Damian, with a great reputation in the East and at Byzantium, after whom Pope Felix IV (526–530) named a Basilica at Rome, and to whom Pope Symmachus had already dedicated an oratory. From these and other indications Mgr. Batiffol concludes very ingeniously, and not without reason, that the *Communicantes* dates from this last-named Pope (498–514). Nevertheless, it may be objected to this that certain names in this list may perhaps have been added later.

Attention has already been called to the words *Infra actionem* which form the title of the *Communicantes*, and to the alternative *Communicantes* used on certain Feasts.

Hanc igitur oblationem is to-day recited while the priest is holding his hands spread out over the oblations ; which has led some to believe that we have here the Roman *epiclesis*. But nothing in the words of the prayer show this. Moreover, this imposition of the hands is not of ancient date, and would seem to be only a gesture designating the matter which is to serve for the Sacrifice. The *Liber Pontificalis* says that St. Gregory added to this text the *Diesque nostros* with what follows it. In the existing Missal there is an alternative *Hanc igitur*, the words of which are the same for Easter and Pentecost, reminding us that on these two Feasts Baptism was given to the catechumens. But in the Gelasian Sacramentary a large number of variants to the *Hanc igitur* existed—nearly fifty; which St. Gregory suppressed when he re-edited the book. All these variants are interesting, though we cannot study them here in detail.[1] The prayer to-day closes with a doxology, after the words added by St. Gregory; but in some of the variants this did not exist, and the *Hanc igitur* is united to the following prayer :

Quam oblationem ; this might easily have been attached to the *Hanc igitur*, of which it seems a continuation. Some liturgiologists consider this prayer as the *epiclesis*. To this opinion the same objections may be sustained as in the case of the *Hanc igitur*, for it is not an *epiclesis* in the true sense of the term, since there is no invocation of God the Holy Ghost. The signs of the Cross, here so frequent, are intended (as also in the *Te igitur*) rather to emphasise the words of the prayer than as a blessing. (See Excursus, *Gestures in the Mass*, p. 220.)

THE CONSECRATION.—With the *Qui pridie* we come to the really central and essential part of the Roman Mass. It is not only the recital of the Eucharistic Institution, reproducing the actions and the very words of Our Lord at the Last Supper ; it is a prayer which completes the preceding prayers ; its aim is really to work the Mystery of Transubstantiation just as it was accomplished by the actual words of Christ on the eve of His Passion. It would be easy to prove it, but it is enough to refer our readers to a chapter of Mgr. Batiffol's book on the Eucharist, *Saint Ambroise et le Canon Romain*.[2]

[1] See especially the conclusions drawn by Mgr. Batiffol, p. 231 *seq*.

[2] Pp. 335–370. We note with pleasure that in this chapter the author refers many times to the work of Dom Cagin, *Eucharistia*, where may be found, in a rather more complicated form, a learned explanation of all this part of the Mass.

THE MASS AT ROME

We can only, as before, make a few remarks on the text. First of all we notice that, if the words used follow the story of the synoptic Gospels, they do not reproduce it literally. The *sanctas ac venerabiles manus suas* repeated in both Consecrations is not in the Gospel. Nor are the words, *pro nostra omniumque salute pateretur*, said on Holy Thursday. It has been thought that these are additions made in the fifth century, against pre-destinationists.[1] The *Mysterium fidei* is also an addition not yet satisfactorily explained. But with many exegetists the tendency on the contrary is to discover in the Gospel text the influence of ritual practices existing previous to the compilation of the Gospels.[2]

The other Latin liturgies are in agreement with the Roman Church in beginning this recital with the words *Qui pridie* ; while the Greek and Eastern rites follow the text of St. Paul : *In qua nocte*. This agreement of the Latin liturgies on so important a point is no feeble argument in favour of the division made in Chapter II between Eastern and Western liturgies.[3]

Another and even more essential divergence between East and West is this : if it is clear that the liturgies of the latter group, headed by the Church of Rome, teach by this importance given to the recital of the Institution that the Consecration of the bread and wine takes place at this moment, it is also true that in certain Eastern liturgies the text of some of the *epicleses*, which are placed after the Consecration, seems to mean that the Mystery of Transubstantiation is,

[1] Dom Morin, *Une particularité inaperçue du qui pridie*, in *Revue Bénédictine*, 1910, p. 513 *seq.* Cf. also on the words *novi et æterni testamenti* (in the formula of Consecration), *Rassegna Gregoriana*, 1903, Vol. II, p. 190 *seq.*

[2] Brinktrine in particular adopts this opinion.

[3] This is a fact upon which Dom Cagin has thrown a strong light in *Paléographie musicale*, Vol. V.

according to them, wrought by the virtue of God the Holy Ghost.[1]

Who can refuse to see the true bearing of this difference and, from the dogmatical point of view, to admit the advantages of the Roman compilation?

Unde et memores, Supra quæ, Supplices Te.—We may consider these three prayers of the *Canon* as forming a single whole, especially as they end with a single doxology. The technical name of this whole is *anamnesis*, because according to the Greek etymology it *recalls* the different Mysteries associated with the Sacrifice of Our Lord; His Passion, Death, Descent into hell, Resurrection, and Ascension. It is thus the history of our redemption summed up in a few words.

It has a mysterious sense not always understood, and which we must try to explain. It is the real meaning of the Mystery of the Mass. We, servants of God and His holy people, offer to God a pure, holy, spotless Host, the blessed Bread of Eternal Life and the chalice of Eternal Salvation. There can be no doubt, whatever may have been said by certain Protestant interpreters, that in this we must see that the elements have become the Body and Blood of Christ, as is said in the prayer *Supplices Te: the Body and the Sacrosanct Blood of the Son of God.*

The *De tuis donis ac datis* is found in analogous terms in other liturgies, notably in the Eastern. It contains a profound meaning. It is a thought often expressed in the Old Testament, especially in the Psalms, that all that he has, man holds from God, who created the world to be his domain: the rain from the skies which waters the earth, plants and the fruits of trees, animals, birds,

[1] Cf. also Mgr. Batiffol, *L'Eucharistie*, p. 371 *seq.*, and the two articles already mentioned on *Epiclèse* in DACL and *Dict. de théol. cath.*

fish—all these are subject to man, *omnia subjecisti sub pedibus ejus.* Of this universe God constituted him the king. Hence man has laid on him a strict duty to worship God by praise and sacrifice. In offering Him the fruits of the earth, or animals, he only, as it were, performs a work of restitution ; he offers that which he has received, *hostiam de tuis donis ac datis.* This is specially true of that Sacrifice which has supplanted all the rest, where the Victim pure and holy above all others is offered, the Son Whom the Father sent to save man. Thus we offer our sacrifice to the Father, praying Him to accept it as He did those of Abel, of Abraham, of Melchisedech, types of the One True and Complete Sacrifice ; that He will transport it by the hands of His *Holy Angel* to His Divine Throne ; and that all those who have partaken of the Body and Blood of Christ may be filled with His Benediction and Grace.

It is a mysterious prayer, as has been said, and it has given rise to many interpretations. Besides that of those who, deceived by the simplicity of the expressions, have misunderstood the lofty bearing of the whole, and thus failed to see anything more than an earthly sacrifice and earthly gifts, previous to a Consecration which according to them did not take place at the *Qui pridie,* or of others who suppose that one or other of these prayers formerly preceded the recital of the Last Supper and is thus included in the zone of the *Offertory,* there is another difficulty : that of the intervention of the *Holy Angel.* Some take this to mean the Holy Spirit ; others, the Word Himself, the *Angel of Great Counsel.* But for the largest number a mere Angel is here meant ; perhaps St. Michael, the *Angel of the Sacrifice.* However, the text of *De Sacramentis,* already quoted (p. 39), decides this question clearly by putting the plural, *Angelorum Tuorum.* It must also be remembered that in certain prayers of the Roman liturgy mention is made of the *Holy Angel* sent by God, who is not the Word. But, on the whole, the meaning of this *anamnesis* can be compared without much difficulty with certain ancient *anaphoræ*, notably with that of Hippolytus, which joins the Eucharistic prayer to the *epiclesis* and calls down the blessing of God upon those about to partake of the Body and Blood of Christ. Thus we have here an echo of the most ancient Eucharistic traditions.

The *Memento of the Dead*, following the *anamnesis*, is surprisingly placed. This prayer has all the characteristics of a later insertion—a statement difficult to deny. To find it in this particular place is unexpected ; nor is it announced by anything which goes before.

The *Nobis quoque* which comes after it is not less astonishing. But the apparent incoherence is explained by those who admit that this *Memento* is an addition subsequent even to the time of St. Gregory. It was at least not said primitively (or so it would seem), except in Masses for the Dead. Numerous examples of Sacramentaries or Missals in which the Mass does not contain this addition are mentioned by Dom Cagin, Ed. Bishop, Batiffol, and others.

It is really the Diptych of the Dead, just as we have had the Diptych of the Living before the Consecration ; the natural place of both being in most liturgies, at the *Offertory*.[1] However this may be, the text of the prayer itself is none the less interesting. In the *locum refrigerii, lucis et pacis* the proof is clear that some of the Dead, in their place of waiting, do not yet enjoy those blessings which were asked for them, and this again proves the belief in Purgatory.

The list of fifteen names mentioned in the *Nobis quoque peccatoribus* has, like that of the *Memento of the*

[1] Cf. our article *Diptyques* in DACL.

76

Living, been studied wisely by Mgr. Batiffol, who arrives at the same result in both cases : he believes this prayer to have been drawn up under Pope Symmachus (498–514). We find here the Roman Martyr St. Alexander, a son of that other Roman Martyr, St. Felicity, whose tomb that Pope restored ; and Agnes of Rome, whose Basilica in the city he restored from its ruins ; and St. Agatha, Martyr of Catania, for whom Symmachus built a Basilica on the Aurelian Way. Besides these Saints we have St. John (Baptist), who is at the head of all the lists of Saints, and whose absence here in the Mass might have caused surprise ;[1] St. Stephen, the first Martyr, whose presence is not less justified ; SS. Matthias and Barnabas, whom we were less likely to expect to find here, but who complete the list of the Apostles given in the *Memento of the Living*, for Matthias took the place of Judas in the Apostolic College, and Barnabas is frequently attached to it by a special title.

Then follows St. Ignatius, the great Martyr thrown to the wild beasts in the amphitheatre of Rome ; Marcellinus and Peter, two Roman Martyrs, buried in the catacomb *Ad duas Lauros* ; St. Perpetua, one of the group of the great Martyrs of Carthage ; St. Lucy, a Sicilian Martyr always connected with St. Agatha ; and, lastly, three more Roman Martyrs, Agnes and Cecilia, both well known, and Anastasia, titular of a church in Rome, who at that time was also an object of popular devotion.[2] Discussions have latterly arisen as to the name of St. Felicity. At first sight the name Perpetua, which immediately follows, would lead us to believe that she was that Felicity who suffered martyrdom in company with

[1] The *Suscipe Sancta Trinitas*, where he is also mentioned, is of later date.

[2] On these churches see the works of P. Grisar, already mentioned, and Charles Dumaine, *Les saints du canon de la Messe*, Paris, 1920.

Perpetua. But when everything is taken into consideration it seems that here it is rather a question of the Roman Martyr, mother of seven other Martyrs, of whom St. Alexander was one.[1]

Per Quem hæc omnia.—After the two prayers of the *Memento of the Dead* we have next the *Per Quem*, as unexpected in this place as they themselves in theirs, and a *crux* for liturgiologists. Without going through all the various interpretations of this text, let us simply say that *Per Quem* seems to have been inserted here to make a transition between the close of the *Memento of the Dead*, which already broke into the Eucharistic prayer, and the final doxology of the *Canon, Per Ipsum.*

Hence we must not be too much surprised at the terms of this prayer, which is really but the close of another ; nor must we seek to explain its bearing too strictly. The *Hæc omnia*, which has always been a difficulty, originally designed in this prayer (whatever was the place it then occupied) all the gifts offered by the faithful, not excepting those supreme Gifts which are the Body and Blood of Christ.

But we must insist on the doxology which issues from these difficulties, and takes us up to a very high level. As has been seen already in the texts of SS. Justin and Hippolytus, the Eucharistic prayer of the second and third centuries ended with a doxology to which the people responded *Amen.* This was a solemn act of Faith in the whole Eucharistic Mystery just unfolded before their eyes. Therefore this doxology is clothed with importance and unaccustomed solemnity, as it should be. It is first an act of Adoration to the Trinity in Whom and by Whom the Mystery is accomplished. It is also a formula admirably summing up the whole of

[1] In recent times many articles have been written on this question, particularly one by Burkitt in the *Journal of Theol. Studies*, 1931, p. 279 *seq.*

Christian worship : Glory and honour rendered to the
Father, by the Son, in the Holy Ghost. The gestures
added later to this doxology still further emphasise its
dignity. At the *Per Quem hæc omnia* the celebrant has
taken the Host and the chalice ; then with the prescribed signs of the Cross he uncovers the chalice, takes
the Host in his right hand to make with it the sign of the
Cross thrice above the chalice and twice before it, after
which he elevates chalice and Host. *Elevans parum*,
says the rubric ; for this Elevation, once not merely the
principal but the only one in the Mass, has become
secondary since the great Elevation has taken place after
the Consecration.[1] The signs of the Cross, multiplied
here, are not intended as blessings, since these would not
be suitable over the consecrated elements ; but rather
symbols to remind us of the Mystery of our Redemption
with the Mystery of the Trinity, which to-day is the
true meaning of the Sign of the Cross.[2]

THE FRACTION AND *PATER*.—Before St. Gregory's day
the Fraction took place before the *Pater*. Dom Cagin
even thinks that the *Per Quem hæc omnia* was the primitive form of the Fraction in the Roman Mass.[3] What is
certain is that St. Gregory here introduced another considerable change ; he himself tells us why and how he
did it, in a well-known and much-discussed text, upon
which it would seem that most are agreed to-day. Thus,
before St. Gregory, the order was : after the prayers
Per Quem hæc omnia and *Per Ipsum* the Fraction, a
rather complicated ceremony, took place. After that
the prelate regained his seat and said the *Pater*. To
St. Gregory this appeared shocking. To the Bishop of

[1] See our article *Elévation* in DACL.
[2] On the Sign of the Cross see Excursus, *Gestures in the Mass*,
p. 220.
[3] *Eucharistia*, p. 57.

Syracuse he wrote emphatically : " It does not seem to me decent that we say the *Pater after* the prayer of the *Canon (post precem)*, for we say that prayer, composed by some writer *(scholasticus)*, over the oblation (the Body and Blood of Our Lord), while we do not say over that Body and Blood the prayer *(Pater)* composed by Our Redeemer Himself. For it was the custom of the Apostles to consecrate with that prayer."[1] Light is thrown on this text if we remember that during the Fraction the Pontiff regained his seat, and thus did not say the *Pater*, as he did the other prayers of the *Canon*, over the Body and Blood of Christ. By putting the *Pater* before the Fraction, as it is to-day, it is said over the consecrated elements. What St. Gregory does not say in this letter is that there really were two customs about the *Pater*. In its primitive place, after the Fraction and connected with the Communion, it was a kind of preparation for the latter ; and the words *Panem nostrum quotidianum* may well apply to the Bread Supersubstantial, as it is sometimes called, which was then received. This was the custom in Africa as it was at Rome and in other churches. But in the Greek churches this was not so ; and the *Pater* formed part of the prayers of the *Canon*. St. Gregory, who had been a witness of this practice, wished to transport it, like the *Kyrie*, into the Roman Mass. It would seem as though the Bishop of Syracuse had accused the Pope of following the Greek custom too easily. St. Gregory defends himself, as he had about the use of the *Kyrie*, by saying in this case that among the Greeks the *Pater* is recited at Mass by all the people, while at Rome the celebrant alone said it (just as to-day) ; while the people responded : *Sed libera nos a malo*.

---

[1] On the different interpretations given to this difficult and obscure text, cf. Batiffol, *Leçons*, p. 277, and *L'Eucharistie*, p. 352.

From this text two other conclusions are sometimes drawn : that the *Pater* was not said at the Roman Mass and that it was St. Gregory who introduced it there ; and that the Pope's idea was that the Apostles consecrated the bread and wine by the Lord's Prayer alone. These two assertions cannot be discussed here, but both seem to us equally erroneous. It is very difficult to believe that the *Pater* was not recited in Mass at Rome at the end of the sixth century, when this use was that of all other churches ; would not St. Jerome or St. Augustine have pointed out this fact ? The text of St. Gregory's letter, moreover, does not allow us to suspect it.

As to the prayer used by the Apostles in Consecration, we may say that St. Gregory knew what it was no more than we ourselves.[1]

The *Pater* is preceded by a short prelude and followed by an intercalation ; both are invariable in the Roman liturgy, while in Gaul and Spain they changed at almost every Mass. Both are characteristic of the universal liturgy, especially of the Latin liturgies. The Roman prelude is very simple ; it would seem to be indicated by an expression of St. Jerome. The embolism, or intercalation, is a commentary on the last petition : *libera nos a malo*. Here the name of Our Lady is invoked with all Her titles, *Beata et gloriosa semper virgine Dei Genitrice Maria*, as in the *Memento of the Living*, then the great patrons of the Roman Church, Peter and Paul. The name of St. Andrew, alone mentioned among all the other Saints, has caused it to be supposed with reason that its insertion here is due to St. Gregory, whose

---

[1] On this point we may be allowed to refer to our articles on the *Pater*, *Revue Grégorienne*, May–June, September–October 1928 ; January–February 1929 ; cf. also Bishop–Wilmart, *Le génie du rit romain*, p. 84 *seq*.

monastery on the Cœlian was dedicated to St. Andrew. In other places the name of St. Ambrose was added, that of St. Patrick, and other popular patrons.

At the words *Da propitius pacem* the priest to-day signs himself with the paten and kisses it before slipping it beneath the Host. This gesture must be interpreted by the rites of the Papal Mass, of which it is now but a memory. The paten, with the chalice, is one of the most important vessels used in the service of the Mass. Like the chalice it is usually made of precious metal, generally silver ; both are consecrated with special prayers. In certain museums ancient and priceless patens are preserved, like that of Gourdon, or the glass paten of Cologne. At present the paten has lost some of its attributes, and thoroughly to understand the ceremonies of which it is the object (especially at Solemn Masses) we must go back to the ancient rites. At the Papal Masses the paten, or patens, were confided to the sub-Deacon. The *Sancta* (Eucharistic Species) consecrated at a previous Mass were received and preserved on it, until the moment of Communion, when the Pope placed the Sacred Species in his chalice, as a sign of the perpetuity of the Sacrifice. The rites of the *Sancta* and of the *Fermentum* have now been dropped, but some of the attendant ceremonies have been preserved. At Solemn Masses to-day the sub-Deacon has charge of an empty paten, which he covers with a veil. At the end of the *Pater* he passes it to the Deacon, who in his turn carries it to the Priest, who, at the words *Da propitius pacem*, signs himself with the paten and kisses it, as already stated. This ceremonial is observed even at Low Masses. The celebrant makes the Fraction upon the paten, first dividing the Host into two parts, and then putting a fragment of one part into the chalice with the words *Hæc commixtio*. Thus the two rites of the *Fraction* and the *Immixtion* are still closely united, or, as it might be called, confounded in one rite. That of the *Pax* itself has come to be incorporated in the rite of the *Fraction*, for it is with the words *Pax* † *Domini sit* † *semper vobis* † *cum* that the Priest proceeds to the *Immixtion*. In the Papal Mass they were clearly separated, as will be seen.

FRACTION, IMMIXTION, KISS OF PEACE.—The Breaking of Bread by Our Lord at the Last Supper had so impressed itself upon their minds that two of the disciples recognised Him by the way He broke the bread ; and for a long time the words *Fractio Panis* meant the Mass. At Rome, during the period we are now considering, the ceremonies were resplendent, but in our own days many have been retrenched. Moreover, there is no doubt that St. Gregory's innovation as to the *Fraction* had brought about important changes in this part of the Mass. But before these changes were made, the procedure was as follows : the Pontiff made three signs of the Cross over the chalice before he put the *Sancta* into it. As has been explained, these *Sancta* are a portion of the Eucharist consecrated at the preceding Mass, and kept to be used at the next in order to assure the continuity of the Sacrifice. Then the Pontiff detached a portion of the Host, which he left upon the altar until the end of the Mass ; these portions probably served as *Sancta* for the next celebration. He then left the altar and returned to his throne.

We must not forget that at that time the Hosts were whole loaves. They were distributed to the Bishops and Priests surrounding the Pope, and when a signal was given they broke the consecrated bread so that it might be distributed to the faithful in Holy Communion. All this time the *schola* sang the chant of the *Fraction* (called at Milan the *Confractorium* ; these chants can be studied in the old books there). At Rome, Pope Sergius (687–701) prescribed the singing of the *Agnus Dei*, which thus became a chant of the *Fraction*. It was repeated as often as was necessary while the *Fraction* was taking place. After the ceremony of the Breaking of Bread had been simplified the *Agnus Dei* was only twice repeated, *dona nobis pacem* being substituted for the words *miserere nobis* at the third and last repetition. The *Agnus Dei* is thus later than St. Gregory's time, but there was always a chant of the *Fraction* in this place ; many can be found in the ancient Roman liturgical books.[1] One of the finest is the *Venite populi*, still preserved in certain liturgies.

Beside the *Fraction* we have mentioned another rite, the *Immixtion*, or *Commixtion*. This is accomplished now when the Priest puts part of the Host into the chalice with these words : *May this mingling and hallowing of the Body and Blood of Our Lord Jesus Christ avail us that receive it unto life everlasting, Amen.* This mixture, which now takes place immediately before the *Agnus Dei*, is intended to show that the Body and Blood of Christ remain united, in spite of the apparent separation of the elements. The *Immixtion* was more strongly marked in St. Gregory's time. The formula quoted is in *Ordo I*. By these words and this action the Roman Church affirms anew that Christ is not divided, but entire under both Species. Certain formulas of *Immixtion* point this out more clearly than the formula now in use.[2]

The *Kiss of Peace*, like the *Fraction* and *Commixtion*, has lost much of its solemnity in our own days. Before placing the third portion of the Host in the chalice the Priest, holding it in his right hand and signing with it

[1] Cf. articles by K. Ott, *Il transitorium e il confractorium nella liturgia ambrosiana*, in *Rassegna Gregoriana*, especially p. 211 seq.

[2] Cf. *Immixtion*, DACL, according to the work of Michel Andrieu.

three times upon the chalice, says : *Pax † Domini sit †
semper vobis † cum.* ℟. *Et cum spiritu tuo.* After the first
Communion prayer, *Domine J. C. qui dixisti. . . .
Pacem relinquo vobis,* he gives (at High Mass) the Kiss of
Peace to the Deacon, who gives it to the sub-Deacon,
who in his turn " carries the Peace " to the members of
the clergy in the choir. In the time of St. Gregory and
till the time of Innocent III the *Kiss of Peace* was not
merely exchanged amongst the clergy, as it is to-day, but
amongst all the faithful ; for at that time the people were
still divided into two parts—men on one side, women on
the other—all being expected to receive Holy Communion.
Thus the *Kiss of Peace* after the words of the *Pater* on the
forgiveness of offences and before partaking of the Body
and Blood of Our Lord was an act of deep meaning.

The Roman liturgy is almost alone in putting the *Kiss
of Peace* in this place. In the Mozarabic, Gallican, and
Eastern liturgies it takes place at the *Offertory.* This
conveys quite another idea. The Mass of the catechumens is finished ; they, with the uninitiated and
others who would not communicate at the Mass, had
been sent away. Only the faithful remained ; the
Prayer of the Faithful was then recited, after which the
Kiss of Peace was given. The rite in such a place is
justified. Nevertheless this difference between the
liturgies has naturally been much remarked upon ; and
it is one of the reasons for which the Gallican liturgies
have been classed in a different order from our own
(cf. Chapter II), and their origin sought in the East.
We may, however, ask whether this difference may not
be otherwise explained.[1]

THE COMMUNION.—The rites of the *Pater, Fraction,*
and *Kiss of Peace* in the Roman Mass may be considered

[1] Cf. our article *Baiser de Paix,* DACL.

as a preparation for Communion. This part of the Mass has suffered more change than any other since St. Gregory's time. The Pontiff communicated first, under both Species ; then he distributed to the faithful, first the consecrated Bread, which they still received in their hands, as in primitive times, after having kissed the Bishop's hand. The Deacon then presented the chalice to them, and they drank of it through a tube, *pugillaris*, *fistula*. Later, in the tenth-twelfth centuries, it was thought sufficient to steep the consecrated Bread in the Precious Blood, and to present it thus to the faithful, as is still the custom in the East. When receiving the Communion the faithful responded *Amen*. The whole of this ceremonial goes back to the most ancient period, and Mgr. Batiffol has many texts on this subject—an inscription at Autun of the second century, a passage from St. Cyprian, a passage from the life of St. Mélanie in the fifth century, etc.[1] At Rome, Communion under both kinds was maintained until the fourteenth century. The difficulty which Communion with the chalice presented, the fear of any risk of profanation and a tendency to simplify all rites, brought about many modifications from the tenth century onwards, and finally Communion was given under only one kind. We know what discussions have arisen from the suppression of Communion under both kinds in the time of John Hus (fifteenth century). But at bottom there was here nothing but a precaution of a practical order. Throughout all time it had been believed that Christ was present Whole and Entire under the Species of Bread, and we have examples of Communion under one kind only in the most ancient times.[2]

[1] P. 288 *seq*.
[2] The theological question is treated in all theological books. See particularly the *Dict. de théol. catholique* under these words.

On the other hand, the recital of the *Confiteor, Agnus Dei, Domine non sum dignus*, as well as the three prayers after the *Agnus Dei*, are later than St. Gregory, and hardly appear before the thirteenth century. It has been thought, and not without reason, that this group of prayers must have constituted at first the ritual of the Communion distributed outside Mass ; for example, to the sick.[1]

During the distribution of the Communion the Communion anthem was sung. Primitively this was a psalm, modulated, like those of the *Introit* and *Offertory* on the antiphonic mode. Here again only the anthem has been retained. Psalm xxxiii. was for a long time the one chiefly used, as we have already seen in Africa in St. Augustine's time.[2]

After the Communion the Priest recited a prayer, called in ancient times *oratio ad complendum*, or finished prayer ; it is the third of that category of prayers, the first of these being the *Collect*, and the second the *Secret*. This third prayer is now called the *Post-communion*. It is of the same style and character as the first two. Many of them are of high dogmatic meaning and affirm the faith of the Roman Church in the Eucharist.[3]

DISMISSAL AND LAST PRAYERS.—In the time of St. Gregory the Mass ended after the *Communion* and *Post-communion*. The Deacon dismissed the people with the words *Ite missa est*, and the Pontiff withdrew, giving his blessing.[4] Here there is another difference

---

[1] Batiffol, *loc. cit.*, p. 287. Cf. Chapter IX, where we speak again of these prayers.

[2] The various prayers, *Quid retribuam, Sanguis Domini, Quod ore, Corpus tuum*, are also of later date. Cf. Chapter IX.

[3] Cf. the article *Ad complendum* in DACL.

[4] For the prayers since added, *Placeat*, Last Gospel, etc., see Chapter XI.

between the Roman and the other Latin liturgies. The blessing given by the Priest in a special formula before the Communion does not exist at Rome, and that given as the Pontiff withdrew is quite another thing (as we explain in connection with the Gallican liturgy; cf. p. 153). This blessing, moreover, was at first reserved for Bishops, then in the twelfth and thirteenth centuries ordinary Priests were allowed to bestow it. It originally consisted of these simple words : *Benedicat vos Dominus.* ℞. *Amen.*

On weekdays in Lent, however, there is a prayer, *super populum*, which follows the *Post-communion*. The Priest says *Oremus*, the Deacon *Humiliate capita vestra Deo*, and the Priest then pronounces the formula, which is one of blessing. It was St. Gregory, or one of the compilers of the *Gregorian Sacramentary*, who assigned this form of blessing to Lent, Sundays always excepted. The formulas themselves, however, have not a penitential character. Some are borrowed from the Leonine, others from the Gelasian Sacramentary, both of which have on certain days an *oratio ad populum*. There is the same custom in the liturgy of St. Mark, with the *Humiliate capita vestra Deo*, and also in that of St. James. Lastly, as has been remarked, the Gallican liturgies also had an episcopal blessing, but this was given before Communion. Several collections of formulas for those blessings exist, forming a special liturgical book, the *Benedictional*, and some of these are magnificently illustrated.[1]

CONCLUSION.—This Roman Mass in the seventh century is remarkable for its simplicity, the austerity of its forms, especially if compared with the magnificence and pomp of the Byzantine liturgy, and even with the Mozarabic and Gallican Masses. Edmund Bishop loved to remark that this Papal Mass was both logical and rational. There is little symbolism, there are no useless

---

[1] *Books of the Latin Liturgy*, (Sands, 3s. 6d.), p. 68 *seq.*

rites, but great order and sequence in the ritual. He gave a celebrated conference on this subject on 8th May 1899.[1] But what it is chiefly necessary to point out (though Bishop could not say all he wished on this subject in a single conference) is the excellence of the prayers and the Prefaces of this Missal; the choice of the Epistles, the Gospels, and the other formulas which make of the Roman Missal the most beautiful book of prayer in existence.

May we be allowed to refer our readers to an article written on this subject: *The Excellence of the Roman Mass*, in *The Clergy Review*, 1931, pp. 346–368.

BIBLIOGRAPHY

(Beyond the works cited in the course of this chapter) :—

Dom G. MORIN, *Liturgie et basiliques de Rome au milieu du VIIme siècle, d'après les listes d'évangiles de Würzburg. Revue Bénédictine*, 1911, pp. 296–330.

H. GRISAR, *Histoire de Rome et des Papes au moyen âge*, trad. Ledos, 1906 (Vol. I, pp. 154–167). *Description des églises de Rome au V et VIe siècles.*

ARMELLINI, *Le Chiese di Roma dal secolo IV al XIX.* Roma, 1841.

BATIFFOL, *Le Canon de la Messe a-t-il Firmicus Maternus pour auteur ?* In *Revue des sciences relig. de Strasbourg*, Vol. II, 1922, pp. 113–126, refuting a hypothesis of Dom Morin's.

Liturgia, pp. 501–533.

[1] This is the conference which has been translated (into French) and enriched with notes by Dom A. Wilmart, *Le génie du rit romain*, Paris, 1921.

CHAPTER V

THE AMBROSIAN MASS

The books of the Ambrosian liturgy.—Analogies with other liturgies.

THE Ambrosian liturgy is still practised in the Cathedral of Milan. It takes its name from the great Bishop of that See, St. Ambrose, who died in 397, and who did so much for the liturgy.

THE BOOKS OF THE AMBROSIAN LITURGY.—We have studied elsewhere the books which contain this liturgy.[1] They are Sacramentaries, Pontificals, a manual, some *Ordines*, and lectionaries : in fact, a collection which enables us to reconstitute the Ambrosian Mass. Not one of these is really earlier than the ninth century ; we must confess that the preceding period is rather obscure, and that from the fourth-ninth centuries this liturgy has probably been subject to influences coming from the East, from Rome, and other countries. It has been stated in the book referred to in our note below that the characteristics of this liturgy have been explained in two ways. One party declares that they are strongly influenced by the East ; while Mgr. Duchesne attributes them specially to an Arian Bishop, Auxentius (355–374), who occupied the See of Milan for some years. Another group of liturgiologists, on the contrary, without denying Eastern or Byzantine importations, such as are found even in the Roman liturgy, use every effort to emphasise the analogies between the Ambrosian and Roman

[1] See *Books of the Latin Liturgy* (Sands, 3s. 6d.), pp. 85–88.

liturgies ; affirming that the first is almost identical with the second, especially with a Roman liturgy existing previous to the reforms of Damasus, Gelasius, and St. Gregory.[1] It must be admitted that this last hypothesis has gained ground to-day, and certain coincidences recently noted, concerning Rome and Milan, would seem to strengthen it.

ANALOGIES WITH OTHER LITURGIES.—In this sketch it will be enough to note, as they occur, analogies with Rome on one hand, and with Oriental and Gallican liturgies on the other.

In the Ambrosian rite certain ceremonies were accomplished in the *Basilica major* or *ecclesia æstiva,* and others in the *Basilica minor* or *ecclesia hiemalis.* This custom has been compared with that of the Roman " Stations."

At the beginning of Mass the clergy came to the sanctuary from the sacristy to the singing of the *Ingressa,* which has been compared to the Roman *Introit.* The *Ingressa,* however, is not the chanting of a psalm, as the *Introit* is ; it has only one verse, which is not always chosen from a psalm, and it has no doxology.

The prayers at the foot of the altar are almost the same as those of the Roman Missal, but these prayers as a whole date only from the late Middle Ages.

The *Gloria in Excelsis* was sung as at Rome, but is followed instead of preceded by the *Kyrie Eleison,* which is different from the Roman *Kyrie,* being composed of the first acclamation, thrice repeated by the Priest alone, *Christe Eleison* not being said. This *Kyrie* is again repeated after the Gospel and after the Post-

---

[1] Do not forget what has been said in Chapter II as to the liturgical exchanges and borrowings between the Eastern churches (notably those of Antioch and Jerusalem) and those of the West.

communion. This use seems particular to the church at Milan.[1] The Ambrosian rite has also preserved an old form of prayer, the *preces* or litanies, which are translated almost literally from the Greek.[2] This is found, with a few variations, in the Missal of Stowe (p. 66) under the title : *Deprecatio sancti Martini*. This has been studied in the article *Litanies* in DACL. It would seem that Rome and the other Latin liturgies were acquainted with litanies of this kind.

The celebrant salutes the people with : *Dominus vobiscum*, as at Rome. The prayer which follows is called *Super populum*, a title given by Rome to certain prayers in Lent, and which is also used in the Gallican liturgies. There are three readings or Lessons in the Ambrosian Mass : one from the Old Testament, sometimes replaced by the reading of the Acts or *Gesta* of the Martyrs ; one from the New Testament (Acts or Epistles) ; and finally, the Gospel. These three Lessons are found in the Mozarabic and Gallican liturgies, while those of the Eastern rite have three, and sometimes many more, Lessons. The question is to know whether Rome had not three Lessons also, at one time, as the presence of the *Alleluia* after the Gradual would make us believe. This anomaly is not found at Milan, each reading being followed by a chant. The Gradual is called *Psalmellus*, but has the same characteristics as the Roman Gradual ; the second Lesson is followed by the *Alleluia* ; while the Gospel is followed by the *Kyrie*, and by an anthem of which we shall speak immediately.

The song of Zacharias, *Benedictus*, after the Gospel, seems at first sight a Gallican importation. Not long ago Père Thibaut showed the importance of this chant in

---

[1] Lejay thinks (wrongly, in our opinion) that the second *Kyrie* is only a vestige of the Prayer of the Faithful.

[2] Cf. Duchesne, *Origines du culte*, p. 203.

the Gallican liturgy;[1] yet others, notably the Roman liturgy, have also adopted it, and it has sometimes even taken the place of the *Gloria in Excelsis*.[2]

The catechumens were dismissed before the Offertory. A celebrated formula, as to which we shall have a word to say, is as follows :

> *Si quis cathecumenus est, procedat.*
> *Si quis hæreticus est, procedat.*
> *Si quis judæus est, procedat.*
> *Si quis paganus est, procedat.*
> *Si quis arianus est, procedat.*
> *Cujus cura non est, procedat.*

This formula was discussed at Rome in 1905 during the conferences on Christian Archæology. Mgr. Stornaiolo, who had discovered it in a Vatican codex of the eleventh-twelfth centuries, gave it as a unique example of the *missa*, or *dismissio*, of the non-Catholics before the Mass (of the Faithful). Bannister gave it another interpretation ; in his opinion it was an appeal from the Church to come and be baptized. He himself had found the same formula in the Office of Holy Saturday, after the *Sicut servus*. Cardinal Tommasi had already published two formulas of this kind, found in the Roman books ; Muratori two others, from the Ambrosian rite.[3] The *Paléographie musicale* of the Solesmes Benedictines gave the formula of the *codex urbinatus* (that published by Mgr. Stornaiolo) with the neumatic Ambrosian notation (Vol. VI, pp. 174, 175, and 262). Finally, the same formula was discovered in Beroldus by Mgr. Magistretti, who proved by the

---

[1] *L'ancienne liturgie gallicane, son origine aux Ve et VIe siècles*, (Paris 1929), and our remarks on this subject in *Revue d'Hist. ecclés. de Louvain*, Vol. XXVI, p. 851 *seq.*

[2] Cf. DACL, *Cantiques évangéliques*, col. 1995.

[3] Thomasi-Vezzosi, VII, p. 6 *seq.* ; Muratori, *Antiqu. Medii Evi.*, Vol. IV, pp. 842 and 914.

context that the meaning of *procedat* could not be an appeal to advance, but, on the contrary, an invitation to withdraw, *procedat* being equivalent to *recedat*.[1]

There was an anthem, *post Evangelium*, which, according to Lejay, was connected with the Offertory. However, as has been observed in Chapter IV, a chant after the Gospel cannot be considered as unfamiliar in Rome. After this anthem there was the *Pacem habete, corrigite* (erigite) *vos ad orationem*. This is an ancient rite, which seems clearly to indicate that in the primitive Ambrosian Mass the Kiss of Peace took place here, and even the reading of the Diptychs. On this point, then, this rite was different from that of Rome, in which the Diptychs were recited in the middle of the Canon, and where the Kiss of Peace was given at Communion ; but it does agree with the Gallican, Mozarabic, and Eastern liturgies. This difference is the most important of all between Rome and the other Latin liturgies. Certain liturgiologists have boldly affirmed that it is reasonable to believe that on this point it is the Roman liturgy which has changed, while all the rest remained faithful to the primitive system.[2]

The Ambrosian liturgy has adopted prayers which are not very ancient for the Offertory. Otherwise both ceremonies and formulas are very like those of Rome.

On the paten on which he has placed the Host the Priest says : *Suscipe, clementissime Pater, hunc panem sanctum ut fiat unigeniti corpus in nomine Patris et Filii et Spiritus sancti*. When he puts wine and water into the chalice, he says : *De latere Christi exivit sanguis et aqua pariter, in nomine Patris*, etc.

---

[1] *De la missa ou dismissio catechumenorum*, in *Revue Bénédictine*, 1905, Vol. XXII, pp. 569–572 ; cf. also *Rassegna Gregoriana*, 1905, July–August, p. 338.

[2] Cf. the works of Dom Cagin, Probst, Lucas, and Fortescue, already mentioned; and also DACL, *Baiser de Paix*, and *Diptyques*.

Here there are two prayers, *Suscipe sancte Pater* and *Suscipe sancta Trinitas*, which strongly resemble the Roman formulas. Then comes this prayer, with imposition of hands over the oblations : *Et suscipe sancta Trinitas hanc oblationem pro emundatione mea ; ut mundes et purges me ab universis peccatorum maculis, quatenus tibi digne ministrare merear, domine et clementissime Deus*. All these formulas are of later origin, and can be found in other books of the Middle Ages, with variants.

The prayer, *Super sindonem* (or, prayer over the winding-sheet or Corporal), is, on the contrary, very ancient. It is true that the Roman liturgy has not that prayer to-day, but it has at this moment the ceremony of the Corporal, and further, the *Dominus vobiscum* and *Oremus*, which are not followed by any prayer, which surely indicates that there is a gap here. Many liturgiologists have said, and still say, that what is missing here is the Prayer of the Faithful ; but we are of Bishop's opinion : that it is more reasonable to believe that once at Rome, as now at Milan, the *oratio super sindonem* stood in this place.[1]

The offerings were brought to the singing of the *antiphona post evangelium* ; and this too is conformable with the Roman rite. The celebrant blessed them with this further prayer :[2] *Benedictio Dei omnipotentis Pa✝ tris et Fi ✝ lii et Spiritus ✝ sancti copiosa de cœlis descendat super hanc nostram oblationem et accepta tibi sit hæc oblatio, Domine sancte, Pater omnipotens, æterne Deus, misericors rerum conditor*.

---

[1] Bishop–Wilmart, *Le génie du rit romain*, p. 45 and note 45.

[2] Lejay, who admits that the oblations were presented at the beginning of the Mass (as in the Gallican rite), thinks that the ceremony described above is a reduplication, and consequently an addition, of a later age.

In certain manuscripts the prayer *Adesto Domine* is found at this point.

The blessing of the incense resembles the Roman blessing ; having the same formulas, with one exception. But all these prayers are also of the late Middle Ages.

During solemn Masses at Milan a characteristic ceremony took place. Ten old men (*vecchioni*) and ten old women, who lived at the expense of the Chapter, came in special costume to offer the bread and wine. This, too, is a custom which reminds us of the Roman Offertory. This offering also is accompanied by a prayer, *oratio super oblatam*, which answers to the Roman Collect.[1]

The Ambrosian Preface is framed on the Roman lines, and also concludes with the *Sanctus*. But the Milanese rite has kept a large number of these Prefaces. Lejay has an interesting study on that of the manuscript of Bergamo ; and he distinguishes amongst them the following types :

Prefaces in the form of Collects, ending with the doxology *Per Dominum nostrum*, etc. ;

Prefaces in the form of a narrative, recounting the Lives of Saints ;

Oratorical Prefaces, true rhetorical efforts, sometimes perhaps rather stilted in tone ; and related more closely to the Gallican or Mozarabic style rather than to the sobriety of Rome ;

Antithetical Prefaces, in which two subjects are opposed to each other in a series of contrasts ;

Lastly, Lejay also distinguishes Parallel Prefaces, in which two Saints are compared with each other ; or Eve with Our Lady, or Christ with St. Stephen.

In spite of the oratorical tone of all these compositions,

[1] Lejay considers that this prayer is a reduplication of the *oratio super sindonem* (*loc. cit.*, col. 1406). To me this does not seem exact, each of these prayers having its own well-determined object.

he yet declares that "some of these pieces are really beautiful, and betray a master's hand" (*loc. cit.*, cols. 1413–1414). Two of these Prefaces even contain hexameters, and one, pentameters.

At the present day the Ambrosian Canon, except for very slight variants, is like the Roman Canon, and has been like it for many centuries. In his article on the Ambrosian rite, Lejay has published the entire text of the Sacramentary of Biasca, as well as that of the Missal of Stowe and the Gelasian Sacramentary (*loc. cit.*, cols. 1407–1414). The comparison of these texts is most instructive, but it can be seen at a glance that, excepting for the list of Saints, to which the Ambrosians have added several specially honoured at Milan, and for a few less important variants, the Ambrosian Canon is exactly similar to the Gelasian, which itself is but the Gregorian Canon of our own Missal, with a few very slight variations.[1]

We may agree with certain liturgiologists that the Canon of *De Sacramentis* (which is printed on p. 39) gives us a very much earlier form of the Canon than the Ambrosian ; one, indeed, which goes back to about the year 400. But, as was then said, that text too presents many analogies with the Roman Canon. Lejay, following Mgr. Duchesne here, attempts to go back to an even earlier epoch, in which, he says, "there was no Ambrosian Canon really ; before the adoption of the Roman Canon at Milan the consecrating prayers were still variable in their tenor, as we find them in the Gallican books."[2]

Lejay seeks traces of this primitive Ambrosian Canon in the offices of Holy Week, which, as we know, often preserve the most ancient vestiges of the old liturgies.

[1] Cf. DACL, *Diptyques*.

[2] *Loc. cit.*, col. 1416; cf. Mgr. Duchesne, *Les origines du culte*, 3rd edition, p. 177. But this, we must confess, is at least a hypothesis for the Ambrosian.

Thus, on Holy Thursday, we have a formula which is a pendant to the Gallican *Post pridie*, as follows: after the words of the Institution: *Hæc facimus, hæc celebramus, tua, Domine, præcepta servantes et ad communionem inviolabilem hoc ipsum quod corpus domini sumimus mortem dominicam nuntiamus.*

On Holy Saturday there is a *Vere Sanctus*, just as there is in the Eastern and Gallican liturgies: *Vere benedictus dominus noster Jesus Christus, filius tuus. Qui cum Deus esset majestatis descendit de cælo, formam servi qui primus perierat suscepit et sponte pati dignatus est ut eum quem ipse fecerat liberaret. Unde et hoc paschale sacrificium tibi offerimus pro his quos ex aqua et spiritu sancto regenerare dignatus es, dans eis remissionem omnium peccatorum, ut invenires eos in Christo Jesu domino nostro; pro quibus tibi, domine, supplices fundimus preces ut nomina eorum pariterque famuli tui imperatoris scripta habeas in libro viventium. Per Christum Dominum nostrum, qui pridie.* Here the *Vere Sanctus*, as in the Gallican and Eastern liturgies, joins the *Sanctus* to the *Qui pridie.*

There is yet another variant of the *Vere Sanctus* on Holy Thursday: *Tu nos, domine, participes filii tui, tu consortes regni tui,* etc.[1]

In the Canon of Biasca the formula of consecration is followed by these words: *Mandans quoque, et dicens ad eos: Hæc quotiescumque feceritis in meam commemorationem facietis; mortem meam prædicabitis, resurrectionem adnunciabitis, adventum meum sperabitis, donec iterum de cælis veniam ad vos.* This is a variant of the Roman *anamnesis*, evidently of very ancient authorship, which recalls the formula of the *Apostolic Constitutions*

---

[1] All these formulas will be found in Lejay, *art. cit.*, cols. 1416, 1417. It is well known that Dom Cagin has ingeniously endeavoured to find the *Vere Sanctus* in the Roman Mass itself.

(VIII, 12, *P.G.* Vol. I, col. 1104; cf. VII, 25, col. 1017), themselves inspired by the actual text of St. Paul : *'Οσάκις γὰρ ἄν ἐσθίητε* (1 Cor. xi. 26). It is also found in other Eastern liturgies, as those of St. James and St. Basil, in the Missal of Stowe, and in the Mozarabic rite.

In the text of Biasca the Canon ends, like the Canons of all the rites, with a doxology ; but this, slightly different from the Roman doxology, runs thus : *Et est tibi Deo Patri Omnipotenti ex ipso, et per ipsum, et in ipso omnis honor, virtus, laus, gloria, imperium, perpetuitas et potestas in unitate spiritus sancti. Per infinita sæcula sæculorum. Amen.* This is very nearly the same as that of *De Sacramentis,* which in that document follows the *Pater.* According to Lejay this would be its primitive place in the Ambrosian liturgy. Now a doxology after the *Pater* is a primitive custom already found in the *Didache* ; so ancient that it has slipped into certain manuscripts after the Lord's Prayer given by St. Matthew (chap. vi. 13).[1]

As at Rome, the *Pater* is preceded by a short prelude and followed by an embolism which differs only very slightly from the Roman use. The Fraction preceded the *Pater* as it did at Rome before St. Gregory's day. This was also the case with the Gallican liturgies, on this point in agreement with Rome, while the Greeks placed the Fraction afterwards. After the doxology at the end of the Canon the Priest divides the Host, saying : *Corpus tuum frangitur, Christe ; Calix benedicitur,* and breaks off a piece destined to be placed in the chalice, with these words : *Sanguis tuus sit nobis semper ad vitam et ad salvandas animas.* The Commixtion is made with the words : *Commixtio consecrati corporis et sanguinis*

[1] Lejay, *art. cit.,* col. 1418. But we cannot agree with him that this is a feature borrowed from the Eastern liturgies, for it is of far more ancient origin. Cf. on this point the *Pater* in the *Revue Grégorienne,* 1928.

D.N.J.C. nobis edentibus et sumentibus, in vitam æternam. Amen. This rite is accompanied by a chant called *Confractorium.* Lejay mentions one taken from Psalm xxii. 5, according to St. Ambrose (col. 1419).

The *Pax* is given at this moment, as at Rome ; but certain indications allow us to believe that in the primitive Ambrosian rite it was doubtless at the Offertory.

The *Agnus Dei* and the three prayers before the Communion have been adopted by the Ambrosian as they have by the Roman rite ; but they are prayers of a later age.

The ancient formula for Communion was formerly : *Corpus D.N.J.C. proficiat mihi sumenti et omnibus pro quibus hoc sacrificium attuli ad vitam et gaudium sempiternum.* It is unnecessary to remark that this is not a very ancient formula, such as that given in *De Sacramentis,* which is very old. The Priest says : *Corpus Christi,* and the faithful reply : *Amen.*

There is a prayer of Post-communion, as at Rome.

The Mass ends thus : after the Post-communion and *Dominus vobiscum* the *Kyrie Eleison* is said thrice. Then the Blessing : *Benedicat et exaudiat nos Deus. Amen.* The Deacon says : *Procedamus in pace. In nomine Christi.* To this ending has been added the *Placeat,* the Blessing, and the Gospel of St. John.

In this Mass, as we have just depicted it, we find a large number of elements which are identical with the Roman Mass ; either because they have been borrowed from it, or else that both have flowed from the same source. Other features remind us rather of the Gallican and Mozarabic, or even the Eastern liturgies ; and it has already been said that both these opinions have gathered a certain number of supporters. In the future perhaps an even closer study of the documents will produce fresh arguments which will weigh down the balance in one or the other direction. But for the moment we see no sufficient reason to give up that opinion stated in Chapter II. Beyond the reforms imposed by Rome, it seems to us that, during the first few centuries, liturgical unity, understood in its widest sense, gives the key to a certain number of differences, just as it does to analogies between the two liturgies.

In our own opinion it would be more interesting profoundly to study the liturgy of this great church of Milan, which at one moment in the fourth century was " quasi-patriarchal," and of which we have here only been able to give the palest sketch, than it would be to attempt to resolve the above question. Like Antioch, Jerusalem, Alexandria, Rome, Constantinople, Toledo, Ravenna, Aquilea, it was a first-class liturgical centre. Such of its liturgical books as have been preserved, the great churches where this liturgy was celebrated, the great Bishops who were its protectors, all give us the very loftiest idea of it. But we are not now writing the history of the Latin liturgies, an enormous enterprise which would as yet be premature ; we are but endeavouring to study the Mass of the Western Rite under its different forms.

BIBLIOGRAPHY

The Abbé Paul Lejay has published two articles, *Ambrosienne* (liturgy), one in the *Dict. de théol. cath.*, the other, later and more complete, in DACL ; both being under the same title. In his bibliography he mentions the works of CERIANI, MERCATI, MAGISTRETTI, and others upon this subject. To this the following articles may be added :—

In *Liturgia*, p. 801 *seq.*, a chapter on the Ambrosian liturgy.

Books of the Latin Liturgy (Sands, 3s. 6d.), pp. 85-88, on the Sacramentaries, Rituals, Manuals, and Pontificals of the Ambrosian liturgy.

THE MASS OF THE WESTERN RITES

W. C. Bishop, *The Ambrosian Breviary*, in the *Church Quarterly Review*, October 1886, p. 110 *seq.*, published separately. Analogies with the Mozarabic and Gallican liturgies.

Lucas, three articles on *The Ambrosian Liturgy*, in the *Tablet*, 4th December 1897 ; 29th January and 5th February 1898. (Cf. also the *Month*, January 1902, p. 41.) The conclusions of Ceriani, Mercati, Magistretti, and others are adopted, *i.e.* that the Ambrosian liturgy is derived from an ante-Gregorian Roman liturgy.

Archdale King, *Notes on the Catholic Liturgies* (London, 1930).

For Ambrosian (the chant), see the article of Dom Gatard in DACL.

CHAPTER VI

THE MASS IN SPAIN

THE MOZARABIC LITURGY

THE Mozarabic liturgy is that which was followed in Spain before the Arab conquest in 712, and which, after that date, was still generally in use both by those Spanish who had submitted to the Arabs and by those others who, having withdrawn into the northern provinces, were able to retain their independence. The term "Mozarabic" (from *musta'rab*, or *mixto-arabic*, "mixed with the Arabs") only applies in reality to that part of the Spanish population which did submit to the Saracens. It is, strictly speaking, a mistake to use it to qualify the Spanish liturgy, since this existed in Spain previous to the Arab conquest; and, further, because it was also the liturgy of the free Spaniards in the north. Nevertheless, since this name is now well established, and is used by most authors, we think it best to retain it here. Further, the names of Visigothic rite, rite of Toledo, Hispanic, Gothic, or Spanish rite, by which it has been proposed to replace the word *Mozarabic* rite, are none of them in themselves perfectly correct.

In all cases this term denotes a liturgy which has been that of Spain from the beginning of her history; which was maintained in that country until the twelfth century, and which, even after its suppression, was still followed in a few churches, and in the sixteenth century was

103

officially restored in the churches of Toledo, where at the present time it is still practised.

Whatever we may think of its name, the Mozarabic liturgy itself is fairly well known to us. We may even say that, with the exception of the Roman liturgy, it is this which provides us with the greatest number of documents, and gives us the most important information, as may easily be verified by the paragraph in which these sources are enumerated.

This, however, is not the place to discuss the question of the origin and sources of these liturgical documents ; we can but refer our readers to the article *Mozarabe (liturgie)* in DACL. It is enough to say that we are not now reduced (as was the case until recently) to the *Missale Mixtum* of Lesley, but that at present we have the *Liber Ordinum* (Missal and Pontifical) and the *Liber Mozarabicus Sacramentorum*, both published by Dom Férotin, and also the *Comes*, or *Liber Comicus*, published by Dom Morin. Thanks to these various documents we can easily reconstitute the Mozarabic Mass, and go back to an epoch which is almost that of its origin : let us say, the eighth, or even the seventh, century.[1]

THE PRE-MASS, OR MASS OF THE CATECHUMENS

PREPARATION.—The *Missale Mixtum* contains a Preparation for Mass which is given after the Mass for Easter (*P.L.*, Vol. LXXXV, cols. 521–522). It comprehends a number of rites and prayers, washing of hands, four *Ave Maria*, prayers for the amice, the alb, girdle, maniple, stole, and chasuble, an *apologia*, the psalm *Judica me*

[1] On the question of documents, see Bibliography at end of this chapter, and also our articles, *Messe Mozarabe* in *Dict. de théol. cath.*, *Mozarabe (liturgie)* and *Missel* (both in DACL.). In 1928 the Benedictines of Silos published *L'Antiphonaire de la Cathédrale de Léon*, Burgos.

with the anthem *Introibo ad altare Dei*, the confession of sins, the absolution, the prayer *Aufer a nobis*, the signing of the altar with the cross and kissing it (which was formerly the kissing of the Cross present on the altar), and the prayer on extending the Corporal upon the altar and on the preparation of the chalice. Some of these rites and prayers are ancient, as may be seen by a comparison with the Gallican rites ; others are of recent introduction. The preparation of the chalice and the Corporal formerly took place at the Offertory (cf. *P.L.*, *loc. cit.*, col. 339, and Lesley's notes on these passages).

INTROIT.—The Mass begins with the *Officium*, called by the Gallicans *Antiphona ad prælegendum*, in the Ambrosian rite, *Ingressa*, and at Rome, *Introit*, or *Antiphona ad introitum*. It is composed of an anthem, the verse of a psalm, and a doxology, and is taken either from Holy Scripture or from the *Acta* of the Saint whose Feast is that day celebrated (cf. Tommasi, *Disquisitio de antiphona ad introitum Missæ*, and Lesley's note, *P.L.*, col. 234). The doxology differs from that of Rome, and the *Semper* of *Per omnia* is also a feature of the Mozarabic rite. But in outline the Mozarabic *Officium* is closer to the Roman *Introit* than is the Ambrosian *Ingressa*.

GLORIA IN EXCELSIS AND COLLECT.—The *Gloria in Excelsis* is enclosed at beginning and end by *Per omnia semper secula seculorum*. It was sung in this rite on Sundays and Feast Days, as the Fourth Council of Toledo says (canon 12). Etherius and Beatus also state it (*Ord. Elip.*, I, I ; cf. also Lesley's note, *P.L.*, *loc. cit.*, col. 531). Later the Mozarabites omitted this hymn on the Sundays of Advent and Lent. It was also sung by the Gallicans, as may be seen by the Missal of Bobbio, and was followed by two prayers. In the Mozarabic rite, after the final *Per omnia*, the Deacon cried *Oremus*, and the Priest said a prayer. Later on this acclamation of the Deacon was suppressed, but not the Priest's prayer, which varied for the Sundays of Advent, Epiphany, Lent, Easter, Pentecost, and for the Feasts of Saints. The text of these various prayers will be found in the *Missale Mixtum*, *P.L.*, Vol. LXXXV, col. 531 *seq*. The text of the *Gloria* here given is the same as usual, but other forms do exist. (On this point see the discussion between Lebrun and Lesley, *P.L.*, *loc. cit.*, col. 33 ; and also Dom German Prado, *Una nueva recension del hymno Gloria in Excelsis* in *Ephemerides Liturg.*, 1932, pp. 481–486.)

The Collect, here called *Oratio*, is often directly addressed to Christ, as in the Gallican liturgies. Very often it is a paraphrase of the *Gloria in Excelsis*. As a rule it has not the sobriety, the precision, nor the rhythm of the Roman Collect. Often it is merely a kind of pious effusion. We may take as a chance example the prayer for the Feast of St. Stephen (*P.L.*, *loc. cit.*, col. 190). After the *oratio* the Priest says :

> *Per misericordiam tuam, Deus noster qui*
> *es benedictus : et vivis et omnia regis*
> *in secula seculorum. R̿. Amen.*
> *Dominus sit semper vobiscum. Et cum*
> *spiritu tuo.*

READINGS.—On Fast Days in Spain the *Officium* was shortened, and Mass began with the Lessons, as it did formerly at Rome. St. Augustine, too, tells us that in Africa Mass began on Sunday with the reading of Holy Scripture.

We have one Lesson from the Old Testament, one from St. Paul, and the third is the Gospel. The first is called the *Prophecy*, the second the *Epistle*, or *Apostle*, the third the *Gospel*. But this order was not invariable. On

Sundays the Prophecy was omitted, while during Lent
and on Fast Days there were four Lessons, two from the
Old, two from the New Testament. Again, from Easter to
Pentecost the first Lesson was taken from the Apocalypse,
that from the Old Testament being suppressed. The
Gallicans had almost exactly the same custom with
regard to their Lessons. At Rome, on the contrary
(cf. p. 54), the readings were usually two in number, as
they are to-day. St. Isidore tells us that the Prophecy
was read by the Lector (*Epist. ad Ludifrid. Cordubensem.*
As to this custom, cf. Lesley's note, *P.L., loc. cit.*, col. 251).
After the first prayer the Priest saluted the people, and
the Lector from a high place announced the title of the
book, *Lectio libri Exodi*, the people responding *Deo
Gratias*, making the sign of the Cross, and listening to the
Lesson. After it was over they answered: *Amen* (St.
Isidore, *Offic.*, 1, I, c. x., and 1, II, c. xi.). The Priest
added, as he did after the prayer: *Dominus sit semper
vobiscum. Et cum spiritu tuo.*

PSALLENDO.—After the Prophecy is chanted the
Canticle of the Three Children, with the first verse of the
psalm *Confitemini*, as was also the custom in the Gallican
liturgy. The Lectionary of Luxeuil says: *Daniel cum
benedictione*, as also does the author of the Letters of
St. Germain. The same order is recalled by the Fourth
Council of Toledo (can. 14). After the *Benedictus es* the
Priest began to intone the Psalm *Confitemini*, which was
continued by choir and people (see the *Missale Mixtum,
P.L., loc. cit.*, col. 297 and note). According to the MSS.
the *Benedictus es*, which was sung in responses, shows a
large number of variations. The *Psallendo*, which comes
next, is a responsory sung by the Precentor from a
pulpit. St. Isidore calls it *responsoria*, while in Gaul it
was called *Psalmus responsorius* (St. Isidore, *Offic.*,
1, I, c. viii.; Gregory of Tours, *Hist. Franc.*, 1, VIII,

c. iii). It has sometimes been confused with the Roman Gradual, but it differs from this in certain characteristics (cf. Lesley, *P.L.*, *loc. cit.*, col. 257).

TRACT.—The ancient Mozarabic books contain a Tract, *Tractus*, which was sung from the ambone by the Psalmist. Like the Roman Tract it had neither repetition nor interruption, and was sung to a very simple melody. It differed from the Roman Tract, because that of the Gregorian rite follows the Gradual and takes the place of the *Alleluia*, while the Mozarabic Tract holds the place of the *Psallendo* (Lesley, col. 306. Cf. Tommasi, *Responsoralia et antiphonaria Romanæ Ecclesiæ*, p. 32 *seq.*, Rome, 1686).

DIACONAL PRAYERS.—The *Missale Mixtum* contains a rubric after the *Psallendo*, requiring the Priest to prepare the chalice by putting in wine and water, to place the Host upon the paten and put that upon the chalice, and, lastly, to say the *Preces : Indulgentiam postulamus*. But this is a recent rubric, and according to St. Isidore (*Epist. ad Ludifr. Cordub.*) it was the place of the Deacon to prepare the chalice and to say the *Preces* (cf. Lesley, *loc. cit.*, col. 297). In his note Lesley confuses these *Preces diaconales* with the *Prayer of the Faithful*, which is quite different. These diaconal prayers have great interest for the student of liturgical history ; they are a relic of the past, still preserved in the Eastern liturgies, but of which but few traces have survived in that of Rome. They will be found in the *Missale Mixtum*, *loc. cit.*, col. 297.

The Priest then says a prayer in a low voice. The following is the text of that which comes after the diaconal prayer :

Exaudi orationem nostram, domine : gemitusque nostros auribus percipe : nos enim iniquitates nostras agnoscimus : et delicta nostra coram te pandimus tibi Deus peccavimus :

tibique confitentes veniam exposcimus. Et quia recessimus a mandatis tuis : et legi tue minime paruimus. Convertere, Domine, super servos tuos quos redimisti sanguine tuo. Indulge quæsumus nobis : et peccatis nostris veniam tribue : tueque pietatis misericordiam in nobis largire dignare. Amen.

Per misericordiam tuam Deus noster qui es benedictus et vivis et omnia regis in secula seculorum. Amen.

In the Gallican liturgies this prayer is called *Post Precem*.

EPISTLE.—After the singing of the *Psallendo* and the Diaconal Prayers the Priest commanded silence, *Silentium facite*, and the Lector read the Epistle, usually called the *Apostle*, as in Gaul, Italy, Africa, and other countries. He first announced the title, as, for instance, *Sequentia epistolæ Pauli ad Corinthios*, to which the people answered *Deo Gratias*, and signed themselves. But as far back as the time of St. Isidore it was no longer the Lector, but the Deacon, who read the Epistle. The reading ended, the people responded *Amen*, and the Deacon descending from the ambone, carried the book back to the sacristy (cf. Lesley's note, col. 268). The text was not always read in its integrity, and the Mozarabic books contain examples of Lessons where texts are combined or fitted together. (Thus, *P.L., loc. cit.*, cols. 622 and 278.)

GOSPEL.—Like the Epistle, the Gospel was at first read in Spain by the Lector. Then this function was reserved for the Deacon, *ad diaconum pertinere prædicare Evangelium et apostolum* (St. Isidore, *Ep. ad Ludifr.*). This also was the case in Gaul (Gregory of Tours, *Hist. Franc.*, i, VIII, c. iv. IV). The Deacon first said the prayer, *Munda cor meum corpusque et labia mea*, etc., and then went to receive the Bishop's blessing : *Corroboret Dominus sensum tuum*, etc. Having returned to the altar the Deacon said : *Laus tibi*, clergy and people responding : *Laus tibi, Domine Jesu Christe, Rex æternæ gloriæ.* He then ascended the ambone, with the book, preceded by those who bore candles, and perhaps incense, and announced the reading : *Lectio sancti evangelii secundum Lucam,* to which the people answered : *Gloria tibi, Domine,* making the sign of the Cross, and responding *Amen* at the end of the Gospel, which they stood upright to hear. The Bishop kissed the book of the Gospels when this was presented to him, saying : *Ave, verbum divinum, reformatio virtutum et restitutio sanitatum.* (*P.L.,* Vol. LXXXV, col. 269.)

As in the case of the Prophecy and the Epistle, the Mozarabic books do not scruple to omit verses of the Gospel, or to rearrange its text. After the reading the Priest said : *Dominus sit semper vobiscum. Et cum spiritu tuo.*

In private Masses the Priest recited a prayer before the Gospel : *Conforta me, Rex sanctorum,* etc., and also the *Dominus sit in corde meo,* etc., the Deacon saying the *Munda cor meum* (cf. *loc. cit.,* col. 528). But these prayers are of a later age, and are probably borrowed from the Roman liturgy.

LAUDA.—The *Lauda,* which follows the Gospel, is composed of the *Alleluia* and a verse taken generally from a psalm. This place was assigned to it by the Fourth Council of Toledo (cf. also St. Isidore, *Offic.,* 1, I, c. xiii.). In the *Missale Mixtum* it is followed by *Deo Gratias,* but it would not appear that this is primitive (*P.L., loc. cit.,* col. 536). The *Lauda* is sung by the Cantor. This custom of singing a verse after the Gospel is found in other liturgies.

At this point there was formerly (at least on certain days, especially in Lent) a prayer for the penitents, and their dismissal, as well as that of the catechumens (cf. *P.L., loc. cit.,* cols. 307, 308). Here the Pre-Mass ended.

We see that its principal features are very much the same as those of the Gallican, and even the Roman, Pre-Mass. But the Mozarabic rite has preserved more memories of the primitive liturgy.

THE MASS OF THE FAITHFUL

1. THE IMMEDIATE PREPARATION.—In the *Missale Mixtum* the Offertory is composed of the following prayers, which accompany the different acts of the Priest : the offering of the Host and the chalice, the preparation of the chalice and the paten on the altar, etc. : *Acceptabilis sit, Offerimus tibi hanc oblationem . . . et omnium offerentium, In spiritu humilitatis, Adjuvate me, fratres* (*loc. cit.*, col. 113).

Offertory.—The *Sacrificium* which follows these prayers answers to the singing of the Offertory. St. Isidore uses the two words as synonyms. In the letter *ad Ludifr.*, so often quoted, he says *Sacrificium* ; but in *De Offic.*, I, I, 14, he says *Offertoria*. The Gallicans have a chant here, *Sonus*.

Those who were not to assist at the Sacrifice having been dismissed, the Deacons took off the pallium, which up till then had covered the altar, and laid the Corporal upon it. *Quis fidelium*, says St. Optatus, *nesciat in peragendis mysteriis ipsa ligna altaris linteamine operiri* (*Cont. Parmen.*, I, VI). This cloth, sometimes also called *Palla Corporalis*, and made of pure linen, covered the whole altar. It was a general custom which can be proved in Egypt, Gaul, Africa, and Rome, as well as in Spain (Isid. of Pelus., *Ep.*, CXXIII, *Ad Dorotheum comitem* ; Gregory of Tours, *Hist.*, I, VII, c. xxii. ; Optatus of Milevia, *Cont. Parmen.*, I, VI ; *Ordo Romanus*, in Mabillon, ii. n. 9 ; cf. *P.L.*, Vol. LXXXV, col. 339).

While the choir sang the *Sacrificium* the Bishops,

Priests, and Deacons received the oblations of the people
—bread and wine. The men first made their offering, in
order of dignity, then the women, the Priests, Deacons,
clerics, the Bishop himself offering last of all. Great
precautions were taken that the bread should not be
touched by hand. The Bishop and Priests received the
bread upon the *Offertorium*, or *Oblatorium*, a vase of
silver, gold, or copper. At Rome the *Oblatorium* was
replaced by a linen cloth held by two acolytes. The
people themselves were not allowed to touch the offerings, which were presented in a linen cloth. These loaves
of pure wheat might originally have been leavened, but
the use of unleavened bread was established in Spain as
elsewhere (cf. Lesley's note, *loc. cit.*, col. 339).

As to the wine, it was presented in small flagons or
other receptacles. The Deacons poured it all into a great
chalice destined for this purpose. They next took from
the offerings of bread and wine what would be necessary
for Communion, and kept the rest. Those loaves intended for Holy Communion were placed on a paten and
the paten upon the altar ; the wine was put into the
chalice and mixed with water. Sometimes there were
of necessity many chalices and patens upon the altar.
The paten was not given to the sub-Deacon as in the
Roman rite. The Deacons then covered the oblations
with a pallium, which was usually made of silk em-
broidered with gold ; this was called *Coopertorium*,
Palla, or *Palla Corporalis*. There was a prayer, *ad
extendum corporalia*. The other prayers found in the
Mozarabic books for these different acts are of a later
epoch. In Spain, as in Gaul and Rome, these various
acts in primitive days were not accompanied by prayers
(*P.L.*, *loc. cit.*, col. 340, and Lesley's note, *ibid.*).

The Oblation finished, the Bishop returned to his
throne and washed his hands. This is also an ancient

custom, which is attested both by the *Apostolic Constitutions* (i, VIII, c. xi.) and by Cyril of Jerusalem (*Catech. myst.*, V). In Spain it was the Deacon who served at this office, while the sub-Deacon offered water to the Priests and Deacons for the same purpose. The Bishop then returned to the altar, gave the signal for stopping the singing of the *Sacrificium*, and said *Adjuvate me, fratres* ; after which he recited the *Accedam ad te*, which belongs to the class of *Apologiæ sacerdotis* (*P.L.*, *loc. cit.*, col. 113, and article *Apologies* in DACL. On the differences between these rites and the modifications which they underwent in the Mozarabic liturgy during the Middle Ages, see Lesley's note, col. 535).

Missa.—The Priest usually said with the *Dominus sit semper vobiscum* another prayer called *Missa*. It is the first of the seven prayers of St. Isidore (*De Offic.*, i, I, c. xiv.). Etherius and Beatus describe it in these terms : *Prima oratio admonitionis erga populum est, ut omnes excitentur ad orandum Deum* (*Adv. Elipand.*, i, I). It is plainly an opening prayer, the opening of the Mass of the Faithful, a prayer to prepare them for the Sacrifice. It varies according to the Feasts and liturgical epochs, and is addressed sometimes to the faithful, *dilectissimi fratres* ; sometimes to God the Father or to Our Lord (*P.L.*, col. 113 ; cf. 346 and 539). The Missal of Bobbio gives a similar prayer, but this often has no title. Once it is called (as here) *Missa* ; another time *Collectio* ; and twice, *Præfatio*. In the other Gallican Sacramentaries it is called *Præfatio*, or *Præfatio Missæ*. The title *Oratio* is also given to it in the *Missale Mixtum* (*P.L.*, col. 539).

The *Missa* is sometimes an invocation of the Father or the Son ; sometimes a series of pious exclamations ; sometimes again a lyrical chant in honour of the mystery or of the martyr whose Feast the Church is celebrating. Sometimes it is preceded by an *Apologia sacerdotis,*

After the *Missa* the clergy responded : *Agie, agie, agie,* etc. Then the Priest said : *Erigite vos* (*Liber ordinum,* cols. 234, 235, and 186, 191 ; *Liber Sacramentorum Mozarabicus,* p. xx.).

Prayer of the Faithful.—After the prayer the people said *Amen,* and the Priest added these words : *Per misericordiam tuam,* etc. Then, raising his hands : *Oremus,* to which the choir responded : *Agyos, Agyos, Agyos, Domine Deus, Rex æterne tibi laudes et gratias. Postea dicat Presbyter : Ecclesiam sanctam catholicam. in orationibus in mente habeamus . . . omnes lapsos, captivos, infirmos, atque peregrinos in mente habeamus : ut eos Dominus,* etc. In the *Liber Mozarabicus* this prayer is simply called *alia oratio,* or even *alia* (cf. p. xxi.). The choir responded : *Presta eterne omnipotens Deus.* The Priest continued : *Purifica Domine Deus Pater omnipotens . . .* making mention of the Priests who offered, of the Pope, and all Priests and other clerics. The commemoration of Apostles and Martyrs followed, their names being enumerated. In all these prayers the choir intervened with occasional acclamations (*P.L., loc. cit.,* col. 113). The *Liber Offerentium,* called by the Mozarabites the *Little Missal,* contains this prayer under a very much better form, and Lesley's notes must correct that which he gives in col. 113. The *Liber Offerentium* has been included in the *Missale Mixtum* (*P.L.,* cols. 530–569. The *Prayer of the Faithful* will be found in col. 539 *seq.*). These different prayers, from the first *Per misericordiam tuam . . . Oremus,* would seem to tend towards the second prayer of the Mass defined by St. Isidore : *Secunda* (*oratio*) *invocationis ad Deum est, ut clementer suscipiat preces fidelium, oblationemque eorum.* Here indeed can be recognised the principal features of that Prayer of the Faithful, or Litanic Prayer, which in the beginning could be found in all liturgies. The Greek and Eastern liturgies have kept it, but in the Roman it has almost disappeared except in the solemn prayers on Good Friday, which give us the Prayer of the Faithful under one of its most ancient and perfect forms. In the Mozarabic Missal it is not given with anything like the same clearness ; and has probably been retouched again and again. The expression *Ecclesiam sanctam catholicam in orationibus in mente habeamus* recalls that of St. Fructuosus in 259 : *In mente me habere necesse est sanctam Ecclesiam catholicam ab oriente usque ad occidentem diffusam* (in Ruinart, *Acta Mart.*, p. 222).

In the manuscripts the reading of the names appears to be considered as a separate rite, under the title of *Nomina offerentium*. The list of the names of the living was followed by that of the dead. Usually the Deacon, or the Priest himself, read this list ; but sometimes it fell to one of the *Cantores*. *Transfer hæc nomina in pagina cœli, que levitarum et cantorum tuorum officis recitata sunt, in Libro vivorum digito tuo*, we read in the *Liber Mozarabicus* (ed. Férotin, col. 546, and Introduction, p. xxi.).[1]

Oratio post nomina.—This is the name of the prayer which follows. The preceding prayer had comprised the reading of the names of those who offered, and of the dead : *item pro spiritibus pausantium* (*P.L.*, *loc. cit.*, col. 114). It is the third in the order followed by St. Isidore, and he defines it thus : *Tertia autem, effunditur pro offerentibus sive pro defunctis fidelibus, ut per id sacrificium veniam consequantur*. Like the preceding prayers, its text varies according to the Feasts. We may note that here the Memento of the Dead is not separated from that of the living, as in the Roman Mass. Moreover, the Spanish diptychs do not only contain the

---

[1] With regard to all this, see the two articles, *Diptyques* and *Litanies*, in DACL.

names of Apostles and Martyrs, but also those of Old
Testament Saints, Patriarchs, and Prophets (*ibid.*, col.
483 and note). This also was the custom of the Gallican
churches, and Venantius Fortunatus has rightly said :

> Nomina vestra legat patriarchis atque prophetis
> *Quos hodie in templo diptychus edit ebur.*
>
> (i, X, *carm.* vii.)

(See also the prayer *Post nomina* for the Feast of St. Leger,
note 68, p. 283.) We find the same custom in many of
the Greek and Eastern liturgies. St. Cyril of Jerusalem
had said : *Recordamus patriarcharum prophetarum . . . ut
Deus eorum precibus et intercessione orationem nostram
suscipiat* (*Catech.*, V ; Lesley refers in a note to these
different liturgies, col. 483). The prayer *Post nomina*,
in the Gallican liturgies, presents characteristic analogies.
It was the Deacon who read the Diptychs, the Priest
following with the prayer (*P.L.*, col. 375).

In connection with the prayer *Post nomina*, Dom Férotin
rightly calls attention to that *Secret* of the Roman Missal :
*Deus cui soli cognitus est numerus electorum in superna
felicitate locandus . . . et omnium fidelium nomina beatæ
prædestinationis liber adscripta retineat*, which is a true
Oratio post nomina. He is mistaken in calling it a
quadragesimal *Secret* ; it belongs to the Mass of the
Dead, and there can be no doubt as to its Gallican origin,
as well as to that of the Collect and Post-communion
which accompany it (Dom Férotin, *Liber Mozarabicus*,
p. xxi.).

We may also notice the very long *Oratio post nomina*,
which is a homily in itself, drawn up towards the end of
the seventh century by St. Julian of Toledo, and which
was imposed on all Priests by a contemporary Council of
Toledo to end an intolerable abuse. There was a question
as to whether certain priests did not, in the *Oratio post*

nomina, pray for the death of their enemies. The text of
St. Julian's prayer is a long and vehement protestation
against such criminal manœuvres (see the 5th Canon of
the XVIIth Council of Toledo in 694. The prayer is in the
Liber Ordinum, cols. 331–334. Cf. also *Liber Mozarabicus*,
p. xxi.).

Oratio ad pacem.—This is thus defined by St. Isidore :
Quarta post hæc infertur pro osculo pacis. The Kiss of
Peace is placed close to the Communion in the Roman
Mass ; in Spain, as also in Gaul and in the East, it
precedes the Consecration, and even the *Illatio.*

It may be said that it is attached to the Prayer of the
Faithful, of which it was the natural conclusion. Primitively, the Kiss of Peace must have been frequent, and
have formed a part of every synaxis. It must have been
fixed at this place in the Mass at an early date, and it
was also natural that it should precede the Communion.
Perhaps it took place twice in certain churches ; in that
case one of the two rites must soon have been suppressed
as useless. However it may have been in primitive
practice, as to which we have not sufficient information,
we see this singularity mentioned in the Roman rite with
regard to the place of the Kiss of Peace at a very early
date, in contradistinction from the other Latin liturgies,
as well as the Eastern. I have mentioned the following
very significant fact elsewhere : in the *Traditio Apostolica*
of St. Hippolytus, which represents the Roman liturgy
at the beginning of the third century, the Kiss of Peace,
according to general custom, is attached to the Prayer
of the Faithful : *Et postea* (he is speaking of the neophytes
who had just received Baptism) *jam simul cum omni
populo orent, non primum orantes cum fidelibus, nisi
omnia hæc fuerint consecuti. Et cum oraverint, de ore
pacem offerant. Et tunc iam offeratur oblatio a diaconibus.
Didascaliæ Apostolorum fragmenta veronensia latina* (ed.

E. Hauler, Leipzig, 1900, pp. 111, 112). The suppression of the Prayer of the Faithful in the Roman Mass, at the moment when the Roman Canon as we have it to-day was established, must have brought about this change in the place of the Kiss of Peace, as no doubt it brought about many others.

Here, as in many other circumstances the Mozarabic Mass represents customs earlier than those of that of Rome. The *Oratio ad pacem* and the Kiss of Peace were attached to a whole which St. Isidore describes by the words *post hæc, i.e.* the prayers *Per misericordiam, Ecclesiam sanctam, Purifica Domine* (or prayer of oblation), the memorial of the holy Saints, Patriarchs, Apostles, Martyrs, etc., the reading of the Diptychs of the living and the dead with the prayer *Post nomina*. Only then, and quite logically, came the prayer for peace, and the Kiss of Peace (*P.L., loc. cit.*, col. 115). It goes without saying that the title *Oratio ad Patrem is* a typographical error for *ad Pacem*, as Lesley has already noted. In this the Spanish custom was the same as that of the Gallican churches, where an *Oratio ad pacem* followed the *Oratio post nomina*, and preceded the *Illatio* or *Contestatio*. In all these liturgies the text of the *Oratio ad pacem* varies according to the Feasts. In all, those prayers are always about peace, or the oblations. The Greek and Eastern liturgies also have this *Oratio ad pacem* followed by the Kiss of Peace (see these connections in Lesley's note, *P.L.*, col. 505).

According to the *Liber Ordinum* we see that the Deacon intervened at the Kiss of Peace with these words : *Inter vos pacem tradite*. The Council of Compostella (1056) alludes (c. 1) to the same usage (*Liber Ord.*, col. 191 ; cf. *Liber Mozar.*, p. xxi.). While this was going on the choir sang *Pacem relinquo vobis*, or some other anthem of the same kind. The same book gives a formula of

Ad Pacem in which the prayer is preceded by an invocation, as is often the case in this, and also in the Gallican liturgy (*Lib. Ordin.*, col. 236).

2. THE SACRIFICE.—The prayer of the anaphora, or Eucharistic prayer properly so called, begins after all this preparation.

Illatio.—This rite in the Mozarabic liturgy bears the name of *Inlatio*, or *Illatio* ; and St. Isidore defines it in these terms : *Quinta infertur illatio in sanctificatione oblationis in quam etiam Dei laudem, terrestrium creatura, virtutum cœlestium universitatis provocatur, et Osanna in Ecclesiis cantatur*. It is preceded by a dialogue which differs from that in the Roman Mass. The Priest, bending forward with his hands joined, says : *Introibo ad altare Dei ;* the choir : *Ad Deum qui lætificat juventutem meam*. The Priest, laying his hands on the chalice, says : *Aures ad Dominum*, the choir answering : *Habemus ad Dominum*. The Priest then says : *Sursum corda ;* the choir : *Levemus ad Dominum*. The Priest, bending forward with joined hands : *Deo ac Domino nostro Jesu Christo filio Dei qui est in cœlis dignas laudes dignasque gratias referamus*. Here he raises his hands towards Heaven (*P.L., loc. cit.*, col. 115). The Mozarabic *Illatio*, like the Roman Preface or the Gallican *Contestatio*, always ends with the *Sanctus*, and in Spain, as in Gaul, but unlike Rome, the *Sanctus* is followed by a prayer always called *Post Sanctus*. For St. Isidore the *Illatio*, or fifth prayer, comprehends the *Sanctus*, the *Post Sanctus*, and also the Consecration. The sixth prayer is that of the *Post pridie*, or *Confirmatio Sacramenti*. This division seems just, for it marks clearly the close union of all these parts, from the *Illatio* to the end of the Consecration. Again it is better suited to the title *Immolatio*, which is that of the Gallican Prefaces, the word being a good synonym for *Consecratio*.

As to the word *Illatio*, it is characteristic of the Moz-arabic books. Some have attempted to prove that it is a copyist's error for *Immolatio*, which, as has been said, is the Gallican title of the Preface, which can be explained naturally. But it is curious that if it be a copyist's error it should be so universal, for the word is found in all the Mozarabic books. The Preface is called *Illatio* everywhere ; nor do I believe the word *Immolatio* has ever been found there, except once in the *Liber Ordinum*. The question is curious, and perhaps deserves a separate study. *Illatio*, or *Inlatio*, like *Oblatio* (which is a synonym), is almost the exact translation of the word ἀναφέρω, to offer. In the post-classic tongue the word *Inlatio* (from *inferre*) means the action of carrying, like *Invectio*, and is specially applied to the dead (Ulpien) ; it also signifies the paying of tribute. In philosophic language an *Illatio* is a conclusion drawn from premises, *ex duobus sumptis ratione sibimet nexis conficitur illatio* (Capella). In Spain the word is used in the Councils in the sense of gift, present, tribute (Third Council of Braga, can. 2 ; and Seventh Council of Toledo).[1] Thus the term *Immolatio* of the Gallican liturgies is something quite different, which may be a corruption, or, if we like, a paleographic inter-pretation of the word *Illatio*. This is the opinion of Dom Cagin (*Les noms latins de la préface eucharistique*, in *Rassegna Gregoriana*, 1906, pp. 322–358) and also that to which Lesley was inclined (cf. *P.L.*, Vol. LXXXV, col. 507). But so far this is only a hypothesis founded on the similarity of the two words. It remains to be explained why one is exclusively used in the Mozarabic MSS. and the other almost exclusively in the Gallican.

On this point the latter are less exclusive than the former. In the *Missale Gothicum* as well as in the *Missale Gallicanum Immolatio* alternates with *Contestatio* and

[1] Cf. our article *Illatio* in DACL.

Præfatio Missæ ; it is not found at all in the *Missale Francorum*, and only once in the Missal of Bobbio, and then, as it would seem, by accident (cf. *Paléographie musicale*, Vol. V, pp. 100, 101, and 168). The word is absent, as well as *Contestatio*, in the letters of the pseudo-Germain, and it may well be that this is a fresh argument in favour of the recent date of these pretended letters (cf. *Germain, Lettres de Saint*, in DACL). The glossaries and *Thesauri*, Ducange, Forcellini, Freund, and the *Thesaurus linguæ latinæ* of Leipzig give but very insufficient information on this subject, under the word *Contestatio*.

Of the dialogue which precedes the *Illatio* we shall say nothing. It contains what we may call the essential elements which may be found in all liturgies, *Sursum corda, Gratias agamus*, etc., and those which serve as the opening of all Prefaces : *Vere dignum et justum est*, etc. To the sobriety of the dialogue of the Roman Preface the Spanish liturgy, as always, adds ornaments and complications which only serve to overload the text.

We are obliged to say the same thing of the *Illatio* itself. The Mozarabic books offer the richest and most varied collection of *Illationes* ; hardly a Mass but has its own ; some of them comprise many columns of text, and if they were sung, these must have lasted at least half an hour. We will attempt presently to discover their authors. But we may say at once that they form a dogmatic collection which is priceless for the study of theological history in Spain during the Middle Ages, and a collection which, it must be confessed, has as yet been but little studied. It contains pages which do honour to the learning, the depth, and the culture of Spanish theologians from the fifth-ninth centuries. We have treated the question of the orthodoxy of this liturgy elsewhere (see *Liturgia*, p. 816). Here and there we do doubtless find a few singular opinions, but taken as a whole, what riches of doctrine, what fervour of faith and piety! Here are real theological theses, and long panegyrics for the Feasts of Saints, especially for the Saints of Spain, like St. Vincent or St. Eulalia. We will mention only the *Illationes* on the Samaritan, on the man born blind, on fasting, on the Trinity, on the Descent into hell, on the Patriarchs, etc. (The first of these are in the *Liber Sacramentorum*, edited by Dom Férotin, pp. 167, 178, 184, 224, and 290; that on the Patriarchs in *P.L.*, Vol. LXXXV, cols. 271 and 287. See also the *Illatio* on the Trinity, col. 281.)

Naturally the same faults which we have already pointed out in all the other parts of this liturgy are found here; they are those of the Latin literature of Spain, especially from the sixth-tenth centuries—prolixity, verbiage, the abuse of verbal conceits and plays on words—in fact, all those faults which have been decorated with the name of Gongorism.

The Sanctus.—The *Illatio* always ends by a transition to the *Sanctus*. This *Sanctus* of the Mozarabic Mass is not invariable, as it is in the Roman liturgy and most others. In their love of variety the Mozarabic authors often introduced changes. This is the ordinary form:

Sanctus, sanctus, sanctus Dominus Deus Sabaoth: pleni sunt celi et terra gloria majestatis tue: Osanna filio David: Osanna in excelsis. Benedictus qui venit in nomine Domini: Osanna in excelsis (*P.L.*, *loc. cit.*, col. 116).

The singing of the *Sanctus* is assigned to the choir in the Mozarabic books. Formerly both in Spain and in Gaul the *Sanctus* was sung by the people. Thus we have in a *Post Sanctus* the words: *Psallitur* (hymnus iste) *ab angelis, et hic solemniter decantatur a populis* (*Post Sanctus* of the fifth Sunday in Lent, *P.L.*, col. 376). Gregory of Tours says in his turn: *Ubi expeditur contestatione omnis populus sanctus in Dei laudem pro-*

clamavit (*De mir. S. Martini*, I, II, c. xiv.). The Eastern
liturgies formerly had the same custom, as we see by the
Apostolic Constitutions, and by the texts of St. John
Chrysostom and of St. Gregory of Nyssa, quoted by
Lesley (col. 349). The texts quoted prove that it was
sung in Spain half in Latin, half in Greek. The same
usage obtained in Gaul.

Post Sanctus and Consecration.—The title *Post Sanctus*,
both in Spain and in Gaul, always designates a prayer
which is a paraphrase of the *Sanctus*, and which usually
begins with the words *Vere sanctus*. It is a transition
from the *Sanctus* to the Consecration ; and is also found,
though without a title, in the Greek and Eastern liturgies.
In Spain it varied daily (see, for example, *P.L.*, col. 549).

Vere sanctus did not end formerly with a doxology,
but went straight on to *Qui pridie*, by a short formula of
this kind : *Vere sanctus, vere benedictus Dominus noster
Jesus Christus qui pridie*, with the words of Institution.
The *Qui pridie* was the Roman formula, as also that of
the Gallican and all the Latin churches. The ancient
Spanish liturgy followed the same tradition. By a
change wrought in the Mozarabic liturgy at a date which
cannot be fixed, one of the most audacious changes of
which that rite has preserved the trace, the sacred
formula was broken into by the introduction of the
prayer *Adesto Jesu bone*, and by replacing the *Qui pridie*,
one of the most striking and characteristic features of the
Roman and other Latin liturgies, by the *In qua nocte*,
which is the version followed by all the Greek and
Eastern rites. What is perhaps even more extraordinary,
the reformers did not try to conceal the traces of this
change, but continued to call the prayer which follows
the recital of the Institution, *Oratio post pridie* ! We
give here the text of the *Adesto* :

Adesto, adesto Jesu bone Pontifex in medio nostri : sicut

fuisti in medio discipulorum tuorum : sancti † fica hanc oblationem : † *ut sanctificata* † *sumamus per manus sancti angeli tui sancte domine ac redemtor eterne* (here there is a gap in the *Missale Mixtum*). *Dominus noster Jesus Christus in qua nocte tradebatur accepit panem : et gratias agens, bene* † *dixit ac fregit : deditque discipulis suis dicens : Accipite et manducate. Hoc : est : corpus : meum : quod : pro : vobis : tradetur. Hic elevatur corpus. Quotiescumque manducaveritis : hoc facite in meam* † *commemorationem. Similiter et calicem postquam cenavit dicens. Hic* † *est : calix : novi : testamenti : in : meo : sanguine : qui : pro : vobis : et : pro : multis : effundetur : in : remissionem : peccatorum. Hic elevatur calix coopertus cum filiola* (=*palla*). *Quotiescumque biberitis hoc facite in meam* † *commemorationem. Et cum perventum fuerit ubi dicit : In meam commemorationem, dicat presb. alta voce omnibus diebus preter festivis : pari modo ubi dicit in claritatem de celis. Ut qualibet vice respondeat chorus : Amen. Quotiescumque manducaveritis panem hunc et calicem biberitis : mortem Domini annunciabitis donec veniet. In claritatem de celis. ℞. Chorus. Amen* (*P.L., loc. cit.*, cols. 116–117 ; cf. also col. 550, another text).

In the later editions of the *Missale Mixtum* a note has been added to the effect that the form of Consecration here given is only a memorial of the past, but that at the present time the Roman form must be adhered to (*ibid.*, cols. 116, and 550, 551, note *a*).

Dom Férotin gives two new texts of the words of Institution according to the *Liber Mozarabicus* and the *Liber Ordinum*, which present many variants, not only with each other but with the *Missale Mixtum*. It can be seen that Rome did not approve the version given in the *Missale Mixtum* of 1500, and substituted for it the Roman formula. That extremely rare edition of Todole preserved at the British Museum contains, fastened to the vellum, this note : *Forma ista consecrationis ponitur ne antiquitas ignoretur ; sed hodie servetur Ecclesiæ traditio ;* and the Roman formula is then given. (This note is reproduced in *P.L.*, cols. 116 and 550. On all this cf. Dom Férotin, *Liber Mozarabicus*, p. xxv.) In two MSS. quoted by Dom Férotin the words of Institution are preceded by the title *Missa secreta* ; and he gives another example in which the *Post Sanctus* is called *Post Missam secretam*, which clearly show that at that time this part of the Canon was said in a low voice (*ibid.*).

The very tenor of this prayer shows that it interrupts the sequence of the *Vere sanctus*, and repeats the formula *Dominus noster Jesus Christus*. It is quite evidently an interpolation, a fact which has been emphasised by the greater number of modern liturgiologists since Le Brun, Binius, Lesley, Dom Férotin, Dom Cagin, etc. But no protestations seem to have been raised in the Middle Ages ; at least I do not think that any signs of them have been traced up till now. Without seeking for any other explanation, it must simply be stated that at a certain moment, assuredly later than St. Isidore and probably before the tenth century—probably also at Toledo—a Bishop thought well to borrow, from the liturgy of Constantinople, which had already lent so much to Spain, the actual form of Consecration, and this he then substituted for the ancient form which was that of Rome and of all Latin churches (*P.L., loc. cit.*, col. 549).

The actual formula, *Hoc est corpus meum*, is borrowed from 1 Cor. xi. 24 ; while the *quod pro vobis* is the translation of the Vulgate. The Roman formula, *Hoc est enim corpus meum*, conforms to that in the liturgy of St. Mark ; and it seems also to have been that of the Gallican churches, at least, according to the letters of the pseudo-

Germain. The formula for the Consecration of the wine is borrowed from I Cor. xi. 24, and from St. Luke xxii. 20, and St. Matthew xxvi. 28. The words *Hic est calix novi Testamenti in meo sanguine* are those of an ancient Latin version different from the Vulgate ; they are quoted under the same form by Sedulius Scotus and by Gregory II (see the quotation, *P.L., loc. cit.*, col. 551). The Roman formula, *Hic est enim calix sanguinis mei*, etc., was also that of the Gallican churches. The Spanish liturgiologists of that day were not afraid to paraphrase the words of Institution in their own way. (On all this see Lesley's note, col. 551 *seq.*)

It is stated in the rubrics of the recital of the Institution that there was a double elevation. The custom of the elevation is universal, but it was not practised everywhere in the same way. That here mentioned is conformable with the usage established in France in the eleventh century, which thence spread, with certain variants, to Rome and to other churches. The Mozarabic rubric shows that the chalice was covered at the elevation ; that is, covered with the *palla*, or veil, sometimes called the *Offertorium*, because it had been used to collect the offerings of the faithful at the Oblation. This was formerly the Roman custom when the elevation took place at the end of the Canon after the *Per ipsum* (cf. the first *Ordo Romanus* of Mabillon, note 16, and the *Ordo* published by Hittorp).

Another rubric which prescribes the words *In meam commemorationem* and *In claritatem de celis* to be said aloud would give the impression that the actual words of the Institution were to be said in a low voice. But Lesley thinks with apparent reason that this rubric is recent, and that the Spanish, like the French, said these words aloud. As to the words *In claritatem de celis*, they are another peculiarity of the Mozarabic rite. On Holy

Thursday the Epistle was read from 1 Cor. xi. 20–34.
After the words *mortem Domini annunciabitis donec
veniat* they added this variant : *in claritatem de celis*,
taken from the liturgy, but which does not exist in the
Vulgate, or in the Greek, or in any other version with
which we are acquainted (see *P.L.*, col. 409, for the text
of the Epistle, and col. 552 for the rubric).

Oratio Post pridie and *Epiclesis.* — The prayer *Post
pridie*, which follows the Consecration, corresponds with
that called *Post secreta*, or *Post mysterium* in the Gallican
books. St. Isidore speaks of it in these terms : *Ex hinc
sexta oratio succedit, confirmatio sacramenti, ut oblatio
quæ Domino offertur, per Spiritum Sanctum sanctificata,
Christi corporis et sanguinis confirmetur* (*De offic.*, 1,
I, c. xv. ; cf. Etherius and Beatus, who emphasise the
terms *Confirmatio sacramenti*). It should be noted that
the Missal of Bobbio has no prayer *Post secreta*, which is
also missing occasionally in the *Missale Gallicanum* as
well as in the *Missale Gothicum*. But on the other hand
it is always found in the *Missale Mixtum*, and as it varies
daily, and is sometimes very long, we have here, as in the
Illatio, one of those prayers in which the exuberance of
the Spanish Fathers has had free course. Both the
place and the function of this prayer *Confirmatio Sacramenti* are more propitious than those of the *Illatio* for
dogmatic developments. It will be found of great use
in the study of the doctrine of the Spanish church upon
the Eucharist, notably upon Transubstantiation and the
questions connected with it. In reality the prayer
answers to the *Epiclesis* of the Eastern liturgies, and, as
we have remarked elsewhere, the expressions here used
must often be interpreted *cum grano salis*. We can note
only a few of such examples here, as in cols. 117 and 250,
note 7 ; 519, note *a* (cf. also article *Liturgie*, in *Dict. de
théol.*, col. 812, and *Epiclèse* in DACL).

Sometimes, but far more rarely, the *Epiclesis* is found in the *Post sanctus*. (There are some examples of this in Dom Férotin's *Liber Mozarabicus* ; in the same Sacramentary the *Post pridie* is called *Post missam secretam* on the vigil of Easter, a point worthy of remark.) On the other hand, and speaking generally, the *Post pridie* often contains the proof that the Consecration or Transubstantiation is accomplished by the words of Institution. To this interpretation the elevation also bears witness, but it is difficult to fix the date of this rite with the Mozarabites. We may quote, as especially explicit, the following *Post pridie* : *Hec pia, hec salutaris hostia, Deus Pater, qua tibi reconciliatus est mundus. Hoc est corpus illud, quod pependit in cruce. Hic etiam sanguis, qui sacro profluxit ex latere, etc. (Liber Moz.,* col. 313).

The prayer *Te prestante*, which for the rest has no particular title, seems rather the conclusion of the *Post pridie* than a separate prayer. As we shall see, it resembles our *Per quem hæc omnia bona creas*. This is the text :

Te prestante sancte Domine : quia tu hæc omnia nobis indignis servis tuis : valde bona creas : sancti † ficas, vivificas † bene † dicis ac prestas nobis : ut sit [sint] benedicta a te Deo nostro in secula seculorum. R̥. *Amen.*

The Priest then takes the consecrated Host on the paten ; holds it over the uncovered chalice, and says, or sings : *Dominus sit semper vobiscum.* R̥. *Et cum spiritu tuo. Fidem quam corde credimus ore autem dicamus,* and he elevates the consecrated Host to show It to the people. In some places there was sung at this point an anthem : *Ad confractionem panis (P.L., loc. cit.,* col. 117 ; cf. also p. 554 for the explanation of this prayer). Here, as in the Ambrosian Missal, the *Hæc omnia* seems to refer to the consecrated elements of bread and wine, created by God, sanctified by prayer, vivified by Consecration, blessed by the Holy Ghost (*Epiclesis*), and finally given to the faithful in the Eucharist. This at least is the interpretation given to these words by Lesley, who will not admit that of Benedict XIV and other liturgiologists, who say that *Hæc omnia* means the fresh fruits which were blessed at this moment. It is an old quarrel amongst liturgiologists, and one which seems as yet unresolved (Benedict XIV, *De missæ sacrificio*, I, II, c. xviii.). Lesley admits that in certain Sacramentaries these words may indeed apply to a blessing of this kind, but only in a special case. In his opinion the words are too precise, the gestures too solemn to be applied to anything but the elements consecrated in the Eucharist (col. 553, note *c*).

It is a general custom that the Elevation should take place at this moment. Before the eleventh century it was the principal Elevation. We may also notice that in the Roman Missal the prayer is addressed to God the Father, and that it closes with a magnificent doxology which has disappeared in the Mozarabic Mass.

The Credo.—The Spanish were the first in the West to introduce the symbol of Nicea-Constantinople into the Mass. In the East the custom already existed, and in 568 Justinus the Younger made it a law. In 597 the Third Council of Toledo issued an edict : *Ut prius quam Dominica dicatur oratio, voce clara a populo* [symbolum Constantinopolitanum] *decantetur, quo fides vera*, etc. This is a fresh example of the eagerness shown by the Spanish Bishops to follow the customs of Constantinople. From Spain the usage spread into Gaul ; but Rome held out long, and only yielded in the eleventh century. The true place of this symbol is in the rite of Baptism, and it is not an essential element of the Mass. The Gallican churches sang it after the Gospel, at the end of the Mass of the catechumens, and this too is the place given to it by Rome. Like the Greeks and Orientals, the Spanish, by putting it at the end of the Canon, before the *Pater*, rather disturbed the general equilibrium of this part of the Mass ; and, moreover, diminished accordingly the importance of the *Pater*. This story of the insertion of the *Credo* in the Mass is fairly well known ; and we shall say no more about it. (Cf. Mgr. Batiffol, *Leçons sur la Messe*, p. 11. See also Lesley's note, which, as is always the case, is highly instructive, and that of Dom Férotin quoted on the next page. For rather curious variants of the Spanish text—the *Credimus*, the *Omousion*, the *Ex Patre et Filio procedentem*, etc., cf. Lesley, *P.L.*, *loc. cit.*, col. 555 *seq.*, and *Liber Moz.*, col. 37.)

The *Liber Mozarabicus* contains a formula of introduction to the *Credo* : *Omnes qui Christi sanguinis effusione*, etc., which is not met with in any printed book, nor even, according to Dom Férotin, in any MS. (*Liber Moz.*, *ibid.*).

Fraction.—In the Mozarabic rite the Fraction is rather complicated. The Priest divides the Host in the middle, placing half on the paten ; the other half is divided into five parts, which are also placed on the paten. He then divides the first part into four. The nine particles so obtained are arranged in the form of a Cross, and each receives its name : *Corporatio* (or Incarnation), *Nativitas*, *Circumcisio*, *Apparitio* (or Epiphany), *Passio*, *Mors*, *Resurrectio*, and, separately, *Gloria*, *Regnum*. This figure is twice given in *P.L.*, *loc. cit.*, cols. 118 and 557. St. Ildephonsus alludes to the names of these fragments (*De cognitione baptismi*, c. xix. ; cf. *Liber Moz.*, p. xxxiii.). It is unnecessary to say that all these rites are not ancient, any more than it is an ancient practice to make the Memento of the Living here, since at the beginning of the Mass of the Faithful a Memento of the Living and the Dead has already been

made. When the *Credo* is finished the *Pater* is said.
The Fraction of the bread, a rite so important in its
origin that it gave its name to the Mass, has become here,
as in the Celtic liturgies, so complicated as to fall sometimes into mere superstition ; it is usually accompanied
by the singing of the *Confractio*, which is to be found in
most liturgies. In this rite it is called *Laudes ad confractionem.* (Cf. *Liber Ordinum*, col. 239, and *Liber
Moz.*, p. xxiii. Cf. also our article *Fraction*, in DACL,
and *P.L.*, cols. 118 and 557.)

The Pater.—The *Pater* is recited in the Mozarabic Mass
as it is in most liturgies. It is preceded by a prelude
which varies according to the day ; it is almost always
a paraphrase analogous to the Roman prelude, but generally more extensive and more complicated. The *Pater*
ends with an embolism of which we shall presently speak
(*P.L.*, col. 118, cf. 559–591). It is a rather singular thing
that the prelude begins with the word *Oremus*, which is
sung by the Priest. But this rubric is of a later age,
like that which prescribes *Oremus* before *Agios*. In the
church of Spain in ancient times it was the Deacon and
not the Priest who said *Oremus* ; the Deacon, too, made
the other interventions : *Flectamus genua, Erigite vos,
Levate aures ad Dominum, Silentium facite.* St. Isidore
says of the Deacons : *Hi voces tonitruorum, ipsi enim,
clara voce, in modum præconis, admoneant cunctos sive in
orando, sive in flectendo genua, sive in psallendo, sive in
lectionibus audiendo*, etc. (*De offic. eccl.*, I, II, c. viii.).
Etherius also alludes to them (*Adv. Elipand.*, I, I).
The same custom is noted by the pseudo-Germain (cf.
col. 1079).

The presence of the *Pater* in the Mass in most liturgies,
since the fourth century at least, is a well-known fact.
In Spain, however, certain Priests only said it on Sunday.
The Fourth Council of Toledo, therefore, proclaimed it

of daily obligation (Canon 10). But it was not said everywhere in the same manner. In Spain the Priest begins *Pater noster qui es in cœlis,* and the people answer *Amen,* and so on with all the petitions. At *Panem nostrum quotidianum da nobis hodie* they respond : *Quia tu es Deus* ; and after the word *tentationem,* at the end : *Sed libera nos a malo, Amen.* The *Pater* is the seventh and last of the prayers of the Mass according to St. Isidore (*De offic.,* 1, I, c. xv. ; *P.L., loc. cit.,* col. 559 *seq.*).

The embolism is not variable as it is with the Gallicans. It is a paraphrase of the last petition in the form of a liturgical prayer, *Liberati a malo,* etc. (*P.L.,* col. 119). The *Liberati* is sung, like the *Pater* ; the same custom obtains in the rite of Lyons, and even in that of Rome on Good Friday.

Commixtion.—After the embolism the Priest takes from the paten that fragment of the Host which corresponds to *Regnum* (see *Fraction, ut sup.*), holds it over the chalice, and lets it fall therein with the words : *Sancta sanctis et conjunctio corporis Domini nostri Jesu Christi : sit sumentibus et potantibus nobis ad veniam : et fidelibus defunctis prestetur ad requiem.* From Easter to Pentecost he said instead, with a loud voice, thrice these words : *Vicit leo de tribu Juda radix David,* to which the people responded : *Qui sedes super Cherubim radix David, Alleluia* (*P.L., loc. cit.,* col. 119).

The *Sancta sanctis* is an ancient Eastern formula, to which St. Cyril of Jerusalem alluded ; it is preserved in the greater number of Eastern liturgies. It loses a little of its strength here, because it is said in a low voice, and because it forms part of the prayer of *Commixtion.* Lesley rightly supposes that formerly the *Sancta sanctis* was said aloud in Spain and in Gaul, as it was with the Easterns, and that it was followed, as in Gaul, by the singing of the *Trecanum,* a hymn in honour of the

Trinity. With the Easterns also the *Sancta sanctis* is a doxology (*P.L.*, *loc. cit.*, col. 561, note *a*). We may note that Dom Martène has pointed out in two MSS. of Angers the formulas : *Sanctum cum sanctis*, and *Sancta cum sanctis et commixtio*, etc. (*De ant. Eccl. Rit.*, 1, I, c. iv. art. 9).

As for the formula of Commixtion, *et sanguinis* must naturally be added to *corporis*, as *potantibus nobis* suggests. It corresponds with the same rite in the Roman Canon, *Hæc commixtio et consecratio corporis et sanguinis*, etc., and to that of the Ambrosian Canon, which is almost the same. The rite of *Commixtio* itself is ancient, and common to most liturgies, but here, as for the Fraction, a great variety of customs exists. We content ourselves with referring to our article *Messe*, in which these different customs are noticed. The note may also be read in which Lesley describes and compares these rites (*loc. cit.*, col. 561, note *c* ; cf. also *Liber Ordinum*, pp. 239–241, and *Liber Moz.*, p. xxiii.).

Blessing.—The rite of Blessing in Spain, as in Gaul, is placed after the *Pater*. The Deacon warns the people : *Humiliate vos benedictioni. Dominus sit semper vobiscum. Et cum spiritu tuo.* The Priest then blesses them with a variable formula, which is interspersed with *Amens* like the *Pater* (see, *e.g.*, *P.L.*, col. 119).

There are a few differences as to the exterior form of this blessing between the churches of Gaul and those of Spain, but the fact of a blessing at this moment is common to both of them ; and in both cases the rites present striking analogies. The African church had also this custom of Episcopal blessing, as may be seen by the letter of the Council of Carthage to Innocent I against Pelagius and Celestinus, and by letter CLXXXIX of St. Augustine to John of Jerusalem. But neither the Roman liturgy nor those of the Greek and Eastern churches followed this custom. We find, indeed, formulas of Episcopal blessings in the Roman collections, but they are Gallican additions. The Sixth Council of Toledo (c. 18) recalls the practice of Spain in these words : *ut post orationem dominicam et conjunctionem panis et calicis, benedictio in populum segnatur, et tum demum sacramentum corporis et sanguinis Domini sumatur* (Canon 18, *P.L.*, col. 592, note *b*).

Communion.—The Communion in the Mozarabic rite comprehends a collection of rites and formulas which must first be described : The salutation of the people by *Dominus sit semper vobiscum* ; singing of the *Gustate et videte* and other verses, with doxology *Gloria et honor Patri*. During the chanting of the *Gustate* the Priest takes that particle of the Host which answers to the word *Gloria*, holds it over the chalice while reciting *Panem celestem*, and then says : *Memento pro mortuis*, reciting the prayer : *Dominus meus*, etc.

He makes the sign of the Cross with the Host, consumes the particle which was in his hand, covers the chalice, and consumes the other fragments of the Host, following the appointed order. He then places the paten on the chalice, saying : *Ave in evum celestis potus*, etc. He takes the Blood, and says the prayer : *Dominus meus Pater et Filius*, etc. The choir sings *Refecti corpore et sanguine*. The Priest goes to the corner of the altar and recites a prayer beginning with the words of the preceding chant : *Refecti corpore et sanguine*, etc. This is the prayer of Thanksgiving, which closes with the doxology : *Per misericordiam tuam*, etc. (*P.L.*, col. 120 ; cf. also cols. 554, 561, 566, and *Liber Ordinum*, 241, 242 ; *Liber Mozar.*, p. xxiii.).

The Deacon intervenes at the Communion with the order : *Locis vestris accedite*. Each then must take his place according to a strictly established order : higher

clergy, lower clergy, men, women. To each of the faithful he gives a part of the Blood, for Communion was
received under both kinds. The anthem *Gustate* is
called *Ad accedentes*.

Completuria and end of the Mass.—The *Liber Mozarabicus* and the *Liber Ordinum* sometimes contain after the
Communion prayers an *Oratio completuria*, or simply,
Completuria, which recalls the Roman *Post-communion*.
There are many examples of this (*Liber Ordinum*, cols.
272, 273 ; *Liber Moz.*, col. 343, and pp. xxiii. and xxxv. ;
and the Index at the word *Completuria*).

The end of the Mass is thus announced : the Priest
salutes the people with *Dominus sit*, etc. ; the Deacon
says : *Solemnia completa sunt in nomine Domini nostri
Jesu Christi, votum nostrum sit acceptum cum pace. Deo
gratias* (*P.L., loc. cit.*, col. 120). In the *Liber Mozarabicus*
the Deacon says : *Missa acta est* (p. xxxv.).

GENERAL REMARKS.—We shall not point out the
analogies between this Mass and that of the Gallican
rite ; they are so self-evident that many liturgiologists
consider both liturgies as two branches from the same
trunk, or even as derived one from the other.

From this study of the Mozarabic Mass it may be
concluded that this particular liturgy was in a great
measure a national one, like that of Gaul, its sister.
Many of its formulas were written by Spanish prelates ;
certain rites also were created by them. For many
centuries Toledo was the centre of what may truly be
called a national liturgy. If ever a Spanish Abbé Bremond
writes the history of religious feeling in his own country
—as it has already been admirably written for France
—the Mozarabic liturgy will take the most important
place therein, and all will be astonished at the wealth,
variety, and singularity of its formulas.

We shall not stop here to discuss the question of the

orthodoxy of this liturgy, since this has been fully argued by liturgiologists of the seventeenth and eighteenth centuries ; by Edmund Bishop, Dom Férotin, Mgr. Mercati, and Dom de Bruyne. It would take us too far from our subject. We can only give here a Bibliography in which will be found the names of the principal authors by whom the question has been discussed.

BIBLIOGRAPHY

F. Arevalo, *Sancti Isidori opera omnia, P.L.*, Vols. LXI–LXXXIV, and especially Vol. I, *Isidoriana*.

Bianchini, *Thomasii opera omnia*, vol. I (Rome, 1741 ; only volume issued) ; on this work, which includes the *Libellus orationum*, cf. Ed. Bishop, *Spanish Symbols*, in *Liturgica Historica*, p. 165 *seq.*

W. C. Bishop. Under the title *The Mozarabic and Ambrosian Rites* (London, 1924), the Fifteenth Tract of the Alcuin Club, is a collection of four Essays by W. C. Bishop, one of which is entitled : *The Mass in Spain* ; the same writer published an article : *The Mozarabic Rite*, in *Church Quarterly Review*, October 1906, January 1907.

Cl. Blume, *Hymnodia Gothica* (Leipzig, 1897).

A. M. Burriel, *Codex Muzarabicus*, etc.; cf. *Particularités littéraires sur la liturgie mozarabe tirées des lettres MSS. du P.B.*, in the *Journal des savants*, 1787, pp. 9-14.

De Bruyne, *De l'origine de quelques textes mozarabes*, in *Revue Bénédictine*, 1913, vol. XXX, pp. 421-436 ; *Un système de lectures dans la liturgie mozarabe*, in *Revue Bénédictine*, 1922, Vol. XXXIV, pp. 147-155.

Callevaert, *Le carême primitif dans la liturgie Mozarabe* in *Revue bénédictine*, 1926, t. XXXVIII, p. 60.

Cenni, *Antiquitates Ecclesiæ Hispaniæ*.

D. A. Dold, *Eine Parallele zum Liturgie—Fragment 1 aus Cod. Aug. CXCV in der Mozarabischen Liturgie*, in *Revue Bénédictine*, 1927, Vol. XXXIX, pp. 135-136.

Eiguren, *Memoriadescription de los codices notables conservados en los archivos ecclesiasticos de España* (Madrid, 1859).

EUVALD & LÖWE, *Exempla scripturæ visigothica* (Heidelberg, 1883).

FLOREZ, *De la Misa antiqua de España*, in *España Sagrada*, Vol. III, p. 187 *seq* (Madrid, 1748).

(For the question of the orthodoxy of this liturgy, cf. :

ED. BISHOP, in *Journal of Theological Studies*, 1909, pp. 602-603.

ALB. GAYAN, *La Messe mozarabique*, in *Revue des sciences ecclésiastiques*, 1886, pp. 446-456.

C. A. HALE, *Mozarabic Liturgy*, in *Amer. Christ. Church Review*, 1876, Vol. XXVIII, p. 273 *seq*.

P. LEBRUN, *Ancienne et nouvelle liturgie des Églises d'Espagne*, in *Explication de la Messe*, édit. 1726, Vol. II, p. 272 *seq*.

MERCATI, *More Spanish Symbols*, in Bishop's *Liturgica Historica*, p. 203 *seq*. ; and in *Journal of Theological Studies*, Vol. VIII, 1907, pp. 423-430.

To complete this Bibliography see :

JENNER, *Mozarabic Rite*, in *The Catholic Encyclopedia*, which is scholarly, and contains a complete Bibliography.

La Liturgie mozarabe, in *Liturgia*, pp. 814-819.

U. CHEVALIER, *Topo-bibliographie*, at the word *Mozarabe* (*Liturgie*).

DOM CABROL, *Mozarabe* (*La Liturgie*) in DACL.

CHAPTER VII

THE MASS IN GAUL

The Mass of the Catechumens.—The Mass of the Faithful.

IN the volume on *Books of the Latin Liturgy* (Sands & Co., London), pp. 96–103, we have mentioned the different documents by the aid of which the Gallican Mass may be reconstituted and the origins of this liturgy established. On this subject we have also stated that for the description of the Gallican Mass no reliance can be placed on the pretended letters of St. Germain of Paris, though this has been done too often. These letters are not a document of the middle of the sixth century, but an anonymous treatise written a century later (*ibid.*, p. 99). We must therefore, like Mabillon and, more recently, Dom Wilmart (DACL, *Germain, Lettres de St.*), keep solely to the other documents which we possess on this subject, and to the texts of contemporary authors, the most valuable of which is that of Gregory of Tours. A very complete bibliography of all these documents will be found in the article *Gallicanes* (*Liturgies*) of Dom Leclercq, DACL.

THE MASS OF THE CATECHUMENS

The Gallican Pre-Mass, or Mass of the catechumens, was already very fully developed ; it possessed chanted anthems, psalms, canticles, readings, and litanies. It began with an anthem and a psalm, while the Priest went from the sacristy to the altar. This chant, executed by clerics, existed also in the Mozarabic Mass, and answers to the Roman *Introit* and the *Ingressa* of the Milanese rite. Gregory of Tours, whatever may be said to the contrary, makes no allusion to this introductory anthem.

The Deacon enjoined silence, probably in these words : *Silentium facite.* The Bishop saluted the congregation with the formula : *Dominus sit semper vobiscum.* At Rome and Milan the salutation is : *Dominus vobiscum.* But the former greeting is found in the Mozarabic rite.

The letters of the pseudo-Germain announce the solemn singing of the *Aios* in Latin and in Greek at this point. What was this chant ? It is not the *Sanctus*, as has been wrongly believed, and which, also wrongly, has sometimes been called the *Trisagion*. The latter title must be reserved for a chant of Byzantine origin, the history of which is well known. It was introduced there under Theodosius II (408–450), but is perhaps more ancient, and runs thus : Ἅγιος ὁ Θεός Ἅγιος ἰσχυρός Ἅγιος ἀθάνατος ἐλέησον ἡμᾶς. Pierre le Foulon (+477) added these words to it : ὁ σταυρωθεὶς δἰ ἡμᾶς, and there was much quarrelling over this formula, which for its author had a monophysite meaning, and which was adopted by the Syrian Jacobites. On Good Friday, in the Roman liturgy, we have the *Trisagion* under its primitive double form in Greek and Latin, naturally without Foulon's addition. There is yet another form in the Mozarabic liturgy, which does not concern us here (cf. Dom Férotin, *Liber Ordinum*, cols. 737, 760, and 809).

The *Kyrie Eleison* was then sung, once only, by three children. We have spoken elsewhere as to the researches recently made regarding the *Kyrie Eleison*, and upon its use ; we shall therefore merely refer to the article under that heading in DACL.

The singing of the Prophecy which came next means the singing of the *Benedictus*. This point is now finally settled, and the *Collectio post Prophetiam* in the Gallican books is the prayer which followed. On the bearing of this canticle on the Mass we may also refer to our article, *Cantiques (évangéliques)*, in DACL. P. Thibaut has recently called attention to this chant, and its title of *Prophetia*. In his opinion it is exclusively Gallican, and is an allusion to the conversion of Clovis, who became the protector of the Gallo-Roman churches. The *Cornu salutis* may indeed have given rise to the legend of the *Sainte Ampoule* (*op. cit.*, p. 29).

Next comes the first Lesson. According to the pseudo-Germain this is taken from the Prophets or the historical books, and from the Apocalypse during Paschal time; while on the Feasts of Saints their Acts were read, *Gesta sanctorum confessorum ac martyrum in solemnpnitatibus eorum.* The usage of the prophetic Lesson has almost entirely disappeared from the Roman Mass since the fifth century; it was maintained longer at Milan, and on this point the Gallican books confirm the testimony of the pseudo-Germain. The Mozarabic rite has also preserved the ancient use of this Lesson. The importance of the reading of the Lives of the Saints at Mass will be noticed; this point is confirmed by Gregory of Tours and by the Gallican books. In Spain and at Milan the custom was the same.

The second reading at Mass was taken from the Acts of the Apostles and the Epistles. After these two Lessons the Canticle of the Three Children in the furnace was sung, *Benedictus es*, also called *Benedictio*. This fact is confirmed by the same witnesses. The importance attached to this rite is shown by the fact that the Council of Toledo of 633, which was presided over by St. Isidore, laid down that " in all churches of Spain and Gaul, in the solemnity of all Masses, the aforesaid hymn shall be chanted from the Lector's pulpit." Only, in the Mozarabic liturgy the canticle was inserted between the first and second readings. The singing of the *Benedictus es* in the Roman Church on Ember Saturday is an old tradition which recalls this custom. In the Missal of Bobbio a collect *post Benedictionem* is mentioned, but this would seem to be a derogation from the usage attested by many witnesses of a sung Responsory here, which chant must be identified with the *Psallendum*, the *Versus* or *Clamor*, or *Psalmellus*. At Rome, after the Lessons, there was the Responsory and *Alleluia*, sometimes replaced by the *Tractus*. The Council of Toledo just mentioned forbade the custom which had been introduced into several Spanish churches of singing *Laudes* between the Epistle and Gospel. We may take it, with St. Isidore, that this word signifies *Alleluia* (Dom Wilmart, *op. cit.*, col. 1072). This chant, which is another Gallican feature, is also a memorial of the Baptism of Clovis, according to P. Thibaut ; it should be followed by a *Collectio post Benedictionem*, as mentioned in the Missal of Bobbio (*op. cit.*, p. 39).

The pseudo-Germain notes here the repetition of the chant of the *Agios*, or *Trisagion*, an innovation of which no other example is found at this place in the Mass in any liturgy. It was evidently intended to give greater solemnity to the reading of the Gospel, which was about to follow. The author of this document emphasises this intention in the following remarkable terms : *Expeditur processio sancti evangelii velut potentia Christi triumphantis de morte, cum prædictis armoniis et cum septem candelabris luminis . . . ascendens in tribunal analogii . . . clamantibus clericis : Gloria tibi, Domine.* The *tribunal analogii* means an ambone or tribune, raised and decorated, from which the Bishop would preach, and upon which he would appear as a judge upon his tribunal. The acclamation *Gloria tibi, Domine*, or *Gloria Deo omnipotenti*, of which Gregory of Tours speaks, answers the Deacon's announcement : *Lectio sancti evangelii.*

The Gospel was usually followed by a chant. The pseudo-Germain says that the *Trisagion* sung before the Gospel is again taken up and repeated at this point. At Milan the Gospel was followed by *Dominus vobiscum* and a triple *Kyrie* with anthem. At Rome the Pope saluted the Deacon with *Pax tibi*, and then said the *Dominus vobiscum* and *Oremus*. The homily generally followed the Gospel.

Here occur the litanic prayers which may be attached to the Pre-Mass, at least in the Gallican use, since the catechumens were not dismissed until these were said. The pseudo-Germain thus describes these prayers : *precem (psallant levitæ) pro populis, audita (apostoli) prædicatione, levitæ pro populo deprecantur et sacerdotes prostrati ante dominum pro peccatis populi intercedunt.*

There can be no doubt but that we recognise here the diaconal litany referred to in the preceding pages, and which must not be confused with the *Prayer of the Faithful*, as Duchesne and others after him have confused it.[1] Each of these prayers presents analogies, and belongs, we believe, to the class of litanic prayers ; yet they are distinguished by certain characteristics which must be mentioned here as this question has its importance.

These litanies, or διακονικὰ, are recited by the Deacon, and form part of the Pre-Mass. To each invocation made by the Deacon the people respond : *Kyrie Eleison*, and at the end the celebrant concludes with a prayer.

[1] Dom Wilmart, after Edmund Bishop, has insisted on this point. Cf. Ed. Bishop, *Observations on the Liturgy of Narsai*, pp. 117–121 ; *Journal of Theological Studies*, 1910–11, Vol. XII, pp. 406–413 ; and *Liturgica Historica*, pp. 122, 124 ; Connolly, *Journal of Theological Studies*, 1919–20, Vol. XXI, pp. 219–232 ; Dom Wilmart, *art. cit.*, col. 1075. Duchesne, in his fifth edition of *Origines du culte chrétien*, p. 211, note 2, discusses the attribution to Gelasius of the *Dicamus omnes*.

This type of prayer, doubtless created at Antioch, was adopted at Constantinople, and thence transported to Rome and Gaul in the fifth century. The *Supplicatio litaniæ* of which it is question in the Rule of St. Benedict, the *Preces deprecatoriæ*, the *Letaniæ*, the *Kyrie* of the Roman Mass are all derived from this.

We have spoken elsewhere of this diaconal prayer, of its origin and destinies ; many examples of it exist in the Gallican books, such as the *Divinæ pacis*, and *Dicamus omnes*. Both these are given by Mgr. Duchesne in his chapter on the Gallican Mass (fifth edition, pp. 210, 211), to which we may refer our readers. Further, they present the most striking analogies with those we have quoted from the *Apostolic Constitutions*, with the *Deprecatio Sancti Martini* of the *Missal of Stowe*, and the *Deprecatio pro universali Ecclesia*, which good judges continue to attribute to Pope Gelasius (492–496) in spite of the opinion of Duchesne.[1]

The Mass of the catechumens is certainly finished with these diaconal prayers, and the catechumens are dismissed by the Deacon. The formula is not given here, but an equivalent will be found in the Milanese ritual : *Si quis catechumenus procedat, si quis judæus procedat, si quis paganus procedat, si quis hæreticus procedat, cujus cura non est procedat.*[2] St. Gregory mentions another formula : *Si quis non communicet det locum* ; and the Pontifical even yet contains this curious formula at the Ordination of Exorcists : *Exorcistam oportet . . . dicere populo ut qui non communicat det locum.* The pseudo-Germain recalls in this connection the energetic words of the Gospel : *nolite dare sanctum canibus neque mittatis margaritas ante porcos.*

[1] Cf. Duchesne, *op. cit.*, p. 221, note 2 ; and Dom Wilmart, *art. cit.*, 1076 ; cf. also article *Litanies*, in DACL.
[2] Under this formula cf. Ambrosian Mass, p. 93.

All these precautions prove the importance of the
action which is about to take place, and fresh warnings
from the Deacon awaken the attention and respect of
the people. Formerly the formula was *Silentium faciet*,
or *Pacem habete*, as in the Milanese rite. The pseudo-
Germain, who often comments on or interprets the rite,
says that they made the sign of the Cross on eyes, ears,
and mouth, *ut hoc solum cor intendat ut in se Christum
suscipiat*.

THE MASS OF THE FAITHFUL

The *Prayer of the Faithful* is a prayer recited after the
departure of the catechumens by the faithful alone ;
thus it forms part of the Mass of the Faithful. Sometimes it is called the Prayer of the Church, or the Common
Prayer. In the West, especially at Rome, it was recited
in the following way : the Pontiff invited the faithful to
prayer ; the Deacon gave the order to bend the knee ;
the Bishop pronounced the prayer, and the people
responded *Amen*. Ed. Bishop remarks acutely, in this
connection, that this prayer bears the seal of the Roman
Church, in which ecclesiastical authority always main-
tains its rights, the part of the faithful being reduced to
a minimum ; while in the East the initiative of Christian
people is allowed a much wider scope. To such a degree
is this the case that at Rome this prayer might more
correctly be called the Prayer *for* the Faithful. We have
a very well-preserved type of the prayer in the *Orationes
solemnes* of Good Friday. But all other trace of it has
disappeared from the Roman liturgy. Under an analogous form it existed in the Gallican liturgies in the
sixth century, as is proved by a text of the Council of
Lyon under Sigismond (516–523), which alludes to the
Oratio plebis quæ post evangelium legitur (*Concilia ævi
merovingici*, p. 34). But since then it has disappeared,

as it has at Rome, and we find in the Gallican liturgy only diaconal litanies, imitated from those in the Byzantine liturgy.

The offering of bread and wine in Gaul, as elsewhere, was made by the faithful. What must be remarked here, and what to some extent is peculiar to the Gallican Mass, are the honours paid to the oblations, *i.e.* the elements which are to be consecrated. Analogous customs exist in the Eastern liturgies, and there is a temptation to see in this the results of Byzantine influence (Duchesne, *op. cit.*, p. 216 ; Dom Wilmart, *art. cit.*, col. 1080). It is surprising to find the pseudo-Germain describe these elements, in a prolepsis, by the following words : *Procedente ad altarium corpore Christi, præclara Christi magnalia dulci melodia psallit Ecclesia* (*P.L.*, Vol. XXII, col. 93). Gregory of Tours expresses himself in somewhat similar terms when he says that the *Mysterium dominici corporis* was contained in vessels shaped like towers ; wooden towers, sometimes covered with gold.[1] The wine to be consecrated was brought in a chalice : *sanguis Christi . . . offertur in calice.* Water was added to the wine, as in all other rites. The bread was placed on a paten. Reference is made to the veils which covered the oblations : the first, *Palla*, of linen or wool ; the second, which was placed beneath the oblations, of pure linen, *Corporalis palla* ; finally, a precious tissue of silk and gold, ornamented with jewels, which covered them. Although analogous rites are certainly encountered elsewhere, some of those just described seem peculiar to the Gallican churches. In any case, they testify to the care and respect paid to the elements even before the Consecration. (For details, and comparison with other rites, cf. Dom Wilmart, *op. cit.*, col. 1081 *seq.*)

[1] *Glor. Mart.*, 86 ; *Hist. France*, X, xxxi. 13 ; *P.L.*, Vol. LXXI, cols. 569, 781.

THE MASS OF THE WESTERN RITES

The *Sonum quando procedit oblatio* was a special canticle, very closely allied to the *Cheroubicon* of the Greeks. When the oblations were placed upon the altar the choir chanted the Christmas *Laudes* of the Mozarabites : *Alleluia, Redemptionem misit Dominus populo suo ; mandavit im æternum testamentum suum ; sanctum et terribile nomen ejus, Alleluia*. These chants, *Sonum* and *Laudes*, practically correspond with the Offertory psalm used at Rome and Milan.

The reading of the Diptychs occurs here, as it does in most liturgies ; but we have no special information as to this rite in the Gallican churches. The names of the living for whom the Sacrifice was to be offered, and names of other personages, were read at this moment. From the theological point of view this rite is important, because the inscription on the Diptychs is a sign that the faithful were in communion with those whose names were read out. The names of heretics were struck off the list, a practice which often gave rise to bitter controversies. Lastly, the Pope's name was usually in the place of honour (cf. art. *Diptyques*, in DACL). We give as a type the following formula, taken from Duchesne (*Origines du culte*, p. 221) : *Offerunt Deo Domino oblationem sacerdotes nostri* (here the Spanish Bishops are signified), *papa Romensis et reliqui pro se et pro omni clero ac plebibus Ecclesiæ sibimet consignatis vel pro universa fraternitate.* . . . *Item pro spiritibus pausantium, Hilarii, Athanasii,* etc. In the Gallican and Mozarabic rites this reading is followed by a prayer : *Collectio post nomina*. The numerous formulas preserved in the Gallican books should be studied at first-hand, for allusion is made to the effects of the Sacrifice of the Mass (see art. *Mozarabe, Messe*, in *Dict. de Théol. Catholique*). The whole of this rite of the Diptychs is, moreover, deeply interesting, for it is a proof of faith in the intercession of the Church, in the efficaciousness of that Sacrifice, and in the union of all the faithful in the Church on earth and with the Saints in Heaven.

The Kiss of Peace which followed is also accompanied by a prayer, *Collectio ad pacem*. In the Gallican and Mozarabic books this, like the preceding prayer, varies with every Feast. They are a rich collection of texts, often expressive ; it will be sufficient here to quote one example of the *Collectio ad pacem*, that of the Assumption of Our Lady, celebrated by the Gallicans in January. It is taken from the *Missale Gothicum* (*P.L.*, Vol. LXXII, col. 245) :

Deus universalis machinæ propagator, qui in sanctis spiritaliter, in matre vero virgine etiam corporaliter habitasti ; que ditata tuæ plenitudenis ubertate, mansuetudine florens, caritate vigens, pace gaudens, pietate præcellens ab angelo gracia plena, ab Elisabeth benedicta, a gentibus merito prædicatur beata ; cujus nobis fides mysterium, partus gaudium, vita portentum, discessus attulit hoc festivum ; precamur supplices, ut pacem quæ in adsumptione Matris tunc præbuisti discipulis, solenni nuper (doubtless *sollempniter*) *largiaris in cunctis, salvator mundi, qui cum Patre. . . .*

We know that as regards the Diptychs and the Kiss of Peace the Roman liturgy differs in many important respects from the Gallican and Mozarabic rites, which latter on these points approach more closely to those of Constantinople. But we see, from what has gone before, that many ceremonies were borrowed comparatively late (cf. our article *Baiser de Paix* in DACL).

In the Gallican books the *Collectio ad pacem* is followed by an even more important prayer, usually called in these books the *Contestatio*, or *Immolatio* ; it corresponds to the Roman *Preface*, and begins with *Sursum corda* : *Habemus ad Dominum*. The prelude, too, is the same :

Vere dignum et justum est. But these Gallican *Contestationes*, like the Mozarabic *Immolationes*, are characteristically different from the Roman Prefaces. They are, if we may use such a comparison, like locally grown fruit. The Gallo-Roman genius of the sixth and seventh centuries here gave itself free rein. The Latin of that period was no longer the classical language of Augustan Rome ; it is very often prolix ; we find in it antitheses, ornaments, and even verbal conceits which we should desire to see banished from ecclesiastical compositions. The Roman manner, especially at the time of Gelasius and Gregory, has incontestably more discretion, more dignity ; moreover, it expresses a more carefully guarded orthodoxy. But from the point of view which alone interests us here this rich collection of *Contestationes* preserved in the Gallican books is a treasure as yet little explored by theologians. Here may be studied the doctrines of this Church on the Eucharist, Grace, the Incarnation, and Redemption, better perhaps than in any other collection. We can but mention here this source of the history and theology of the Gallican Church, for a detailed explanation would require a long thesis.

As in other liturgies the *Contestatio* ends with the *Sanctus*. But the Gallican and Mozarabic liturgies have another prayer, the *Collectio post Sanctus*, which is a transition from the *Sanctus* to the recital of the Institution. It generally begins with these words : *Vere Sanctus*. Thus in one of the Masses of Mone : *Vere Sanctus, vere benedictus dominus noster Jesus Christus filius tuus qui pridie (P.L.*, Vol. CXXXVIII, col. 866). But usually more ample developments are found, where dogmatic questions are touched upon, as in the following from the same collection (*loc. cit.*, col. 873) :

Hic inquam Christus Dominus noster et Deus noster, qui sponte mortalibus factus adsimilis per omne hunc ævi diem immaculatum sibi corpus ostendit, veterisque delicti idoneus expiator sinceram inviolatamque peccatis exhibuit animam, quam sordentem rursus sanguis elueret, abrogataque in ultimum lege moriendi, in cælo corpus perditum atque ad patris dexteram relevaret, per Dominum nostrum qui pridie. . . .

In the MS. this passage is altered, but we can guess the meaning (see Denzinger's note, col. 873). The *Post Sanctus* also answers to a prayer of the same kind in the Eastern liturgies. That of Rome has no prayer which corresponds to the *Vere Sanctus.*

The recital of the Institution, introduced in the Gallican liturgies by *Vere Sanctus*, follows the text of St. Matthew and St. Mark with the words : *qui pridie quam pateretur.* Here is an instance of complete accord between the rites of Rome and Gaul ; but on this point we can but refer to the remarks of other liturgiologists, especially to those of Dom Cagin, who has drawn his conclusions from this fact extremely well. The Eastern liturgies follow another tradition, and say with St. Paul : *In qua nocte tradebatur.* Spain, it is true, also says : *In qua nocte,* but this is generally attributed to Byzantine influence in a later age. This is all the more likely because the Spanish books called the prayer which follows, *Post pridie.*[1]

The words *Mysterium fidei* also seem to have been adopted in Gaul, as in the Roman formula, and probably under Roman influence.

In Gaul the words of Consecration were accompanied by the sign of the Cross traced on the oblation ; a gesture

---

[1] Cf. on this point Dom Cagin, *Paléographie musicale*, Vol. V., p. 55 *seq.* ; Duchesne, *loc. cit.*, p. 230, note 1 ; Dom Wilmart, *art. cit.*, col. 1085. There has been discussion as to whether these liturgies did not in primitive days contain the incisive words : *pro nostra et omnium salute.* Cf. *Revue Bénédictine*, 1910, Vol. XXVII, p. 513 *seq.*

recognised as possessing the special virtue of accomplishing the Mystery, and which is ratified by Heaven. The pseudo-Germain, speaking of the transformation operated by the Consecration of the bread and wine, alludes to the Angel of God who blesses the Host : *Angelus Dei ad secreta super altare tamquam super monumentum descendit et ipsam hostiam benedicit instar illius angeli qui Christi resurrectionem evangelizavit.* In this connection the story related by Gregory of Tours may well be recalled ; he tells us that St. Martin appeared in the Basilica dedicated to him in that town, and blessed, *dextera extensa,* the Sacrifice offered on the altar, *juxta morem catholicam signo crucis superposito (Vita Patrum,* XVI, 2 ; *P.L.,* Vol. LXXI, col. 1075 ; cf. Dom Wilmart, col. 1086).

The following prayer is of the first importance for the theology of the Mass. It bears the name *Post Secreta,* and elsewhere *Post Mysteria, Post Eucharistiam.* This title, this formula, the miracle of St. Martin just mentioned, the fact that Gregory of Tours calls the words of Consecration *Verba sacra (Glor. Mart.,* 87; *P.L.,* Vol. LXXI, col. 782), and other texts we could mention, sufficiently prove that the words of the Institution were considered as operating the mystery of the Eucharist. But it must be added that this prayer is frequently conceived in terms which would incline a reader to the contrary belief, *i.e.* that Transubstantiation is wrought by the *Epiclesis,* such as that of one of the Masses of Mone (*P.L.,* Vol. CXXXVIII, col. 871, and Vol. LXXII, col. 257). In any case, the collection of these prayers, *Post Secreta* in the Gallican liturgies, is one which should be most carefully studied, in order to realise the faith of these churches in the Eucharistic Mystery.

It has been thought, since the word is *Post Secreta,* that the formula of Consecration was said in a low voice, while the *Contestatio* and *Post Sanctus* were said aloud.

We shall not take up here that question so hotly debated in the seventeenth and eighteenth centuries, by theologians and liturgiologists, as to the Secret of the Mysteries, which we treat elsewhere (p. 216).

The rites of the *Fraction* and the *Commixtion* are attached to the prayer *Post Secreta*. In the primitive Mass the *Fraction* was a rite of the first importance. The name of *Fractio panis* given to the Eucharist at the beginning, the place of the word *Fregit* in the story of the Institution, the insistence of all the most ancient liturgies in this formula upon the words (*corpus meum*) *quod pro vobis confringetur*, and many other indications which could be given are sufficient to prove this fact. There are numerous variants of the rite in the various liturgies. In the Celtic rite, as we shall see, the Irish divided the Host in seven different ways, according to the Feast. In Gaul they divided it into nine particles, in the form of a Cross. Sometimes the particles were arranged on the paten to design a human form. The Council of Tours in 567 forbade this practice as superstitious, and ordained that the particles were to be disposed in the form of a Cross. The meaning of this act is given in the chant of the *Fraction*, called *Confractorium*, or *Ad Confractionem*. We have mentioned some of these in our article *Fractio Panis* (DACL). Here is one of them :

Credimus Domine, credimus in hac confractione corporis et effusione tui sanguinis nos esse redemptos : confidimus etiam quod spe hic mysterium jam tenemus, in æternum perfrui mereamur. Per. . . .

The *Commixtion*, or *Immixtion*, has, like the *Fraction*, a dogmatic bearing. The celebrant soaks one or several of the consecrated particles in the chalice, allowing one of them to fall into it. Under this form, with the words accompanying it in many liturgies, the sole meaning of this rite is to show to the faithful, before Communion, that it is the very Body and Blood of Christ which they are about to receive ; and that their separation under the different species of bread and wine is only apparent. Although at this epoch Communion under both kinds was almost universal, the doctrine that Christ was present, whole and entire, under both species, was none the less of equally universal acceptance. The rites of *Commixtion* or *Immixtion*, which are attached to this part of the Mass, seem, in our opinion, to favour this interpretation (see *Immixtion* in DACL).

The recitation of the *Pater* follows the *Fraction* and *Commixtion*. Its recital during Mass in this place, or at some place very near to these two rites, is an almost universal practice. Some exceptions might indeed be mentioned. The *Apostolic Constitutions* do not speak of the *Pater* ; neither does St. Hippolytus, nor Serapion, nor the *anaphora* of Balizeh. But these are exceptions. The *Pater* has its place, and that a place of honour in the Roman Mass, where it is surrounded with special rites. With the Gallicans, as in most other liturgies, it is, as it were, framed between a prelude or protocol and a conclusion or embolism.

Both of these are variable in the Gallican rite, like the *Contestatio*, the *Post Sanctus*, or the *Ad pacem*. These various rites aim at emphasising the importance of this prayer, taught to His disciples by Christ Himself, the Prayer of prayers. From the beginning its importance has been recognised and attested by the liturgy. The end of the *Pater* was enriched with a doxology, as we see in the *Didache* and in some of the most ancient MSS. of the New Testament ; and we cannot be surprised at that assertion of St. Gregory who, astonished at finding the *Pater* relegated to a place after the close of the Canon, declared that originally this was the prayer by means of which the Apostles consecrated (see pp. 79–81). It has also an honourable place in Baptism and in the other Sacraments.

In the Gallican Mass it is recited by the entire congregation, as was also the custom amongst the Greeks ; while in Africa and at Rome the celebrant alone recited the *Pater* aloud, the people responding *Amen,* or *Sed libera nos a malo.* In Spain we have seen there was a special place for the recitation of this prayer.

Before the Communion the Bishop, or even the Priest, blessed the faithful. This blessing also is important ; it is not confined to the Gallican liturgy, but took place in Africa also, in the time of St. Augustine. It existed, too, in the Eastern liturgies, and even Rome may have known it at one time, though it has been transformed and placed elsewhere.[1]

The meaning of this blessing, a kind of absolution or final purification before Communion, is determined by the accompanying formulas. The Deacon said : *Humiliate vos benedictioni* ; or with the Greeks : *Let us bow down our heads before the Lord.* The pseudo-Germain mentions the following : *Pax, fides et caritas, et communicatio corporis et sanguinis D.N.J.C. sit semper vobiscum.* He says, too, that the blessing given by the Priest must be shorter and less solemn than that given by the Bishop. This is a discreet allusion to the discussions which doubtless took place about this time, since the canons of some of the Councils of the fifth and sixth centuries bear traces of the controversy. The question was whether the right of blessing the people should be reserved to the Bishop alone, or whether (as here) it was sufficient to mark the difference between his blessing and that of a Priest (cf. especially the 44th canon of the Council of Agde, held 506). The formula varied according to the day. In the

[1] Cf. Dom Wilmart, *op. cit.,* col. 1088 ; Dom Morin, *Revue Bénédictine,* 1912, Vol. XXIX, p. 179 *seq.*

MS. collections many episcopal benedictions exist, some of which have been published, and these must not be neglected, since they form part also of liturgical theology (see our article, *Bénédictions épiscopales*, in DACL).

A certain hierarchical order—indeed, a very rigorous one—was enforced for the Communion. Priests and Deacons communicated at the altar ; other clerics before it ; the laity outside the choir. This at least was the Spanish custom. In Gaul the faithful entered the choir and communicated at the altar. Men received the Host upon the bare hand ; while women received It in a linen cloth called the *Dominical* (Duchesne, *op. cit.*, p. 257).

During the Communion a chant was sung : *antiphona ad accedentes*. This, according to the most ancient tradition, was Psalm XXXIII, *Benedicam Dominum in omni tempore*, or at least some of its verses which apply so well to the Eucharist : *Accedite ad eum et illuminamini, Iste pauper clamavit et Dominus exaudivit eum* ; and, above all : *Gustate et videte quoniam suavis est Dominus*. Dom Cagin (*Paléographie musicale*, Vol. V, pp. 22–25) has collected the principal evidence as to this tradition. It is interesting to know that Gaul had preserved it. The pseudo-Germain, amongst others, recalls it, but chiefly to prove that this chant (which he calls the *Trecanum*) is an act of Faith in the Trinity. And indeed, three verses which were repeated in a certain manner, and doubtless ended with the Trinitarian doxology, did teach those who communicated that " the Father is in the Son, the Son in the Holy Ghost, the Holy Ghost in the Son, and again the Son in the Father." P. Thibaut gives an explanation of this obscure text. *Trecanum* is an erroneous transcription of *Tricanon* (in Greek, τρικάνων, three rules, or three bars). Now the Psalm *Gustate et videte* is numbered in Roman figures XXXIII, which

was taken as a graphic symbol of the Trinity, three X's
and three I's which must be written thus :

$$\begin{array}{ccc} X & X & X & I & I & I \\ 1 & 2 & 3 & 3 & 2 & 1 \end{array}$$

This would explain the pseudo-Germain's text on
Circumincession in the Trinity. It is very subtle, but
subtlety never frightened the symbolists of that period.
However, what is incontestable is that these three
verses with a special doxology are indeed a chant in
honour of the Trinity ; and on this point the Mozarabic
rite agrees with that of Gaul. Other chants for Communion accompanied this, or took its place, such as the
beautiful hymn, *Sancti venite*, of the Celtic liturgies. In
the Eastern and Mozarabic rites the Symbol of Nicea-
Constantinople was recited at this moment. What
must always be noticed is the intense care taken to cause
an act of Faith to precede the participation in the Body
and Blood of Christ ; because the Eucharist is, above all,
the mystery of union with Our Lord, and through Him
between the faithful, in Faith and Charity.

After the Communion was said a prayer, the text of
which varied. The Post-Communions preserved in the
Gallican books are well worth study, for they express
the faith of these liturgies in the Real Presence, and in
the effects of the Sacrament upon the soul.

After these prayers the faithful were dismissed, as in
other liturgies. The formula in the Roman rite is *Ite,
Missa est* ; in the Missal of Stowe it is *Missa acta est, In
pace*. The Ambrosian rite has *Procedamus in pace, in
nomine Domini* ; while the Mozarabites have an even
more solemn formula. The Eastern liturgies have yet
others ; and it was not until much later that, in certain
rites, the reading of the Gospel of St. John and other

prayers were added after this dismissal, a custom which causes the latter ceremony to lose all its meaning.

The part played by the Gallican liturgy did not end with its disappearance. In the history of the liturgy from the ninth-fifteenth centuries Gaul's place was a very important one—it might be said, almost the most important of all. It was in Gaul that the Gelasian and Gregorian Sacramentaries, as well as the greater number of the *Ordines Romani*, have been retouched, modified, and finally moulded into that form which may be studied in the Missals of the ninth-thirteenth centuries, which are in reality Gallicano-Roman. An influence almost equally considerable was exercised in that country upon the Pontifical, the Ritual, Breviary, and other liturgical books. This history of the liturgy is not yet written, but it can be said that each day some fresh work on the subject confirms this general impression. We must also take into consideration the numerous initiatives undertaken in that country which were in the end adopted in other lands, even by Rome herself, such as the institution of new Feasts, and of more solemn rites.

None the less, it is infinitely to be regretted that, as regards this liturgy which in the splendour of its forms could rival the Mozarabic, the Ambrosian, or even the liturgy of Rome, we are reduced to a few fragments, doubtless of great interest, but which are mere *membra disjecta*, as the poet calls it. What a pity that one of our old Basilicas, that of Rheims, for instance, or Sens, did not play the same *rôle* as Toledo or Milan, and thus keep till our own day that collection of rites and customs of which to-day only a few relics are left ![1]

[1] We shall have a word to say as to the neo-Gallican liturgies of the seventeenth and eighteenth centuries on p. 203. But they have in reality little to do with the Mass.

BIBLIOGRAPHY

H. Lietzmann, *Ordo Missæ Romanus et Gallicanus* (Bonn, 1923).

J. B. Thibaut, *L'ancienne liturgie gallicane* (Paris, 1929); and on this book our article : *Les origines de la liturgie gallicane*, in *Revue d'Hist. eccl. de Louvain*, Vol. XXVI, 1930, p. 951 *seq.*

Liturgia, pp. 793-800, *La liturgie gallicane*.

H. Netzer, *L'Introduction de la Messe Romaine en France sous les Carolingiens* (Paris, 1910).

In DACL. *Gallicanes* (*Liturgies*), a very complete bibliography by Dom Leclercq. Cf. also the article *Germain, lettres de Saint*.

CHAPTER VIII

THE CELTIC MASS

THE title " Celtic liturgy," or rather " Celtic liturgies "
(the plural is used on account of the various forms which
this liturgy takes), designates the rite which was in use
amongst the populations of Ireland, Wales, and Cornwall,
Scotland, and Armorican Brittany. I have stated elsewhere what may be thought as to this expression " Celtic
liturgies." For, as a matter of fact, in the sense in which
the term is used to describe the Mozarabic or Gallican
rites, there is really no Celtic liturgy.

THE CELTIC LITURGICAL BOOKS

The Celtic monks, missionaries, and travellers, whom
we may consider as the authors of the above, had no
intention of composing a new liturgy, or even one which
differed from those already existing. What they did
was to take what suited them from one or the other rite,
and then to combine these various elements. That in
itself is not enough to constitute a new liturgy. It is
none the less true that their liturgical books, transcribed
and arranged as they are by Celtic copyists, have a very
real interest. We have made a study of them in another
volume, entitled *Books of the Latin Liturgy* (Sands & Co.,
London), pp. 107–112.

Of these books the most important is a Sacramentary,
or Missal, the *Missal of Stowe* ; and in it the Celtic Mass

may be studied. Some critics have placed the date of this MS. as far back as the eighth, or even the seventh, century. Certain doubts may be felt as to this great antiquity ; but whatever the date of the MS., it certainly describes a liturgy older than the ninth century.

THE CELTIC MASS

In the *Missal of Stowe* the preparation for the Mass comprehends a confession of sins, a long litany in which are found the names of all the Irish and Celtic Saints, and a *Apologia sacerdotis*, or prayer of preparation for Mass. This feature is not confined to the Celtic rites ; and we have studied elsewhere these liturgical *Apologies* (cf. article, *Apologies*, in DACL).

It would seem that the preparation of the oblations took place before the entrance of the celebrant, as in the Gallican rite. It comprised several prayers, as follows : in pouring water into the chalice : *Peto Te, Pater ; Deprecor Te, Fili ; Obsecro Te, Spiritus Sancte ;* in pouring the wine : *Remittat Pater, Indulgeat Filius, Misereatur Spiritus Sanctus.* Another Celtic book, the *Leabhar Breac*, notes that a single drop, both of water and wine, should be allowed to fall as the Name of each Person of the Trinity was pronounced. We first notice here the insistence, found nowhere else in the same degree, on emphasising each Person of the Blessed Trinity in the Eucharistic Mystery.

The setting of the Pre-Mass is almost the same as that of the Roman rite : a prayer, the *Gloria in Excelsis*, one or several Collects (which Celtic priests habitually multiplied to an extent which sometimes caused the faithful to protest), an Epistle taken from St. Paul, a Gradual chant, and the *Alleluia*. A celebrated litany, the *Deprecatio Sancti Martini, Dicamus omnes*, was said here.

This is borrowed from the Eastern liturgies, which have prayers of the same type ; the above litany is merely the translation of a Greek text. It has indeed been adopted by other Latin liturgies.[1]

Two prayers followed this. Then the chalice and oblations were partially unveiled, probably by the removal of the first veil ; they were not completely uncovered until the Offertory. The formula, *Dirigatur Domine*, was sung thrice ; then one veil of the chalice was taken away, and the prayer, *Veni, Domine, Sanctificator omnipotens, et benedic hoc sacrificium præparatum tibi, Amen*, was said three times.[2]

The Gospel followed. One of the fragments discovered by Bannister gives as that for the Circumcision an apocryphal Gospel of James, the son of Alphæus.[3] The *Credo* included the *Filioque*, but as an addition to the primitive text, and with several variants. After the Gospel there was a chant, which perhaps corresponds to the Mozarabic and Gallican *Laudes* and to St. Benedict's *Te decet laus*.

The Offertory included the complete unveiling of the chalice, which was elevated, sometimes with the paten ; and different formulas given in the *Missal of Stowe*, which have no particular characteristics.

Then came the *Memento of the Dead*, with the reading of the *Diptychs*. This is the Mozarabic and Gallican use. The following is the characteristic formula :

Has oblationes et sincera libamina immolamus tibi domine ihesu christe, qui passus es pro nobis et resurrexisti tertia die a mortuis pro animamus (animabus) *carorum*

---

[1] This very interesting but not specially Celtic text will be found in Duchesne, *Origines*, edition 1908, p. 202.

[2] For all this cf. Dom Gougaud's article in DACL., cols. 3008, 3009.

[3] Cf. *Journal of Theological Studies*, 1907–8, Vol. IX, pp. 414–421.

nostrorum N. et cararum nostrarum quorum nomina recitamus et quorumcumque non recitamus sed a te recitantur in Libro vite.

The Preface begins with *Sursum corda.* The text given in the *Missal of Stowe* is a combination of the *Trisagion* and the Roman Preface of the Trinity ; it also deserves to be quoted. We have already noted this insistence of the Celtic Mass upon confessing the Trinity.

Pater omnipotens . . . qui cum unigenito tuo et spiritu sancto Deus es unus et immortalis, Deus incorruptibilis et immortalis, Deus invisibilis et fidelis . . . te credimus, te benedicimus, te adoramus et laudamus nomen unum in æternum et in sæculum sæculi, per quem salus mundi, per quem vita hominum, per quem resurrectio mortuorum, per quem mæstatem tuam laudant angeli, etc.

The *Sanctus* is paraphrased like the Preface :

Benedictus qui venit de celis ut conversaretur in terris, Homo factus est ut delicta carnis deleret, hostia factus est ut per passionem suam vitam æternam credentibus daret per dominum.

Like the Gallican and Mozarabic books, those of the Celtic rite usually have a *Post sanctus.* The Canon of the *Missal of Stowe,* under the title of *Canon dominicus papæ Gilasi* (edn. Warren, p. 274 *seq.*), is famous among liturgiologists. This precious text, which by some is believed to be the most ancient text of the Roman Canon, contains the *Te igitur,* the *Memento of the Living,* and other prayers of the latter rite, but with notable variants, the chief of which are as follows :

Te igitur clementissime pater . . . una cum beatissimo famulo tuo, n. papa nostro, episcopo sedis apostolicæ, et omnibus orthodoxis atque apostolica fidei cultoribus, et abbate nostro, N. episcopo.

Hic recitantur nomina vivorum.

Memento etiam, domine, famulorum tuorum, N . . . qui

tibi offerunt hoc sacrificium laudis pro te suisque omnibus, pro redemptione animarum suarum, pro stratu (sic) *seniorum suorum, et ministrorum omnium puritate, pro integritate virginum, et continentia viduarum, pro æris temperie, et fructum* (sic) *fecunditate terrarum, pro pacis redetu et fine discriminum, pro incolimitate regum, et pace populorum, ac reditu captivorum, pro votis adstantium, pro memoria martirum, pro remissione peccatorum nostrorum, et actuum emendatione eorum, ac requie defunctorum, et prosperitate itineris nostri, pro domino papa episcopo, et omnibus episcopis et presbyteris et omni ecclesiastico ordine, pro imperio romano et omnibus regibus christianis, pro fratribus et sororibus nostris, pro fratribus in via directis, pro fratribus quos de caliginosis mundi hujus tenebris dominus arcisire dignatus est, uti eos in æterna summæ lucis quietæ pacis divina suscipiat, pro fratribus qui varis dolorum generibus adfliguntur, uti eos divina pietas curare dignetur, pro spe salutis et incolimitatis suæ, tibi reddunt vota sua eterno Deo vivo et vero communicantes, in natale domini et diem sacratissimam.* . . .*

(Then follows the enumeration of other feasts—Circumcision, Epiphany under the title of *Stella*, Holy Thursday as *Natalis calicis domini nostri*, Easter, Ascension, and Pentecost.)

Et memoriam venerantes imprimis gloriosæ semper virginis. . . .

Hanc igitur oblationem . . . quam tibi offerimus in honorem domini nostri ihesu christi et in commemorationem beatorum martirum tuorum, in hac æcclesia quam famulus tuus ad honorem gloriæ tuæ ædificavit, quesumus, domine, ut placatus suscipias, eumque, adque omnem populum ab idulorum cultura eripias, et ad te Deum verum patrem omnipotentem convertas, diesque nostros in tua pace disponas, atque ab æterna damnatione nos eripias, et in electorum tuorum iubeas grege numerari per, etc.

Quam oblationem te, deus, in omnibus, quesumus, benedictam, ascriptam, ratam, rationabilem, acceptabilemque facere dignareque nobis corpus et sanguis fiat dilectissimi fili tui domini nostri ihesu Christi.

Qui pridie. . . .

Hæc quotiescumque feceritis, in mei memoriam facietis, passionem meam predicabitis, resurrectionem meam adnuntiabitis, adventum meum sperabitis, donec iterum veniam ad vos de cælis.

Passages which bear an analogy with this formula can be found in the *Apostolic Constitutions*, in the liturgies of St. James and St. Basil, in the Ambrosian and Mozarabic liturgies, etc.

Irish treatises upon the Mass emphasise the importance of the formula of Consecration. The Priest bows thrice at *Accepit Jesus panem* ; the people prostrate themselves when he offers the bread and wine to God. This prayer has been called the *periculosa oratio*, and none must dare to break silence. The *Penitential of Cummean* inflicts a penance of fifty strokes upon the Priest who has hesitated once in speaking these words. In some Missals the word *Periculum* is written in the margin. Unfortunately to all these marks of attention and respect, so well justified, must be added certain other features which sometimes betray a meticulous and complicated piety. According to some treatises the celebrant had to take three steps forward and three backward, " *a triad which recalls the three ways in which man sins, that is, by thought, word, and deed, and the three ways in which he is renewed in God.*"[1]

After the Consecration we have the prayers *Unde et memores sumus*, *Supra quæ propitio*, *Supplices Te*, as in the Roman Canon. The *Memento of the Dead* presents a

[1] Cf. also Dom Gougaud, *loc. cit.*, col. 3011 ; and our article *Messe*, in *Dict. de théol. cath.*, cols. 1381–85.

very interesting formula also, which has analogies with
the Mozarabic and Gallican prayers :

*Memento etiam, domine, et eorum nomina qui nos
præcesserunt cum signo fidei, et dormiunt in somno pacis,
cum omnibus in toto mundo offerentibus sacrificum spiritale
deo patri et filio et spiritui sancto sanctis ac venerabibus
(sic) sacerdotibus offert senior noster, n. præspiter, pro se, et
pro suis et pro totius ecclesiæ cetu catholicæ ; et pro com-
memorando anathletico gradu venerabilium patriarcharum,
profetarum, apostolorum et martirun, et omnium quoque
sanctorum, ut pro nobis dominum deum nostrum exorare
dignentur.*

To this formula must be joined another, which in
Warren's edition is separated from it in mistake by a
list of names (pp. 238–240).

*Et omnium pausautium qui nos in dominica pace
precesserunt, ab adam usque in hodiernum diem, quorum
deus non nominavit et novit, ipsis et omnibus in christo
quiescentibus locum refrigerii,* etc.[1]

Then *Nobis quoque* with *Patricio* after *Petro* and *Paulo* ;
Per quem hæc omnia. . . .

We do not think, with certain critics, that it is necessary
to see the most ancient form of the Roman Canon in this
formula. The addition *diesque nostros*, made by St.
Gregory ; that of *Pro fratribus in via directis*, borrowed
from the Rule of St. Benedict, and other indications are
opposed to this view. As with the other Celtic prayers,
the author has made a mixture of fragments culled from
different sources ; but there can be no doubt that some
of these fragments are very ancient, as, for example, the
two *Mementos*.

The rites of Fraction, Immixtion, and Communion in

---

[1] The *Quorum deus nomina scit*, or analogous formulas, have
been pointed out by Le Blant, in his *Inscriptions funéraires de la
Gaule, Inscr. chrét. de la Gaule*, p. 563, and notes.

the Celtic Mass present no less interesting features. On these points there was great liberty.

Following the *Per quem hæc omnia*, the rubric of the *Missal of Stowe* adds *ter canitur*, and in Irish : " *here the oblations are raised above the chalice, and half the bread is plunged into the chalice."* This is the rite of Intinction, practised in the Syrian liturgy. The versicle *Fiat domine misericordia tua super nos quemadmodum speravimus in te* follows.

Then the Fraction takes place. " *The bread is broken,"* says the Irish rubric. This is the usual place for the Fraction in the Latin liturgies, even in the Roman Mass before St. Gregory's time. The versicles which follow comment on the actions of the Priest, and emphasise the special importance of the rite. *Cognoverunt dominum, alleluia, in fractione panis, alleluia.* This is the *Confractorium*, or *Antiphona ad confractionem* of the Ambrosian and Mozarabic rites, and of which a few vestiges remain in certain Roman books.[1] With regard to the Fraction it has been shown that in the Celtic, and perhaps in other churches, a Priest here joined the celebrant, if the latter were a simple Priest, to break with him the Body of the Lord. It was the Confraction. But were the celebrant a Bishop he broke the Host alone.[2] These other versicles of the Fraction followed :

Panis quem frangimus corpus est domini nostri ihesu cristi. Alleluia.

Calix quem benedicimus (alleluia) sanguis est d. n. I. C. (Alleluia) in remissionem peccatorum nostrorum (Alleluia).

Fiat domine misericordia tua super nos. Alleluia. Quemadmodum speravimus in te. Alleluia.

Cognoverunt dominum. Alleluia.

Credimus, domine, in hac confractione corporis et

[1] Cf. our article *Messe*, in *Dict. de théol. cath.*, col. 1400.
[2] Cf. Dom. Gougaud, *loc. cit.*, col. 3011.

effusione sanguinis nos esse redemptos et confidimus, sacramenti hujus adsumptione munitos, ut quod spe interim hic tenemus mansuri in celestibus veris fructibus perfruamur, per d., etc.

The Host was divided in seven different ways, according to the Feasts : into five parts at Common Masses ; into seven on the Feasts of Saints, Confessors, and Virgins ; into eight on the Feasts of Martyrs ; into nine on Sundays ; into eleven on the Feasts of Apostles ; into twelve on the Kalends of January, and on Holy Thursday ; into thirteen on the Sunday after Easter and on the Ascension ; and into sixty-five on the Feasts of Christmas, Easter, and Pentecost. The particles were arranged in the form of a Cross, and each group received a part of this Cross according to grade. Everything here seems to have been invented to distract attention at the very moment when it should have been concentrated on the One Essential Object. Happily those chants of the Fraction already mentioned led to more serious thoughts.

As in the greater number of liturgies the *Pater*, said after the Fraction, is set between a prelude and an embolism, which differ little from the Roman formulas ; the name of St. Patrick is read after those of SS. Peter and Paul. There is a blessing here, as in the Mozarabic and Gallican rites, and it runs thus :

Pax et caritas D.N.I.C. et communicatio sanctorum omnium, sit semper vobiscum. ℟. *Et cum spiritu tuo.*

The Kiss of Peace was then given, as in the Roman Mass. The *Missal of Stowe* contains at this point many anthems on Peace, mingled with anthems and chants for Communion.

The Commixtion of the Body and Blood was carried out as in the Roman rite. The Communion was encircled with rites and chants which gave it great solemnity. We mention a few : *Novum carmen cantate, Omnes sancti venite, Panem cœli dedit eis, Sinite parvulos venire ad me, Venite benedicti Patris mei.* Psalm xxxiii., of almost universal tradition at Communion, was also sung. The famous hymn, *Sancti venite, Christi corpus sumite*, preserved in the *Antiphonary of Bangor*, is of lofty inspiration, and would cause the wearisome prolixity of some other prayers to be pardoned.

The text of the Post-communions is borrowed from the Roman books. The dismissal was given in these words : *Missa acta est. In pace.*

Beyond a few formulas and rites which seem particularly to belong to the Celts, it can easily be seen that nothing really original can be found in this Mass. What does distinguish it is the almost equal mixture of Roman and Gallican rites, with a few features borrowed from the Mozarabites, the Ambrosian liturgy, or from the Eastern rites. It is composite. And the rite of Baptism, which we need not study here, presents the same characteristics.

BIBLIOGRAPHY

Celtiques (Liturgies) in DACL, the very complete article by Dom Gougaud, with a good bibliography at the end. Cf. also in the same dictionary the articles *Bobbio (missel)* and *Bangor (antiphonaire de).*

Liturgia, p. 822, an article by Dom Gougaud on the Celtic liturgy ; and his work : *Christianity in Celtic Lands*, Chapter IX, *Liturgy and Private Devotion.*

THE PRIMITIVE LATIN LITURGY

This title is ambitious. It would indeed be over-bold to attempt to reconstitute the Latin liturgy as it was before the seventh century. But, taking all the liturgies together—the African, Gallican, Mozarabic, Ambrosian,

Celtic, and Roman, which have just been studied in the preceding chapters—a few general features may be noticed as standing out clearly, and these will throw some light upon the first-named.

(1) The Pre-Mass was composed of three Lessons (there are actually two in the Roman liturgy) ; each was usually followed by chants or psalmody, and by a prayer. The chants and psalmody comprise verses of the Psalms, in the form of responsories, or anthems. The *Alleluia* and *Gloria in Excelsis Deo* or another canticle also belong to it, as does a special prayer, the Diaconal litanies with the *Kyrie Eleison*.

(2) The Pre-Mass terminated with the dismissal of the catechumens and others outside the fold.

(3) The Mass properly so called began with the *Prayer of the Faithful*, of which some traces still survive.

(4) The Offertory presents analogous characteristics in all these different liturgies.

(5) The reading of the *Diptychs*, whatever its actual place was, also formed part of it.

(6) The Preface, preceded by a dialogue and ending with the *Sanctus*, was often freely improvised in these churches ; but it always began with the same theme : *Vere dignum et justum est*, etc.

(7) The *Sanctus* was followed by the *Benedictus qui venit*, while in the East the *Sanctus* is composed of the formula of the Prophet Isaias, and as a rule admits of no complement.

(8) The *Vere Sanctus*, which existed amongst the Mozarabites and Gallicans, is seemingly absent from Rome.

(9) The *Qui pridie* was attached to the *Sanctus*, or the *Vere Sanctus*, by a short formula, of which the book *De Sacramentis* gives an example which is probably the most ancient.

(10) The *Anamnesis* followed the Consecration in most rites.

(11) The *Post pridie* and *Epiclesis*, which hold so large a place in the Gallican and Mozarabic liturgies, have quite disappeared in that of Rome. But was it always so ? The *Anaphora* of the *Paradosis* of Hippolytus, composed at Rome in the third century, has an *Epiclesis*, which, however discreetly worded, is none the less an invocation of the Holy Ghost ; while certain ancient texts seem to allude to a Roman *Epiclesis*. But while the Roman Church always tended to abridge, and even to suppress entirely, that of Spain on the contrary amplified, developed, and multiplied formulas and rites.

(12) The same thing may be noted with regard to the Fraction. While Rome simplified the rite and suppressed the anthem *Ad confringendum*, both these were singularly complicated in Spain and among the Celts.

(13) The Pater, with prelude and embolism, usually had its place here.

(14) The same differences and the same analogies may be remarked in the rites of Communion and Dismissal.

(15) The composition of the Latin liturgical books presents similar characteristics, while in the East such books are subject to other laws.

All this evidently shows that each church had its own tendencies, which appear to separate them one from another in the accomplishment of liturgical functions, though they betray a common origin, and display even more numerous analogies in the primitive period.

The comparison of the calendars, the divisions of the liturgical year, of the *cursus* of the Office, and of the administration of the Sacraments will lead, we think, to the same result.

CHAPTER IX

THE ROMAN MASS, FROM THE EIGHTH TO THE SIXTEENTH CENTURY: ADDITIONS TO THE MASS OF ST. GREGORY

THE DOCUMENTS.—THE MASS.—The Preparation for Mass and the Prayers at the Foot of the Altar.—The Chants, Collect, and Proses.—The Prayers of the Offertory and of the Censing.—The Secret.—The Preface.—The Canon.—The Communion.

THE DOCUMENTS

IN our fourth chapter we described the Roman Mass in the seventh century. From the seventh-sixteenth centuries it was to undergo rather important modifications. Not that there were any essential changes along its principal lines: the Canon remained invariable. But there were a certain number of additions in other parts of the Mass.

These are all of Gallican origin, a term which must be understood in its widest sense, for some of these additions came from Switzerland and Germany as well as from France. We shall only mention them here, as we shall return to this subject in Chapter XI, in which the whole Roman Mass is recapitulated.

We have very sufficient material for the study of this period. In the first place the Sacramentaries and Missals. We have elsewhere described the transformation of Sacramentaries written for the celebrant alone, containing only those parts of the Mass which he had to recite, into full Missals, in which are united all the Epistles, Gospels, and chants of the Mass; a transformation brought about through many causes, but chiefly through the multiplication of Low Masses.[1]

There are other documents not less useful : the *Ordines Romani*, which describe the Roman Mass with its various ceremonies. As has been said, these documents succeed each other from the seventh-sixteenth centuries, and just as we have had *Ordo I* to guide us in our description of that Mass in the seventh century, so we have those of a later epoch for the following period : the *Ordo Romanus III* (ninth-tenth centuries), the *Ordo Romanus VI* (tenth-eleventh centuries), and the *Ordo XIV*, which was that of the Roman Curia in the fourteenth century, exactly at the time when certain important changes were being made.[2]

Finally we have, especially since the ninth century, treatises on the Mass. At the Carlovingian Renaissance a strong impulse was given to liturgical studies. Alcuin, Amalarius, Agobard, Florus of Lyon, Rhaban Maur, and Walafrid Strabo all wrote on various subjects, but especially on the Mass ; unfortunately their works are all rather symbolic than historic, and only give very little really important information as to their chief subjects. Rupert, in the twelfth century, is a mere compiler without any originality, while Honorius of Autun in the same century wrote more especially for edification. Bernold, in his *Micrologue* (eleventh century), is of greater value, and Beleth, Jean d'Avranches, above all Durand de Mende in his *Rationale*, deserve serious study. But the most important of all is Cardinal Lothaire, who became Pope Innocent III (1198–1216), and who wrote the treatise *De sacro altaris mysterio*, which describes the Roman Mass at this period. These different works on the Mass have been collected since the sixteenth century

---

[1] Cf. *Books of the Latin Liturgy* (Sands, 3s. 6d.), p. 31 *seq.*
[2] Upon *Ordines Romani*, cf. p. 43.

by authors like Cochlæus, Hittorp, and others ; but all
such volumes need re-editing, and the different treatises
on the Mass in the Middle Ages ought to be classed
methodically.[1]

THE PREPARATION FOR MASS AND THE PRAYERS AT
THE FOOT OF THE ALTAR.—Before the Introit the Psalm
Judica me, the *Confiteor*, the versicles *Aufer a nobis*, the
Oramus te, Domine, were added ; and, in Solemn Masses,
the censing of the altar.

Psalm xlii. is indicated in the ancient Missals as a preparation for Mass since the eleventh century. It is well
chosen for such an office ; and the anthem *Introibo ad
altare Dei*, taken from the text of the Psalm, emphasises,
as is intended, the principal verse which usually deter-
mines the use of a Psalm.

The Confession of Sins before Mass is mentioned in the
Didache, and other ancient liturgical books. It is an
apostolic practice. The formula here employed was the
Confiteor, in the form which prevailed from the tenth-
eleventh centuries, and which had been used ever since,
though with numerous variations. It was followed by
several versicles and responsories taken from the Psalms ;
and these too are one of the most ancient forms of
liturgical prayer.

Then came the *Dominus vobiscum*, and the Priest
mounted to the altar where he said the beautiful prayer
Aufer a nobis, from the Leonine Sacramentary. The
Oramus te which followed it is less ancient, as the use of
the singular is enough to show (eleventh century) ; this
prayer recalled the fact that relics of the Saints were
beneath the altar (to-day they are enclosed within the

---

[1] Cf. Dom Wilmart, *Expositio Missæ* in DACL, and our *Introduction aux Études Liturgiques* (Paris, 1907).

stone of the altar). The kissing of the altar was a very
ancient practice (p. 232).

The censing of the altar which now took place is of
Gallican origin, and was only later adopted at Rome.

CHANTS, COLLECTS, AND PROSES.—The Introit and
other chants or anthems for Offertory and Communion
underwent no change ; nor did the Gradual and Alleluia,
or the Tract. But to the *Alleluia* was added the Prose ;
while Tropes were sometimes added to the *Kyrie, Gloria
in Excelsis,* and *Agnus Dei.*

Proses were originated, it is thought, in the ninth-
tenth centuries, and the name of their inventor is Notker,
a monk of St. Gall. In any case, they had a great success
in Switzerland, Germany, France, and in most of the
Latin countries ; it is sufficient to open certain MS.
Missals of the eleventh-fifteenth centuries to see how
these Proses had increased and multiplied. A Trope
was a given liturgical text with additional notes and
words added to it. Naturally, the only parts sung
suited this kind of ornament very well. The *Kyrie,* the
Benedicamus Domino, the Introits, and other chants all
received Tropes, or, to use the current expression, were
stuffed (farcis). As, for example, *Kyrie fons bonitatis,
Pater ingenite, a quo bona cuncta procedunt, eleison.*
Léon Gautier, who has made a special study of these
Tropes, is very severe in his judgment, and compares
them to mushrooms which threaten to stifle the liturgic
text. It is almost unnecessary to say that Rome never
favoured this kind of composition ; and that without
condemning the Tropes or the Proses or the Mysteries,
she allowed France, Germany, and the other Western
countries to revel in this style of pastime, which gave
great joy to the simple, religious population, but nevertheless threatened to compromise the dignity of the
liturgy.

The Collect, too, underwent no change ; and the greater number of those recited to-day existed in the same form in the Sacramentary of St. Gregory, or even in those of Gelasius and Leo (fifth-sixth centuries). For the Credo, cf. p. 129.

THE OFFERTORY PRAYERS AND THE CENSING.—The prayers introduced since the tenth-eleventh centuries were the following :

> *Suscipe, Sancte Pater ;*
> *Offerimus Tibi, Domine ;*
> *In spiritu ;*
> *Veni sanctificator ;*
> *Suscipe, Sancta Trinitas ;*
> *Orate fratres ;*
> *Suscipiat.*

The use of the singular, the style of these prayers, and the intention of explaining all the gestures which previously were made in silence, suffices to class all these in the second zone of Eucharistic devotions. But this does not mean that they are not often inspired with the breath of true piety.

The Priest, when offering the Host upon the paten, addressed the Father, begging that the Sacrifice might produce all its effects. The *Suscipe Sancte Pater* is, however, an ancient prayer of the ninth century. The prayer when mixing the wine and water, *Deus qui humanæ substantiæ*, is one of the most beautiful of the Leonine Sacramentary, and of very great dogmatic importance.

The chalice, like the Host, was offered with a special prayer, *Offerimus Tibi*, and again *In spiritu humilitatis*. The terms of the *Veni sanctificator* and its accompanying blessing have caused some to believe that there was an *Epiclesis* here. But this is a mistake, and the prayer, moreover, is of a period when little interest was taken in that question.

At Solemn Masses the censing of the oblations, the altar, the clergy, and the faithful was accompanied by different prayers : *Per intercessionem, Incensum istud, Dirigatur, Domine, Accendat in nobis.* Censing under this form is also of Gallican, or even Carlovingian, origin. As we have seen, Rome in the seventh century was acquainted with the use of incense burned in a *thymiamaterium*, but there was no censing, neither at the Gospel, nor of the oblations or clergy. Mgr. Batiffol has outlined very clearly the different stages in these customs (*loc. cit.*, p. 153 *seq.*). The invocation of St. Michael at this moment has given rise to a good deal of discussion, and St. Gabriel, on whom this function more especially devolved, was sometimes substituted for him. But St. Michael's name can be justified here, for he was the Angel of the Sacrifice. The censing of the Gospel is of the same period.

In all these prayers at the censing may be noted the care taken to emphasise each act of the celebrant with prayer. The presence of the Ablution, with Psalm xxv., *Lavabo*, in this place can easily be explained by the ancient ceremonies of the Offertory, as well as those of the censing. It still remains, even in Low Masses, as if in memory of the past.

The *Suscipe Sancta Trinitas*, which again is not in the Roman style, where each prayer is always addressed to the Father by the Son in the Holy Ghost, is yet ancient, and dates from the ninth century, though it had so many variants that it sometimes appears like a prayer over the *Diptychs*. Its place, like its text, has varied. We may make the same remark about the age and use of *Orate fratres* and of *Suscipiat*. The *Dominus vobiscum*, which should naturally precede the *Secret*, as it does all prayers of this kind, was suppressed on account of the use of *Orate fratres*.

But if all these prayers have been added to the Offertory, it was, on the other hand, simplified. The faithful no longer offered the bread and wine, but the collection, which was made at this moment, and the custom (which does not prevail in England) of giving blessed bread are memories of it. At Solemn High Masses the Corporal, chalice, paten, and Host were prepared by the Deacon. At Pontifical Masses the Prelate left his throne at this moment and proceeded to the altar, which he kissed, then censed, and lastly performed the different rites of the Offertory. At Low Masses the Priest was charged with all this, and he said in a low voice the prayers just enumerated. At Solemn Masses the custom of singing the verse of a Psalm remained ; this represents the ancient Offertory chant. The collection of Offertories is an interesting one ; for the Psalm has sometimes been substituted a text taken from another part of Holy Scripture, as, for example, the beautiful Offertories *Sanctificavit Moyses*, *Vir erat in terra Hus*, *Recordare mei* (eighteenth, twenty-first, and twenty-second Sundays after Pentecost), and *Domine Jesu Christe*, from the Mass for the Dead, etc.

THE SECRET.—This still remained the culminating point of the Offertory ; before this time it was the only prayer at the offering (cf. p. 62). But it has followed the same law as that of the Collects, the number of which corresponds to that of the Secrets. The greater part of the most ancient Secrets were preserved, many being anterior to the ninth century. Happily the same can be said of the other formulas of this kind, both Collect and Post-communion ; for the genius of composition was lost after the Golden Age of the Roman liturgy, and Mgr. Batiffol gives an amusing example of the errors into which modern composers sometimes fall (*loc. cit.*, p. 117). Many similar examples could be found in other prayers of the same period.

THE PREFACE.—These, which were reduced to the number of ten in the Gregorian Sacramentary (there are 267 in the Leonine, and even then the Sacramentary was not complete !), suffered no change. It is said that the Preface of the Blessed Virgin was added by Pope Urban II in 1095, to beg the help of Our Lady for the First Crusade.

THE CANON.—This again remained unchanged, as it had from the time of St. Gregory.

THE COMMUNION.—This too was simplified, since the faithful no longer brought with them the bread and wine ; unleavened bread was used, often under the form of a small Host ; and Communion under the species of wine was suppressed.

But certain prayers were added. In the first place the first three Communion prayers :

> *Domine, Jesu Christe, qui dixisti ;*
> *Domine . . . qui ex voluntate ;*
> *Perceptio corporis tui.*

These three were all prayers of private devotion, as the singular number proves ; they have slipped into the Missals since the eleventh century. The first is a prayer for the Peace of the Church, inspired by the *Te igitur* ; the third is a commentary on a thought which was very frequent in ancient devotions : *Perceptio corporis tui non mihi proveniat in judicium.* All three are directly addressed to God the Son, as is often the case in the Gallican and Mozarabic liturgies, while those of Roman origin are always addressed to the Father *by the Son.* Other prayers of this kind can be found in the Missals of the Middle Ages, but these were the most popular, and for the sake of their ring of true devotion they deserved

M

to pass into the Roman Missal. The prayers which follow :

> *Panem cœlestem ;*
> *Domine, non sum dignus ;*
> *Corpus Domini ;*
> *Quid retribuam ;*
> *Sanguis Domini ;*
> *Quod ore ;*
> *Corpus tuum ;*

form a little collection of prayers from various sources, the greater number of which are intended to emphasise and explain each phase of the Communion of the Priest ; the first and third for that under the species of bread, the fourth and fifth for that under the species of wine, while the seventh is for the Ablutions. Among these prayers the *Domine, non sum dignus* is a well-known passage from the Gospel (St. Matt. viii. 8), the *Quod ore* is a Roman Post-communion of the Leonine Sacramentary, and the *Corpus tuum* a Gallican Post-communion.

The little ceremonial for the Communion of the faithful is also later than St. Gregory's day, when Communion was given with no other words but *Corpus Christi* and *Sanguis Christi*, to which the communicant responded *Amen*. The ceremonial is doubtless that used when Communion was given outside Mass, more especially to the sick. It is made up of duplicates, that is, of prayers already used in Mass : the *Confiteor, Ecce Agnus Dei, Domine, non sum dignus, Corpus Domini nostri Jesu Christi custodiat animam tuam in vitam æternam, Amen*.

The end of Mass was also enriched (if we may use the term) by the following prayers : *Placeat Tibi ; Benedicat vos ;* Last Gospel.

The *Placeat* recalls the *Suscipe, Sancta Trinitas* of the Offertory, but is of much less ancient date, and as was said when we spoke of the latter prayer, its style betrays an origin which is not Roman. In the ancient Roman formulary the singular number was never used ; but the prayer is found in the Missal of the Roman Curia ever since the eleventh century.

The *Ite, Missa est* is, on the contrary, a very ancient formula of dismissal ; we have found it in all the Latin liturgies, and, in one form or another, in those of the East. *Benedicamus Domino* took its place in certain Masses which were followed by another Office ; the faithful then were not dismissed, but, rather, invited to remain in church. We have also spoken of the last Blessing, and of the Gospel of St. John, which at first was a private devotion, but which was adopted by the Roman Missal.

In the period which followed, sixteenth-twentieth centuries, there are very few additions to be noted : three Prefaces, and the prayers added by Leo XIII at the end of Mass.

Among the most notable additions during the time with which this chapter is occupied are the Masses on the Thursdays in Lent, under Gregory II (715–731). In the time of St. Gregory I there was neither a Station nor a Mass for these days. One of his successors (Gregory II) desired to fill in this gap, and provided a Mass for all Lenten Thursdays. But the most superficial study of them will show that the composition of these Masses does not at all harmonise with the rest of the Lenten liturgy ; and that the greater part of the items of which they are made up were borrowed from other Masses.[1]

If we wish to keep count of all the other additions brought to the Roman deposit since the time of St.

[1] Thanks to a statement of this kind relative to the Communions for the Thursdays in Lent, Dom Cagin has ingeniously drawn up a fresh argument in favour of the authenticity of the Gregorian Sacramentary (*Un mot sur l'antiphonale missarum*, Solesmes, 1890. Author not named).

Gregory, the ceremonies introduced into the Roman Missal of the ninth-sixteenth centuries must not be overlooked : the blessing of candles on 2nd February ; the blessing of palms ; part of the ceremonies of Holy Week, beginning with the *Exultet* ; and the celebration of Feasts like All Saints, *Corpus Christi,* Trinity Sunday, the Immaculate Conception. But all this is part of the general history of the Roman liturgy, or Missal, and it is only attached very indirectly to our subject.

Before closing this chapter we must note the character of the changes produced in the Mass during this period. These changes affect particularly the beginning of Mass, the Offertory, Communion, and conclusion ; the Canon was respected. The additions mentioned are for the greater part prayers of private devotion, formerly said by the Priest in the sacristy—in any case, outside Mass. These, little by little, slipped into Low Masses, and thence into the Missal. The Mass which up till the ninth century was a public ceremony of which all the prayers are in the plural, became, through the multiplication of Low Masses, very often a private devotion. This does not mean that the Low Mass dates from the ninth century; we have, on the contrary, examples of it in the fourth and even earlier centuries (cf. p. 237). But the Roman Mass, as described from the seventh-ninth centuries was the Mass celebrated by the Pope ; the Bishops and clergy who surrounded him *concelebrated* with him, and all the people united with him. It was a solemn and public ceremony of the whole Christian community ; and, as if to insist on this unity, the *fermentum,* or part of the Sacred Species, was sent to those Priests of the *tituli,* or Roman parishes, who, for some reason or another, were unable to be present at that Mass. Yet they participated in it by uniting their Consecration to that of the Pope.

Another characteristic to note in these additions is the tendency to emphasise and explain a gesture by a formula. If it be true, as De Vert says, that the formula calls forth the gesture, just as the sign of the Cross is added to the word *Benedicere* to bring out its meaning, the opposite was also true in the course of the late Middle Ages. In the place where the gesture had been sufficient, as for the Fraction, the Communion, the Kissing of the Altar, etc., formulas were added ; here an *Aufer a nobis*, there the *Oramus Te*, elsewhere the *Quod ore sumpsimus*, etc.

If we did not know by other evidence that these additions were not of Roman origin, we could guess it from the style of the prayers (singular instead of plural) ; and from some other features, such as prayers addressed directly to God the Son, to the Trinity, etc.

(For Bibliography, cf. Chapter IV.)

CHAPTER X

THE RITES DERIVED FROM THE ROMAN MASS FROM NINTH-SIXTEENTH CENTURIES

The rite of Lyon.—The Carthusians.—Benedictine liturgy.—
Cistercians. — Carmelites. — Dominicans. — Franciscans.—
Præmonstratensians.—The Roman liturgy in England.

IF a special place has been given in these chapters to the
Roman Mass, it is not only because this liturgy is that of
the whole Latin church with the few exceptions mentioned ; it is also because it is the most ancient of all,
or at least that about which exist the most ancient and
numerous documents. Again, it appears incontestable
that the Roman liturgy excels all others in its dogmatic
authority, and even in its literary beauty.

If the Mozarabic, Gallican, and Eastern liturgies show
a trace of lyrical inspiration ; if they are more dramatic
in character, more fervent in piety than that of Rome ;
if this latter has perhaps less originality and brilliance,
it makes up for it by the possession of qualities which are
those of the Roman genius ; those which strike us in the
architectural monuments of Rome : solidity, grandeur,
strength, and a simplicity which excludes neither nobility
nor elegance.

This remark is especially deserved by the ancient
Roman liturgy of the fifth-seventh centuries, for this was
its Golden Age. Two hundred years after the time of
St. Gregory, in the ninth century, the sceptre had passed
to other lands : to France, England, Switzerland,
Germany, and Spain. It was in those countries that
liturgical initiative was found, that new Feasts and fresh

rites were created, new formulas composed, a more rational system instituted for the distribution of liturgical books, as well as fresh technical methods of decorating and illuminating them. In consequence of political circumstances Rome was about to lose all she had gained as to the liturgy ; and it was not for two or three hundred years that she would recover her sceptre.

But by a rather curious stroke of fortune all the new customs originated in the countries just mentioned came back to Rome. They returned there under the covers of the Missal, the Pontifical, Ritual, Breviary, and those other books called Roman, but which are really and more justly Gallicano or Germano-Roman. And, from the eleventh century onwards, Rome got back all her advantages. The reawakening of her liturgical activity was manifested by the efforts of Pope Alexander II (1061–1073), and later by those of St. Gregory VII (1073–1085) to establish the Roman liturgy in Spain instead of the Mozarabic. This episode is instructive ; the latter Pope in his letters on this subject to the Kings of Aragon, Castile, and Navarre reminds them energetically of the Papal right to the charge of Divine worship, and also to that of establishing the Roman liturgy in all Catholic countries, especially in Spain.

Another indication of the supremacy of the Roman liturgy is that it was adopted by the new Orders, Carthusians, Præmonstratensians, Dominicans, Franciscans, and even by the Carmelites, who had an ancient liturgy of their own ; and very soon all these Orders were to become active agents for its spread through all the countries of the West ; not, however, without having occasionally modified it. In this great work the Franciscans played the most important part.

The Roman Curia, which until then had celebrated the same Offices as those of the Roman Basilicas, notably of that of the Lateran, which was the cathedral church of Rome, and considered the mother and mistress of all churches, separated itself from these at the beginning of the twelfth century, and fixed its own Office for the Breviary. The substance of this Breviary was actually that of the Lateran, but it differed on several points, and, above all, it was very much abridged. The same thing happened in the case of the Missal. The subsequent history of these books is rather curious. Innocent III (1198–1206) revised them. In 1223 St. Francis of Assisi ordained that the Franciscans should henceforth adopt the Roman Office ; for hitherto they had simply followed the Office of whatever province they had chanced to find themselves in. This was a means of establishing amongst the Friars Minor that liturgical unity which had previously suffered a great deal. But the liturgy they adopted both for Mass and Office was neither that of the Lateran nor of the Roman Basilicas, but actually that of the Roman Curia, established at the beginning of the twelfth century. This fact was big with consequences for the future. The activity of the Franciscans at that time was prodigious ; and in all the countries through which they passed as missionaries they established this use of the Missal and Breviary which they themselves followed ; though they slightly modified it, especially in the case of the Franciscan Feasts. In 1277 Nicolas III ordered it to be used by the Roman Basilicas ; Gregory IX, from the year 1240, had thought of imposing it on the Universal Church ; but that important duty devolved on St. Pius V (1566–1572). In the sixteenth century the Council of Trent, having declared that the liturgical books required revision, confided the task to the Pope, who undertook a work at once difficult and complicated. In 1568 the correction of the Breviary was completed ; in 1570, that of the Missal. Every church which could not prove a local use of at least two hundred years was obliged to adopt the Breviary and the Roman Missal.

But long before this date, since the thirteenth, and even the eleventh century, the Religious Orders, both new and old, had adopted a liturgy directly derived from the Roman, especially for Mass.

This point deserves an explanation. We speak sometimes of the Dominican or Franciscan liturgy, or again, that of Lyon, or of the Carmelites, as well as of the English *Uses* of Sarum, Hereford, York, etc. But these terms are rather misleading, for such liturgies are not autonomous, with clearly defined characteristics, like those described in Chapters III–VIII. Not only are they all derived from the Roman liturgy, but some of them are purely and simply that liturgy just as it existed from the eleventh-thirteenth centuries before it underwent certain reforms or suffered the changes imposed upon it subsequently. The Orders and churches in question did not accept these changes, so that the student to-day finds himself in presence of a liturgy which is that of Rome between the eleventh and thirteenth centuries, with a few insignificant exceptions. And as we are about to see, this is specially the case with regard to the Mass.

THE RITE OF LYON.—It is unnecessary to say that we reject the hypothesis according to which this rite was brought from Asia by St. Pothinus and St. Irenæus. In studying the origins of the Gallican liturgy we have stated that this *Johannic* thesis has no solid foundation. Nor can it be said that this is the old Gallican liturgy, better preserved in this church than in others. Like all the other Gallican churches, Lyon was obliged to accept the reforms of Pepin and Charlemagne, and to adopt the Roman liturgy, with the addition of certain ancient local uses. But to-day it is generally agreed that the part played by Gallican influence in the rite of Lyon may be increasingly reduced, as indeed is the case with all the other Franco-Gallican rites from the tenth century onwards.

History tells us that towards 789 Charlemagne caused Leidrade, one of his *Missi Dominici,* to be elected Archbishop of Lyon ; and that he charged him to reorganise public worship on the lines of the customs of the Palatine chapel at Aix-la-Chapelle. The cause of the difference which still exists, on a few points, between the rite of Lyon and those of some other churches, is that the ecclesiastics of Lyon jealously preserved the liturgy given them by Leidrade, without accepting the changes and reforms adopted in the course of the centuries by the Roman Curia. It was not till the eighteenth century that De Montazet, Archbishop of Lyon (1758–1788), unfortunately replaced the venerable liturgy of his church by a neo-Gallican one. Therefore in the nineteenth century Lyon, like all the other churches which had adopted these liturgies, had to come back to that of Rome, though she succeeded in saving some of her ancient usages. Thus she has more numerous Proses : to the fifteen Prefaces of the Roman Mass Lyon adds eight. The prayers at the beginning of Mass, the *Suscipe Sancta Trinitas* and some others, present a slightly different text ; the *Libera nos* after the *Pater* is sung at High Mass, as on Good Friday, while after this prayer a blessing is given, as in the old Gallican rite ; the beautiful chant of the Fraction *Venite, populi* has been preserved ; Pontifical Mass is celebrated with especial solemnity, etc.

THE CARTHUSIANS.—It is a rather curious fact in liturgical history that the Carthusians have preserved the ancient rite more faithfully than the Lyonnais themselves. The liturgical revolution mentioned as having taken place in the eighteenth century was not felt by the Carthusians. This Order, founded in 1084 by St. Bruno, in the mountains of the Chartreuse, had taken the liturgical uses of Grenoble, Vienne, but specially those of Lyon. Its founder, who at first had followed the Rule of St. Benedict, kept some of its practices. These different usages were codified at various periods in the Constitutions which have been preserved, and of which the most complete are the *Statuta Antiqua*. The prayer *Pone, Domine, custodiam ori meo*, and another, *De latere Domini*, recited at Mass, are derived from the rite of Lyon. On certain Feasts three Lessons at the Pre-Mass have been retained. The wine is poured into the chalice at the beginning of Mass, as in the Dominican rite. The oblations of bread and wine (after they have been offered) are covered with the Corporal, as was the custom before the use of the *Palla* had been introduced. *Domine, Jesu Christe* is the only one of the three prayers said before the Communion ; those present in choir remain standing during both Consecration and Communion ; the Mass terminates with *Ite, Missa est*. Before the fourteenth century the Mass of the Dead had a different text from the *Requiem*. Some Benedictine uses have been preserved in the Breviary ; while others seem to have been derived from the rite of Lyon. For a long time the Carthusian calendar remained the same as the old Roman one ; it was only after a very long period that Feasts instituted after the thirteenth century were admitted, and then not without difficulty. In the sixteenth century some reforms were brought about, either as to the correction of the ancient books, or as to bringing them into line with the new rules.

BENEDICTINE LITURGY.—On the whole it may be said that the Benedictines have always followed the Roman practice for the Mass. Instituted in the first part of the sixth century, it appears probable that they first followed the Gelasian Sacramentary, adopting the Gregorian in the next generation ; this latter being the work of St. Gregory, who was himself a disciple of St. Benedict.

But for the daily Office it is quite a different matter. St. Benedict, while doubtless borrowing a certain number of customs from the Roman Office then in use, organised the Psalter and the Day and Night Hours according to a particular plan which has been followed by the Benedictine Order throughout the centuries, till the present day. Liturgiologists are still discussing what has been the respective influence of one use upon another ; but this question cannot be entered into here.

CISTERCIANS.—As is well known, the Cistercians are a reform of the Benedictine Order. Their founder, St. Robert of Molesmes, wished to return to the primitive observance of the Rule in 1098. To this end he rejected all constitutions or additions made since the sixth century. His principle was the same for the liturgy : to bring back the Office as St. Benedict had instituted it. This principle was a good one, but difficult in application, for it was not exactly known in what the *cursus* of St. Benedict's time consisted. Therefore from the beginning there was a good deal of uncertainty. Then scandal was caused by certain suppressions, and in the twelfth and thirteenth centuries they came back to their first attempts as far as the Office was concerned.

As to the Mass, it has been said that the Benedictine Order followed the use of Rome from the beginning. But the Cluniac monks had accepted modifications made since the ninth century, and had introduced a very great solemnity into both Mass and Office. The Cistercian reform consisted in the suppression of all which seemed superfluous, and as concerned the sacred vases and ornaments, in the return to the greatest simplicity.

Thus it was not till quite late, at the beginning of the eighteenth century, that the different liturgical colours were admitted. A certain number of Feasts was also suppressed in the calendar. In the seventeenth century the General Chapters ordered a general revision of the liturgical books, and more ancient rites were abandoned.

CARMELITES.—This rite presents a special case. It is that of the church of the Holy Sepulchre at Jerusalem, which was imposed on the Carmelites about 1210 by St. Albert, Patriarch of Jerusalem, and which they kept for a long time. It is nothing but a Gallicano-Roman use, brought to Jerusalem by the Crusaders. The Office gave a particular place to all which could recall the Holy Land, such as the Mystery of the Resurrection, or devotion to Our Lady, and had besides several other special customs. In the course of ages the Carmelite liturgy underwent various modifications. The Ordinal of Master Sibert de Beka (d. 1332), which has been most carefully published, preserves all the ancient uses conformably to the rite of the Holy Sepulchre. It is in this document that the Carmelite liturgy should be studied.

DOMINICANS.—This Order had no special liturgy at its beginning, but adopted that of the provinces through which the Friars first spread. To prevent the inconvenience of this variety the Order sought, from the year 1245, to establish liturgical unity. To this end efforts were made in 1244, 1246, and 1251. Finally Humbert de Romans, the Master-General (1254–1263), was charged with this revision. He accomplished an enormous work ; and in fourteen volumes published the Lectionary, Antiphonary, Psalter, book of Collects, Martyrology, Processional, Gradual, a Missal for the high altar and one for the other altars in the church, a Breviary for the Choir and a portable Breviary, a book of the Epistles and another of the Gospels. When in 1568 and 1570 St. Pius V imposed the corrected Missal and Breviary on the whole Church, the Dominicans were allowed to retain their own use, which dated back more than 200 years.

This liturgy is not, as has been thought, a Gallican, and more specifically, a Parisian liturgy. It is simply Roman, dating from the thirteenth century, and has not evolved as the actual Roman liturgy has done ; thus retaining all the ancient customs elsewhere fallen into disuse. Thus a thesis which at first sight appears paradoxical has been advanced, to the effect that the Dominican liturgy is more Roman than that of Rome herself. This, however, is the case with the greater number of these rites, which did not accept the transformations of the Roman liturgy.

FRANCISCANS.—It has been already explained how the Franciscans adopted the liturgy which was that of the Roman Curia at the opening of the thirteenth century. To this they added certain special uses, beginning with the Feasts of the Saints of their Order : St. Francis first ; then St. Clare ; St. Antony of Padua ; St. Louis, King of France ; the Stigmata of St. Francis ; St. Elizabeth of Hungary ; St. Paschal Baylon ; St. Bonaventure. Some of the Feasts of Our Lord and of Our Lady owe, if not their actual institution, at least their speedy popularity to the Franciscans. Such are the Holy Name of Jesus, the Immaculate Conception, the Visitation, and the Presentation. Each Religious Order, each diocese has its own Feasts, its own Patrons, which they celebrate with great solemnity ; they are the *Proper*, as it is called, of the diocese or Order.

What should be particularly noted about the Franciscans is that, having adopted the liturgy of the Roman Curia, they made a " second edition of it," as Mgr. Batiffol remarks ; and this was almost the same as that imposed upon the whole Church for Breviary and Missal by St. Pius V.

PRÆMONSTRATENSIANS.—The Order of St. Norbert, being an Order of Canons, was bound to give special attention to the liturgy. Its Founder adopted that of Rome, just as it was practised in France at the beginning of the twelfth century, at Prémontré, in the diocese of Laon. Until the eighteenth century they kept it piously ; and their books are mentioned as being one of the purest sources of the Roman liturgy of the twelfth century. Thanks to this antiquity they too benefited by the exception made by St. Pius V in 1570 in favour of ancient customs. Unfortunately, in the eighteenth century the French Præmonstratensians succumbed to the general temptation, and modified their books in the neo-Gallican sense. In other countries, however, the ancient books were preserved.

THE ROMAN LITURGY IN ENGLAND.—Celtic rites had dominated in England until the arrival of St. Augustine of Canterbury (596). But with the Roman monks the Roman liturgy was established without difficulty wherever Christianity was firmly settled in the land ; and the Anglo-Saxons followed it faithfully. Their Bishops and Abbots made frequent journeys to Rome, either to procure the necessary singing-books and those of liturgical interest, or to study the rites more closely. The Norman Conquest of 1066 changed nothing in this regard, for, like all the other French provinces, Normandy had long been conquered by the Roman liturgy. Thus the various rites called the Use of Sarum (Salisbury), York, Bangor, Hereford, and other places, are, like those of the different Orders we have just been studying, only the Roman liturgy previous to the fourteenth century, with a few rare local customs added to it.

BIBLIOGRAPHY

Liturgia, Encyclopédie populaire des connaissances liturgiques (Paris, 1930), contains a chapter on the different Western liturgies and on those of the Carthusians, Carmelites, and other Religious Orders.

DACL, cf. the articles *Carmes, Chartreux, Cisterciens*, and also *Bretagne (Grande), La liturgie de la*.

ARCH. A. KING, *Notes on the Catholic liturgy* (London, 1930), on the Roman and various Eastern and Western rites.

Our articles *Missel* and *Missel romain* in DACL.

CHAPTER XI

THE MASS, FROM THE SIXTEENTH TO THE TWENTIETH CENTURY: WHAT IT IS TO-DAY—RECAPITULATION

THERE is no lack of witnesses for this period. Here, as elsewhere, the invention of printing brought about a revolution. Not that the second state of things destroyed the first, but it must be remembered that up till then the Missal and all other liturgical books had been copied by hand. Each copy was private property; and thus very often underwent some modification in the course of time. However, these liturgical MSS. were the models copied by the first printers, who drew inspiration from the caligraphy of the copyists and religiously respected their text, especially during that first period from the middle of the fifteenth up to the sixteenth century. The original printed books are imitations of these MSS.; their very characters singularly resemble that Gothic writing then generally in use.

The earliest printed copies, up to 1600, are *incunabula*; and the most precious amongst these precious books are the liturgical volumes, Psalters, Missals, Breviaries, etc.

But these first printed books usually reproduced the text of the MS. exactly as it was written; no attempt being made to correct it. The multiplication of copies of the Missal, for example, brought out very clearly the differences and variations of its text according to the province in which it was used. This point was noted at the Council of Trent, and it was resolved to reduce all these texts to one. The Fathers began with the Breviary and the Missal ; and to Pius IV was confided the task of correction and unification. But this great work was not finished until the days of St. Pius V, who in the Bull *Quo primum* of 29th July 1570 announced a Missal with an invariable text. Clement VIII and Urban VIII caused new editions to be made ; but the only changes were the addition of some new Feasts and the modification of a few rubrics.

This Missal of 1570 itself reproduced without much alteration one more ancient, the first precious original Missal of 1474. This in its turn conforms to a great extent with an MS. text of about 1200, which was perhaps written or inspired by Innocent III himself.[1] The text, *Incipit ordo Missalis secundum consuetudinem Romane Curie*, is itself a revelation. The title of the existing Missal is, simply, *Missale Romanum*. That of the *Curia Romana* was the book used by the Court of Rome from the twelfth-fourteenth centuries ; it differed on several points from the Roman Missal used in the Roman churches, notably at St. Peter's and the Lateran. The same may be said of the Breviary used by the Curia, also slightly different from that of the Roman churches. The Missal and Breviary of the Roman Curia were adopted by certain Religious Orders, especially the Franciscans, as was stated in a previous chapter ; and these Friars were the chief factor in their diffusion throughout Christendom.

We may therefore consider the text of the Roman Missal, especially as regards the Ordinary of the Mass, as fixed from the end of the sixteenth century : if a precise date and official example be asked, by the Missal of St. Pius V in 1570. Thus it seems opportune at this point

---

[1] This famous *editio princeps* has been recently reprinted by the Henry Bradshaw Society (London, 1899–1907).

to give a chronological table of the Mass in which can be seen, at least in some degree, the different states in which it existed from the fifth-twentieth centuries, distinguishing the different epochs as far as possible.

5TH–9TH CENTURIES.	9TH–13TH CENTURIES.	13TH–20TH CENTURIES.
Station (7th cent. says Mgr. Duchesne; 5th–6th, Dom Morin and others).	Prayer of preparation.	
	Apologiæ sacerdotis.	
	Ps. xlii. or others.	
	Confiteor (10th cent.). Versicles.	
Greeting of the officiating Priest.	*Aufer a nobis* (Leonine, 5th cent.).	
Pax vobis, or *Dominus vobiscum.*		
Kissing of altar.		
	Oramus te (11th cent.).	
	Censing of altar.	
Introit.		
Kyrie Eleison and Litanies (5th – 6th cent.).	Tropes of *Kyrie* (10th, 11th cent.).	
Gloria in excelsis Deo.	Tropes (10th–11th cent.).	
Pax vobis, Oremus, Collect. (One only.)	Many collects from 11th cent. onwards.	
[Prophecy].		
Epistle (Apostolic Lesson).		
Gradual (responsorial Psalm, 5th cent.).		
Alleluia (5th cent.). Tract.	Proses : *Victimæ* (11th cent.).	
	Proses : *Veni Sancte* (11th cent.).	
	Proses : *Dies iræ* (13th cent.).	

5TH–9TH CENTURIES.	9TH–13TH CENTURIES.	13TH–20TH CENTURIES.
	Proses: *Lauda Sion* (13th cent.).	
	Proses : *Stabat* (14th cent.).	Only inserted in 18th cent.
Gospel.	*Munda cor meum* (11th cent.).	
Dominus sit in corde tuo.	*Sequentia sancti ev.* (9th cent.) (in Gaul).	*Per evangelica dicta* after 1570 (in MSS of 12th and 13th cent.).
	Gloria tibi Dne : *Dominus vobiscum.* Censing of Book. *Pax tibi.* } 13th cent.	
	Credo (about 1012–1024, at Rome), but from 7th cent. elsewhere.	
Diaconal litanies, dismissal of catechumens, penitents, and others (7th cent.).	Suppressed.	
Dominus vobiscum. Oremus. Collect *super sindonem.*	Suppressed.	
Prayer of the faithful.	Suppressed.	
Kiss of Peace ?	Suppressed.	
Offertory chant (5th–7th cent.).		
Offering (leavened bread and wine).	Unleavened.	
Water mixed with wine (2nd–3rd cent.).	Offering of money (10th cent.). Kissing of altar (13th cent.). Censing of oblations (11th cent.).	
Ablution (7th cent.).	*Per intercessionem. Incensum istud.*	

196

5TH–9TH CENTURIES.	9TH–13TH CENTURIES.	13TH–20TH CENTURIES.
	Accendat.	
	Lavabo (11th cent.).	
Secret Prayer.	*Suscipe Sancte Pater.*	
	Deus qui humanæ subst.	
	Offerimus tibi.	
	In spiritu.	
	Veni sanctificator (in Stowe, 7th–8th cent.).	
	Censing.	
Not of Roman origin.	*Per interc.* *Suscipe sancta Trinitas* (9th cent.). *Orate fratres* (9th cent.). *Suscipiat* (11th cent.).	*Orate p̣ . . ne fratres* (1474).
Dominus vobiscum. *Sursum corda,* etc. Preface.		Preface of the Blessed Virgin.
		Addition of Prefaces in 20th cent.
Sanctus (? 5th cent.). *Benedictus qui venit* (? 5th cent.). Canon.[1]		
Te igitur. Memento of Living. *Communicantes.*[2] *Hanc igitur oblationem.* *Quam oblationem.*	5th– 6th cent.	
Additions by St. Leo and St. Gregory.		
Qui pridie.	Elevation of the Host, about 1200. Elevation of the chalice (14th cent.). Other ceremonies (13th–14th cent.).	

[1] On the silence of the Canon and the signs of the Cross, cf. Excursus, pp. 216, 231.

[2] *Communicantes* under Symmachus, *Memento* in 416.

5TH–9TH CENTURIES.	9TH–13TH CENTURIES.	13TH–20TH CENTURIES.
Unde et memores. *Supra quæ.* *Supplices.* } 4th and 5th cent.		
Memento of the Dead (probably later than preceding prayers, at least, in this place).		
Nobis quoque (aloud) (7th cent.).		
Per quem hæc omnia.	Signs of the Cross at this moment (? 10th cent.).	
Fraction (5th, 6th cent.).[1]		
Prologue of *Pater*. *Pater*. Embolism of *Pater*.		
Fraction, Commixtion. Kiss of Peace.	*Hæc Commixtio.*	
Agnus Dei (687–701).	Reduced to three invocations with *dona nobis pacem*.	
	Domine J.C. *Domine J.C.* *Perceptio.* } Numerous variations.	
Communion anthems (6th, 7th cent.).	*Domine non sum dignus.*[2] *Corpus D.N.J.C.* *Quid retribuam.* *Sanguis.* [*Quod ore*]. Leonine. *Corpus tuum.*	
Collect, or *Ad complendum*, or Communion prayer.		Purification with wine and water (14th cent.).
	Confiteor. *Agnus Dei.* *Domine non sum dignus.*	For the Communion of the faithful (13th cent.).

[1] Changes introduced by St. Gregory, cf. p. 79–80.
[2] All these prayers are of Gallican origin and present variations.

5TH–9TH CENTURIES.	9TH–13TH CENTURIES.	13TH–20TH CENTURIES.
	Communion under both kinds till the 13th century and later.	
Prayer, *Super populum* (? 6th, 7th cent.).		
Ite, Missa est (6th–8th cent.).		Kissing of the altar, 1570.
	Placeat (10th, 11th cent.).	
Bishop's blessing after Mass.		*Benedicat vos.*, 1570.
		Last Gospel, 1570. Prayers at end of Mass. (Leo XIII.)

The foregoing table presents a synchronism of the Roman Mass as it was about the fifth-ninth centuries, with the additions received until the twentieth century. We shall now show the existing Mass with its divisions ; a table which will make it easy to understand the whole, as well as the dependence of the different parts.

FIRST PART

PRE-MASS, OR MASS OF THE CATECHUMENS

A. *Introduction, or Prelude.*

    Preparation in the sacristy.

    Prayers at the foot of the altar, sign of the Cross, Psalm xlii. *Confiteor*, versicles, and prayers at the altar. (Censing of altar at Solemn Masses.)

B. *Chants, Prayers, Lessons.*

    Introit, *Kyrie, Gloria in excelsis.*

    Collects.

    Reading of the Epistle.

    Gradual. *Alleluia* (Tract or Prose).

    Gospel.

    Credo.

THE MASS OF THE WESTERN RITES

SECOND PART

MASS OF THE FAITHFUL OR EUCHARISTIC SACRIFICE

C. *Offertory and Offertory Prayers.*
    Offertory chant. Secret. Preface.
    Sanctus.

D. *Canon.*

   Prayers of the Canon, Consecration, Prayers of
       Canon continued, and final doxology.
   Pater, Fraction, Immixtion.

E. *Communion.*

   Communion Prayers, *Agnus Dei*, singing of Com-
       munion, Post-communion.

F. *Close of Mass.*

   Blessing.
   Last Gospel.
   Prayers after the Mass.
   Thanksgiving in sacristy.

Lastly, as the fitting conclusion of this exposition, we
shall give a few explanations as to some of the more
recent portions of the Mass from the sixteenth-twentieth
centuries, the other necessary explanations being found
in the various chapters of this book.

PREPARATION FOR MASS

Except in the case of Pontifical Masses, when the
Prelate recites these prayers on his throne, reading them
from a special liturgical book, the *Canon* of Bishops and
Prelates, the *Preparatio ad Missam* takes place to-day
in the sacristy. St. Pius V gave a place to these prayers
in his Missal, and the words which follow the title,

Pro opportunitate sacerdotis facienda, indicate that they are not of obligation, but are left to private devotion. This preparation is fairly ancient ; it is found, with variations, in MS. Missals from the eleventh century onwards. The devotions chosen by St. Pius V consist of Psalms lxxxiii., lxxxiv., lxxxv., cxv., and cxxix., followed by the *Kyrie, Pater,* some versicles, and seven prayers. This form of prayer conforms to the use of the ancient Roman or monastic psalmody. It is almost the same as that primitively adopted for the Little Hours. A long prayer follows, divided according to the days of the week ; and then two others, one of which is attributed to St. Thomas. The prayer *Summe sacerdos* held an important place in the history of private devotion in the Middle Ages ; it was called the "Prayer of St. Ambrose," but has been claimed as the work of Jean de Fécamp (twelfth century).[1]

PREPARATION OF THE CHALICE.—For Low Masses it is usually the Priest himself who prepares in the sacristy the chalice, Corporal, paten, Host, and the veil of the chalice ; and who carries them to the altar at the beginning of Mass. At Solemn and Pontifical High Mass it is the Deacon who spreads the Corporal on the altar, and places the chalice and Host upon it, as we have seen was the custom in the seventh century (cf. p. 60).

In the Eastern and Gallican rites this preparation is made at the altar or credence at the beginning of Mass. It is also the custom of the Dominicans and other Orders.

ORDINARY OF THE MASS

The *Ordo Missæ* is to-day united to the Prefaces and Canon : the whole, for the convenience of the Priest, being placed towards the middle of the Missal between

---

[1] Dom A. Wilmart, *L'Oratio S. Ambrosii du Missel romain, R. bénéd.,* XXXIX, 1927, p. 317 *seq.* See also DACL, *Apologies.*

Holy Saturday and Easter Sunday instead of at the beginning. This *Ordinary of the Mass* is, taken as a whole, the same as that of the seventh century, as it has been described in Chapter IV, with the exceptions of the additions which have been pointed out as made between the ninth-twentieth centuries.

PRAYERS AT THE FOOT OF THE ALTAR.—Psalm xlii., *Confiteor*, versicles, *Aufer a nobis*, *Oramus te*, and censing (cf. p. 172).

CHANTS, PRAYERS, AND LESSONS :
> Introit (cf. p. 50).
> *Kyrie* (p. 49).
> *Gloria in excelsis* (p. 51).
> Collect (p. 52).
> Lessons (Epistle and other Lessons) (p. 54).
> Gradual (p. 55).
> *Alleluia* (p. 56).
> Tract (p. 57).
> Proses (p. 173).
> Gospel (p. 58).
> Credo (p. 129).

OFFERTORY (p. 59).

PREFACE (p. 64). All the Prefaces and special *Communicantes* are given at this place in the Ordinary of the Mass.

CANON OF THE MASS :
> *Te igitur* (pp. 69).
> Memento (p. 70).
> *Communicantes* and other prayers (p. 70).
> Consecration (p. 72).
> *Anamnesis* and other prayers (p. 74).
> Memento of the Dead (p. 76).
> *Nobis quoque* up to doxology (p. 76).
> *Pater* (p. 80).

Fraction, Commixtion (p. 83).
Agnus Dei and Kiss of Peace (p. 84).
Communion of the Priest and the faithful (p. 85).

LAST PRAYERS :

Quod ore.
Corpus tuum.
Post-communion.

CLOSE OF MASS.—Dismissal. *Placeat tibi.* Blessing.
Last Gospel. Prayers after Mass.

When withdrawing, the Priest repeats the canticle
Benedicite.

THANKSGIVING IN THE SACRISTY

The Thanksgiving which in the Missal follows the
Preparation is also said in the sacristy. Like the latter
it is contained in the *Canon of the Prelate,* and at Pontifical
Masses is said at the throne. It is composed of the
canticle *Benedicite,* of Psalm cl., and of three prayers.
There follow, at choice, a prayer of St. Thomas, another
of St. Bonaventure, and the *Adoro Te.* (As to this last,
cf. Dumoutet, *Revue Apolog.,* 1931, p. 121 *seq.*)

NOTE ON THE NEO-GALLICAN LITURGIES

The Gallican liturgy spoken of in Chapter II, which
was as orthodox as the Mozarabic liturgy, must not be
confused with the neo-Gallican rites, which are on the
contrary a " liturgical deviation." It has been said how
the Roman had taken the place of the Gallican liturgy
in the times of Pepin and Charlemagne. Ancient Gallican customs, however, remained, and the Roman books,
Missal, Breviary, Pontifical, and Ritual underwent a
certain number of modifications in Gaul from the ninth-
fifteenth centuries. But in substance the Roman liturgy

was preserved, and Rome, far from prot~s~ing against these new uses, accepted a great many of them, as we have also seen.

In the sixteenth century the Council of Trent, greatly concerned to note the liturgical differences, and even errors, which had slipped into certain Missals and Breviaries, entrusted to the Popes the care of a general revision of these books. The names of St. Pius V, Gregory XIII, Clement VIII, Paul V, and Urban VIII are attached to this reform. The Bull *Quod a nobis* (1568) imposed the corrected Breviary on all churches which could not claim a use of at least two hundred years ; the Bull *Quo primum* (1570) imposed the Missal on the whole Church under the same conditions. The other liturgical books, Ritual, Pontifical, Ceremonial, Martyrology, were also corrected during the following years. France gladly accepted these directions, and took part in the reawakening of liturgical studies. It was only later, in the last third of the seventeenth century, that the movement, justly called " the liturgical deviation," began to take shape.

Certain Bishops, inspired by their Jansenist or Gallican sentiments, desired to reform the Missal, Breviary, and other liturgical books contrary to the law obtaining at that time. The Ritual of Alet, the Breviary of Vienne, the Missal and Breviary of Paris and of other dioceses were remade, and, unfortunately, in more than one case, Jansenist or Gallican errors slipped into these books. Another disadvantage was the introduction of notable differences in the liturgy in different dioceses ; and at the time of the French Revolution the confusion was at its worst. It was Dom Guéranger, Abbot of Solesmes, who in 1830 began the war against these liturgies, and who showed that, without speaking of the errors they contained, they were all illegitimate from birth. This struggle was crowned with success, and little by little the different dioceses came back to the Roman liturgy. The Bull *Inter multiplices*, published in 1853 by Pius IX, may be considered as the last act in this history.

BIBLIOGRAPHY

On the original (first edition) Missals, BOHATTA-WEALE, *Bibliographica liturgica. Catalogus missalium ritus latini ab A. 1474 impressorum, Londini* (Quaritch, 1928). Cf. also *Books of the Latin Liturgy*, in which (p. 151) we give a notice of other works on the ancient Missals. Cf. also p. 156, and the works of DELISLE, EBNER, LEROQUAIS, and others mentioned in the bibliography, p. 236.

On the Neo-Gallican liturgies, besides the great work of Dom Guéranger, *Les institutions liturgiques*, ed. 1, Vol. II, cf. *Liturgia*, p. 872, where other works on this subject are mentioned. The Abbé Bremond takes up this question in his volume, *Prières de l'ancien régime*, and, with his well-known talent, gives it new life. What must be regretted is that the reform was effected with so little intelligence in too many dioceses. Many of the Proses and ancient rites might have been allowed to survive, even by the desire of Rome. But for lack of competence, all the old rites and prayers were swept away, even those which could claim an antiquity of many centuries. Thanks to the use of Propers granted to the dioceses a part of this destruction may perhaps be repaired.

CHAPTER XII

EXCURSUS

I. The Different Names of the Mass and the Word *Missa*
in Particular.—II. The Chants of the Mass : Parts sung
by the Cantors, *schola*, or people ; parts sung or recited aloud
by the Priest, and those recited in a low voice. The Gregorian
chant.—III. Attitude of the Faithful and Liturgical
Gestures during Mass.—IV. The Books of the Mass.—V.
Different Sorts of Masses.

I. THE DIFFERENT NAMES OF THE MASS AND THE WORD *Missa* IN PARTICULAR

THE word *Missa* has given rise to numerous dissertations mentioned in the Bibliography, and to long philo-
logical discussions. The reason for this is that the term
was evolved before it was used to design the Mass. It
would seem that the following are the chief stages
through which it has passed. One of the clearest texts
is that of St. Avitus, Bishop of Vienne (d. 518). Gonde-
baud asks him the meaning of the word *Missa* ; he
replies that *Missam facere* means *dimittere*, or dismiss,
and that the expression was used by Romans in audiences
at the palace and in sessions of the tribunal to denote that
the sitting was over.[1] The phrase was even used by them
to denote the end of their sacrifices and religious offices.

The custom of giving a signal to show that an Office
is ended is natural enough, and indeed necessary in a
numerous assembly. The Christians no doubt accepted
it, and Tertullian already speaks of a *Dismissio plebis*.[2]

[1] *Ep.* i. ; *Ad Gond.*, c. 1.
[2] *De anima*, c. 9. The text of Pope Pius I (142–57) does not
seem to be authentic.

St. Ambrose also uses the term *Missa* in this sense
(*Eph*. xx. 4) ; and I know not why it should be contested,
for it appears quite clear (cf. Lejay, article mentioned in
Bibliography). St. Augustine uses the word *Missa* in
the sense of *Missio, Dismissio* (dismissal), at the close of
the Office. From this Mgr. Batiffol justly concludes
that the *Ite, Missa est*, which has the same meaning,
dates from the same period. The same sense is given to
the expression in the *Peregrinatio Etheriæ*, in the Rule of
Aurelian, in Cassian, in St. Benedict. It is the end, not
only of the Mass but of every Office. For already in the
latter writers, especially in Cassian, the word has taken
on this extended meaning and designs every Office,
Missa Canonica, a canonical Office, and *Secunda Missa*,
the evening Office.

In the sixth century we have texts in which *Missa*
means Mass. Thus in Antoninus of Placentia, about 575
—*Missas faciebant*—they said Mass. The same meaning
is given in contemporary authors of that age, Gregory
of Tours, St. Gregory the Great, and Cæsarius of
Arles.[1]

But why *Missa* instead of *Missio* ? It is not a past
participle of *mittere*, for it cannot be explained in that
sense. *Missa* has been made out of *Missio*, just as
Collecta has been made out of *Collectio* ; there are many
examples of this practice, especially in the liturgy.
Missa is thus simply a popular expression which,
taking the part for the whole, has ended by designating
the Eucharistic Sacrifice. Some authors, finding this
etymology rather below the dignity of this function,
have sought a higher origin and meaning in a Hebrew
word which signifies Mission or Message. It is the
message of earth to Heaven ; of man to God. This is the

[1] These texts will be found in Kellner and in the other authors
cited.

meaning which Amalarius gives it in the ninth century. But we are not in the realm of philology here.

In the terminology of the Gallican and Mozarabic liturgies in the seventh century, *Missa* also means a prayer. The *Præfatio Missæ* is the prelude of a prayer. The second Council of Milevia had already said : *Missæ, vel orationes Missæ.*[1] *Missa secreta*=words of Consecration.

For those whom this meaning of *Missa* does not satisfy there is no lack of synonyms with a much loftier signification.

Eucharistia or *Eulogia*.—These two terms, the first of which means thanksgiving, the second, blessing, were once of equal value, and were used indifferently to design the Eucharist. Thus, in the synoptic Gospels, Jesus *blessed* the bread and *gave thanks*. This, of all blessings the most efficacious, was doubtless made by the laying on of hands, or, if we like to follow certain other interpreters, by a sign of the Cross, which prophetically signified the Bloody Sacrifice of the following day. This is one of the essential elements of the Consecration : the Priest at Mass blesses and consecrates the bread and wine by a sign of the Cross.

But the term *Eulogy*, blessing, early fell into disuse, and merely meant the bread or other objects blessed at Mass at the same time as the bread and wine. The other term, *Eucharist*, has lived longer. In the Gospel the *Gratias agens*, giving thanks, is heavy with meaning. Every time He blessed bread (as in the multiplication of the loaves) Our Lord gave thanks. The prayer over the bread before taking a meal is a traditional Jewish custom. This people had felt the necessity of thanking God for

[1] Mansi, IV, 330. A good collection and explanation of these terms will be found in Thibaut, *Liturgie Gallicane*, pp. 49–51 ; *Liturgie Romaine*, pp. 50, 51, 88, 99, 122 *seq.*

His benefits more strongly than any other ancient race. In the books of the Old Testament, especially in the Psalms, this duty of gratitude to God is expressed. The first duty of the creature is to thank God who has given to the earth wheat and the vine, fruits, and all things which contribute to the nourishment of mankind. But the blessing of blessings henceforth is the very bread and wine which Jesus Christ has transformed by His blessing into His Body and Blood. The most ancient *anaphora*, especially that of the *Apostolic Constitutions*, reminds us that the Eucharist is the great Sacrifice, and the most efficacious means in man's possession to *render thanks to God*.[1]

The *Supper* (*Cœna*, repast, supper), and more especially the Last Supper, is a term which we need hardly explain. It was at this Last Supper, taken with His Apostles on the evening of Holy Thursday, that Our Lord instituted the Eucharist (cf. Chapter I, p. 4). But since the sixteenth century, as Protestants have used the words " Last Supper " in a narrow sense, excluding all relation with the Sacrifice of the Cross, they have almost dropped out of Catholic language. However, the Church has retained a lively remembrance of the Last Supper, and during Holy Week, Holy Thursday, the anniversary of this great event, is marked in the liturgical year by exceptional solemnity. The prayers of the Canon, *Communicantes*, *Hanc igitur*, recall the *Diem sacratissimum quo Dominus noster Jesus Christus pro nobis est traditus*, the *Diem in qua Dominus noster Jesus Christus tradidit discipulis suis Corporis et Sanguinis sui mysteria celebranda*. The *Qui pridie* itself contains this curious variant : *Qui pridie quam pro nostra omniumque salute pateretur, hoc est hodie, accepit panem*, etc. The Priest consecrates two Hosts, one of which is re-

[1] Cf. *Eucharistie, Eulogie*, in DACL.

served for the next day's Mass; this is carried processionally into a chapel, where It is exposed for the adoration of the faithful during the day and all that night, and on Good Friday, the day following, is brought back to the high altar with the same ceremonies, and is consumed at the Mass of the Presanctified. This is the only day in the whole year on which this Mass is celebrated in the Latin Church.[1]

The term *Sacrifice, Holy Sacrifice*, is also used; the Mass being for Christians the only Sacrifice, as we have explained (p. 75). It is that which has replaced all others; where Jesus Christ, Priest and Victim, renews the Sacrifice of the Cross, and offers Himself to God the Father for the salvation of all.

The Mass is also often called *The Sacrament*, or *Sacraments*, especially by the Fathers and in the liturgy, because it is at the same time Sacrifice and Sacrament, the chief of all, since it is the Sacrament of the Body and Blood of Our Lord Jesus Christ, source of all Sacraments. We often find in prayers the words: *Sacramenta quæ sumpsimus*, or analogous expressions.

The Oblation, Offering (*Offerre*), is also a very ancient term used at Rome, in Africa, and elsewhere, the Mass being the greatest of all Offerings, the Sacrifice of sacrifices. The Church offers it by her Pontiff; and we have seen with what insistence she urges the faithful to unite their offering with that of the Priest.

The words *Fractio Panis* have been explained in another place (cf. p. 83).

[1] Fr. Thurston, S.J., justly remarks that the altar and tabernacle in which this Host reposes is wrongly called *sepulchre*. There is a confusion here, the sepulchre being really a tomb in which a third consecrated Host was also laid on Holy Thursday. This was brought back in procession on Easter Day to figure the Resurrection. This Mystery was represented in many churches in the Middle Ages.—*Lent and Holy Week*, p. 299 (London, 1904).

EXCURSUS

Liturgy.—In the East this word is used specially to design the service of the Mass. Primitively it had a much more extended sense ; it was a general public function, more especially a religious service. In Christian language it designates all religious services, though in the East it is confined to the Mass.

Other terms are less popular, yet they express some aspect of the Eucharist. Mgr. Batiffol explains very well the meaning of the word *Dominicum* (*convivium*), used in Africa, and even at Rome, in the time of St. Cyprian.[1] St. Paul had already spoken of the *dominica cœna*, or *mensa Domini* (1 Cor. xi. 20 ; x. 21). (κυριακὸν δεῖπνον, τραπέζη κυρίου.) It is a table, reminding us of the Last Supper wherein Christ instituted the Eucharist ; it is a banquet in which all those present are called upon to take part. This characteristic of the Eucharist has perhaps become slightly effaced in the course of time ; but in ancient days it was a living memory ; and the frescoes in the catacombs recall it.

BIBLIOGRAPHY

O. Rottmanner, *Ueber neuere und ältere Deutungen des Wortes Missa,* in *Theol. quartalsch.* (Tübingen, 1889, pp. 531-557).

H. Kellner, *L'Année ecclésiastique* (tr. J. Bund), Paris, 1910, pp. 111-121, *Digression sur le nom de Messe.*

H. Kellner, *Wo und wann wurde " Missa " stehende Bezeichnung für das Messopfer,* in *Theol. quartalsch.,* 1901, LXXXIII, pp. 427-443.

P. Lejay, *Revue d'histoire et de littérature relig.,* Vol. II (1897), p. 287, and VIII (1903), p. 512 ; and *Ambrosien* in DACL, col. 1400 *seq.*

Fortescue, *The Mass.* An appendix on the names of the Mass.

Mgr. Batiffol, *Leçons sur la Messe,* pp. 166 *seq.,* 175, 183.

DACL, *Actio, Eucharistie, Eulogie.*

[1] *Op. cit.,* p. 171 *seq.*

At the Synaxis, or primitive gathering, psalms and canticles were sung (cf. p. 12). The Christians inherited the custom of singing after reading from the Jews. St. Paul himself alludes to these chants in many passages of his Epistles (Eph. v. 19 ; Col. iii. 16). The lessons themselves, as well as the prayers, were also probably sung, or declaimed, in a melodic tone.

The actual practice is as follows : at the Pontifical or Solemn High Mass certain parts are sung, or ought to be sung, by the people : *Kyrie, Gloria in Excelsis, Credo* ; while others are reserved to the cantors, or to the *schola*, and others again are said in a low voice. These points must be studied more in detail so as to establish the necessary distinctions :

1. Parts sung by the cantors, the *schola*, or the people.
2. Parts sung or recited aloud by the Priest, and parts said in a low voice. (The Secret of the Mysteries.)
3. The Gregorian chant.

1. PARTS SUNG BY THE CANTORS, THE *Schola*, OR THE PEOPLE.—Another distinction must be made between the chants belonging to this category. The Introit, Offertory, and Communion have an almost identical origin ; they are sung during a procession, or during movement to and from the altar ; they were instituted in the fourth and fifth centuries, and are composed for the same end and in the same way ; they are Psalms with an anthem. To-day they have been abridged and reduced to almost a single verse. But their origin must not be forgotten, and Mgr. Batiffol has very clearly shown by the example of the Introit for the Epiphany that the choice of Psalm lxx. can only be explained by

EXCURSUS

the verses which are now omitted.[1] The same procedure
may be applied to many of the verses of the Offertory
and Communion. The singing of these pieces must
necessarily have had special characteristics, and resemble
the psalmodic style.

But this was generally rare, and it would seem that
the music which was wedded to the words dates from a
period when these distinctions were hardly known ; it is
not always easy to distinguish an Introit and an Offertory
from a Gradual and an Alleluia by the chant which
belongs to it. The Communions, however, especially
those for Lent, often have a purely syllabic melody,
which betrays a more ancient origin. This psalmodic
chant has been better preserved at Vespers and the
other Offices. But if there is to-day hardly any difference
between the different chants of the Mass, such was not
the case formerly. Originally the anthem, or Psalm
with antiphon, was the Psalm sung by two choirs, each
in its turn repeating an alternate verse until the end was
reached. The *Responsory*, or *Responsorial Psalm*, is
sung by one or more cantors ; the choir or the faithful
taking up one of the verses as a refrain. Probably to
simplify matters and to allow even those who did not
know the Psalm to take part in the singing, a single verse
was chosen as anthem, and this served for a refrain.
This is the case with certain anthems of the Roman
Vespers, which must represent an ancient custom.
Certain Psalms, cxxxv. in particular, with its refrain
Quoniam in æternum misericordia ejus, point out that this
practice originated in the most distant past.

The *Gradual* (cf. p. 55) is quite distinct from the
chants with antiphons of the Introit, Offertory, and
Communion. It is a Responsory, or Responsorial Psalm,
and is thus sung by one or several cantors, the people

[1] *Leçons sur la Messe*, p. 115.

answering by a refrain which is one of the verses of the Psalm. That for Matins (Psalm xciv.) preserves one of the most perfect examples of this practice, probably borrowed, like that of the Lessons, from the services of the synagogues. In any case, it belongs to the same category as the Responsories which follow the Lessons at Matins, and which St. Benedict at the end of the fifth century apparently borrowed from the Roman Church. The Gradual chant is ornate, often difficult, and we can understand why it was reserved to experienced cantors. It also has a special dignity; it is sung from the ambone, or from the steps of the sanctuary. At one time, until the days of St. Gregory, it was reserved for Deacons alone, like the Gospel.

The *Alleluia* is a case apart. At least originally, it is in reality neither anthem nor responsory. The existing custom of incorporating it with the Gradual is not primitive. It is an acclamation, like *Amen, Hosanna, Deo Gratias, Benedicamus Domino*; and Cardinal Pitra has said that its history is a long poem.[1] As such it was sung frequently, and in various circumstances. This no doubt is the reason why its place in the Mass is not always the same in the different liturgies. There were variations even at Rome (cf. p. 56). At present it follows the Gradual, and is usually attached to a Psalm, of which a single verse has been preserved. The *Alleluia* is followed by a *Jubilus*, that is to say, by a somewhat prolonged melody on the final *a*.[2]

When it is suppressed under circumstances already stated it is replaced by the Tract, whose origin is not less obscure. Yet the words *Tractus, Tractim* were familiar to St. Benedict in the fifth century, and used to

[1] We have summed this up in our article, *Alleluia*, in DACL.
[2] Cf. *Jubilus* in DACL. On the Gradual and *Alleluia* cf. DACL. J. de Puniet, *La liturgie de la Messe*, p. 126 *seq.*

denote a Psalm sung without refrain or repetition but consecutively, and as a whole (Fr., *trait*). It is indeed still executed in this form, the only difference being that it is sung by two choirs in alternate verses, so that now it resembles the chant with antiphons. The Tract, in the Gregorian Antiphonary, has preserved its psalmodic appearance better than the other chants of the Mass.

The Proses do not go back to an earlier date than the tenth century. Composed to complete the *Jubilus* of the *Alleluia*, they multiplied prodigiously in the Middle Ages, and hundreds may be counted in the collections which have been made of them. While much in these poems is mediocre, some of them are real masterpieces, like those which the Church of Rome ended by adopting. They form a literature which it would be a mistake to neglect, and the Proses of Hugo de Saint-Victor, to take but one example, are finished models, complete with technical knowledge, and of the loftiest theological teaching.

Even in the seventeenth century a few true humanists set to work to compose hymns for the neo-Gallican breviaries ; and the Abbé Bremond, in his tenth volume (*Du sentiment religieux*) has made war on their adversaries. Happily for us this subject is outside our present scope, since the hymns in question were written for the Office and not for the Mass.

The *Kyrie, Gloria in Excelsis, Credo, Sanctus, Agnus Dei, Dominus vobiscum, Ite, Missa est,* and *Benedicamus Domino* are not taken from the Psalms, like the other chants of the Mass, and thus do not form part of the psalmody, properly so called. They are sung in various ways, and the rules to which they are submitted are much broader. This explains the numerous melodies with which they have been adorned, examples of which may be found in liturgical MSS. from the ninth-fifteenth centuries. They have also often served as themes for polyphonic compositions.

2. PARTS SUNG OR RECITED ALOUD BY THE PRIEST, AND PARTS SAID IN A LOW VOICE.—At present, and since the tenth century at least, the Priest must recite all the prayers of the Mass, including (at High Mass) the parts sung by the people or the ministers, Epistle, Gospel, *Kyrie, Gloria in Excelsis*, etc. The rules for Low Mass prescribe what has to be said aloud. At High Masses the Priest sings the prayers, Preface, and *Pater* ; the Gospel and *Ite, Missa est* are sung by the Deacon ; the Epistle by the sub-Deacon ; while the Priest also intones the *Gloria in Excelsis* and *Credo*. But the Canon is said in a low voice, even at High Mass, with the exceptions of the Preface, the *Pater*, and of *Nobis quoque peccatoribus*, which the Pope always said aloud, as the signal for the prostrate sub-Deacons to rise.

But why should the Canon be said in a low voice ? It is a question which seems to-day of secondary importance ; and we can scarcely explain why there was formerly so much discussion about it. But the *Secret of the Mysteries* was the subject of a celebrated controversy in the seventeenth and eighteenth centuries, and we can see, in the ninth volume of the Abbé Bremond, with what skill and talent he fights against those who, with Dom Guéranger, made a question of orthodoxy of this rubric.

It is clear that primitively, according to the description given in Chapter I, the Eucharistic prayer properly so called (from the dialogue of the Preface to the final doxology to which the faithful responded *Amen*) was said in an audible voice, and very probably was declaimed, on a *melopœia* doubtless resembling that of the Preface or the *Pater*. That at least is what the terms of this prayer would appear to indicate, based as they are on a

lyric tone which seems to call for a chant. Ancient
texts which corroborate this hypothesis are not wanting.
In any case there is nothing mysterious in the words ;
nothing that calls for concealment. The author of
De Sacramentis quotes them in a work not specially
addressed to the initiated ; another example is that of
Melanie of Jerusalem, who was able to hear every word
of this prayer ; and there are many others of the same
sort.[1] But it is none the less true that this was otherwise
at another period, and that the *Secret of the Mysteries*, of
the Eucharistic Mysteries, is not an empty word. Pope
Innocent I (in 416) speaks of this part of the Mass as
falling under the law of the Arcana, *Arcana agenda*,
something which must not be written about. St.
Augustine when he speaks of the Eucharist uses great
reticence in his language, and speaks of those things only
known to the initiated, the baptised. The discipline of
the Arcana is no myth ; it was observed for centuries,
though not everywhere, nor always in the same way.[2]

On this point it is curious to observe the variations of
Catholic devotion in different periods and countries.
Edmund Bishop has already pointed out the opposition
between East and West ; the latter erecting its altar
upon steps in the midst of the sanctuary, as if to expose
it to the eyes of all ; the former, on the contrary, hiding
it behind a screen (*iconostasis*), and concealing with a
curtain the Priest who accomplishes the great Mysteries.
In any case, a law prescribes that the Canon, especially
the words of the Institution, shall be said in a low voice.

[1] Mgr. Batiffol, *loc. cit.*, p. 206 *seq.*

[2] We need scarcely recall Mgr. Batiffol's dissertation on the
Arcane : though he is careful to restrain its scope, he is yet obliged
to admit its existence. We may add that another author, Père
le Brun of the Oratory, whose scholarship none will deny, is not
afraid to devote a treatise of 350 pages to pointing out the
genuineness of this practice in his great work on the Mass, *Du
silence des prières de la Messe* (Vol. IV).

"This mysticism is more Eastern than Roman," says Mgr. Batiffol (p. 21). And yet, at a given moment, doubtless under the influence of Byzantium, Rome became inspired with the same ideas. The Popes hung curtains which hid them from the view of the faithful around the altar. An *Ordo* (II) prescribed the saying of the Canon in a low voice. We can but indicate the question here, since it is only indirectly related to our subject ; moreover, we have treated of it elsewhere.[1] We must not be too much astonished at these fluctuations in Catholic piety. The *Mysterium Fidei* may be envisaged under many different aspects. At one time veneration, respect, and—let us say the word—a kind of fear surrounds this Sacrament, and prostrates the faithful before It in adoration. To-day they are carried away by Its mercy and Its love. At one time the law of the Eucharistic fast, so strict at present, scarcely existed ; at another, devotion constrained the Priest to celebrate Mass several times a day ; at yet another, on the contrary, exclusive of all Jansenist influence, there were those who deprived themselves of Holy Communion out of respect for the great Mystery.

In that book of the Abbé Bremond already quoted the quarrels of Gallicans, Jansenists, and Ultramontanes on this subject can be studied. To-day, thank God, men's minds are pacified. If the Church formerly made a law regarding the *Secret of the Mysteries*, she is no longer so severe, and the compilers of the best authorised prayer-books for the faithful can translate the whole of the Mass without the least uneasiness. Still, there remains that ancient rubric which prescribes that the Priest shall recite the Canon in a low voice, while he must sing, or say aloud, the Preface and the *Pater*.

3. THE GREGORIAN CHANT.—We need not here study the question of the chant, since this has been done in

[1] Cf. the article *Amen* in DACL.

another volume.[1] We shall only say what seems to be
strictly necessary in order to understand the part played
by this chant in the Roman Mass.

The Gregorian chant, the origin of which is obscure, is
revealed in many MSS. from the ninth century onwards
under the form of *neumes*, or musical signs which it has
been possible to decipher by comparing them with other
MSS. of a later age, in which these signs are written in
such a way as to indicate their tonality. But even in the
most ancient manuscript which contains these *neumes*,
that is, of the ninth century, it is possible to see that
there is nothing new in this chant. It is indeed in the
second stage of its evolution. It has its rules, its laws,
a well-established programme, and a learned technique.
The attribution of this chant to St. Gregory was attacked
in the nineteenth century by those who believed it should
rather be traced to Gregory II (d. 731) ; but their
arguments are more specious than solid. It is true that
the MSS. in which this system of notation is found go
back no farther than the ninth century, and that from
thence to the time of St. Gregory there is a gap of two
hundred years—truly, a very long time. But these
objections have been answered. The single fact that the
MSS. of the chant of the ninth and tenth centuries are
unanimous upon so many different points would alone
be a strong argument that this tradition comes from the
same source : the tradition dating back to the eighth
century, which has never hesitated as to the Roman and
Gregorian origin of this chant. It might even be said
that it was anterior to this Pontiff, and that St. Gregory
only did for the Antiphonary what he did for the Sacramentary which bears his name : he made rules and orders
for it, and, no doubt, simplified it. He reorganised a
schola existing before his day, and gave it new life.

[1] Cf. Aigrain, *Religious Music* (Sands, 3s. 6d.).

Some have even thought that the Ambrosian chant, so closely related to the Gregorian, often betrays this earlier state. What must be noticed is the excellence of the Gregorian chant during the first period of its history, its golden age, from the sixth-ninth century. The *schola* became a school of masters, among whom came those who wished to study the true principles of the Gregorian chant : the disciples thus formed spread later through other Latin countries. This explains why the annotated MSS. from the ninth-twelfth centuries present as a whole the same musical system in which variants are very rare. This has been most rigorously proved in the collection *Paléographie Musicale* published by the monks of *Solesmes*.[1] Still more recently an Anglican Bishop, famous for his liturgical prowess, recognises that the Roman Church has supplanted all other Latin liturgies by her *Cantilena* rather than by her liturgical compositions.[2]

BIBLIOGRAPHY

See *Religious Music* (Sands 3s. 6d.), by ABBÉ R. AIGRAIN, and *Liturgia, The Gregorian Chant*, by Dom. M. SABLAYROLLES, pp. 440-478. In the bibliography of the last-named the works of WAGNER, GASTOUÉ, Dom POTHIER, etc., are cited. Cf. also more recently : TH. GEROLD, *Les Pères de l'Eglise et la musique* (1932).

III. THE ATTITUDE OF THE FAITHFUL AND THE LITURGICAL GESTURES DURING MASS

To-day it is hardly necessary, in view of the very large number of studies devoted to this question, to

[1] To furnish documents for this publication the Fathers of Solesmes brought together a unique collection of photographs of annotated MSS. of the ninth–fifteenth centuries, from Italy, France, Germany, Spain, England, etc.

[2] W. H. Frere, *Studies in Early Roman Liturgy*, I, The Kalendar, Oxford, 1930.

insist on the importance of gestures or attitude in connection with the liturgy. We have, moreover, made a separate study of it ourselves, elsewhere.[1] As the Mass is the essential function of the liturgy, it is not astonishing that most of the liturgical gestures belong to it, nor that the Church has very carefully determined both their form and their number. Certain general rules for prayer were already established in the time of St. Paul, who alludes to them many times in his Epistles. For public prayer each must wait his own turn ; must speak intelligibly when he does speak. Women were not allowed to speak at all (1 Cor. xiv.).

We know from other witnesses, especially Tertullian, in texts often quoted, that Christians prayed standing, their eyes raised to Heaven, their hands stretched out. No one knelt on Sunday, nor during the fifty days between Easter and Pentecost. Frescoes in the catacombs represent *Orantes* in the posture described. One such shows a Priest standing before a *triclinium*, his hands outstretched in a gesture of blessing, while beside him a woman stands upright.

Certain rubrics in the ancient liturgical books remind us of these old customs, for some are still preserved in the existing Missal. Thus, the Deacon at certain moments commands the faithful to kneel down, to bow the head, to rise ; he dismisses them at the end of Mass—*Flectamus genua, Levate, Humiliate capita vestra Deo, Ite, Missa est.* In the Greek and Eastern liturgies these rubrics are much more numerous. Some of these gestures, as has been stated, are marked in the ancient Sacramentaries ; but as the gestures at Mass, especially those of the officiant, are both numerous and detailed, they would have overloaded these books. Moreover, at that epoch (fourth and ninth centuries) the tendency was to multiply liturgical

[1] See Bibliography at end of this chapter.

books, so as to have one for each function : book of the Priest, or Sacramentary ; book of Epistles for the sub-Deacon ; of the Gospels for the Deacon ; book for the cantors, etc. One such book was devoted to explaining processions : the order to follow, the places to be taken and kept, and the other movements during Mass. These are the *Ordines*, and especially the *Ordines Romani*, which are of the highest value in liturgical history (cf. *Books of the Latin Liturgy*, p. 81). These *Ordines Romani*, or Roman Orders, specially describe the Papal Mass ; but as we have already said, this Mass was the same as that of a Bishop, or a simple Priest, except for the number of ministers who assisted at it, and for the solemnity of the ceremonies. Only in Low Mass has the number of the latter been suppressed ; and several of those ceremonies still preserved can only be explained by reference to Pontifical High Mass.

This fact being laid down, we can divide our subject, which has never been studied very methodically so far, into a few paragraphs in which we shall try to throw light on the existing rubrics by the ancient customs.

1. Attitude of the faithful during Mass.
2. Processions, Stations, and general ceremonies.
3. Gestures of the officiant and his ministers during Mass.

1. *Attitude of the faithful during Mass.*—In certain frescoes in the catacombs, which seem to be a representation of the Eucharist, we see guests seated around a table as if for a feast. At the Last Supper, when the Eucharist was instituted, Our Lord and His Apostles were, according to the best exegetists, seated, or half lying on couches, according to the general custom. At the *Agape* described by St. Paul, the faithful were either seated or lying down.

But this position was hardly practicable during the celebration of the Eucharist as soon as the number of the faithful was greatly increased ; moreover, the respect due to this function would have been quite enough to impose another attitude. To pray standing was the most usual thing with the Jews, and even with pagans. This position indicated not only respect and deference for the person to whom the prayer was addressed, but it was also, in prayer, an attitude of adoration.

The faithful thus heard Mass standing ; the practice of kneeling being reserved, from the second and third centuries, for days of vigil, for times of penitence, or for certain specially solemn moments, as during the Prayer of the Faithful at the Offertory. A sentence spoken by the Deacon, still preserved in our Missal, warned the faithful : *Flectamus genua* ; while after some moments of recollection he said : *Levate.* The celebrant then pronounced the prayer—*Oremus*—being, as he was, charged in a certain sense to sum up and present to God all the intentions of the people. It was also a rule at this time that on Sundays and during the joyous fifty days from Easter to Pentecost, there should be no kneeling. We are yet reminded of this custom by the fact that during the Ember Days of Pentecost, and on its vigil, the *Flectamus genua*, heard during the penitential seasons, is omitted.

It was not customary to sit during the Mass. The Bishop alone was seated, on his throne, which was not an ordinary seat, but rather a symbol of his functions. The seat of that Bishop of the beginning of the third century at Rome, to which we owe the celebrated *anaphora* already mentioned, is a monument of the highest importance, on which have been written the titles of his various works. Antiquity has preserved the remembrance of other Chairs of this distant period, such as that of St. Peter at Rome, the *Cathedra Petri*, which has always been celebrated.[1]

I think, however, that those texts of Tertullian and others in which Christians are represented standing with outstretched arms during their prayer have been interpreted too rigorously. Such a prayer would mean that the word was used in its deepest sense, for the prayers, and doubtless for the whole of the Mass of the Faithful. But they must have sat down for the Lessons of the Pre-Mass, which were often long. Certain texts of St. Augustine refer to this subject ; he says he will not fatigue the people with a long discourse, as they are all standing. In some places it was allowed to take a staff into the church, to be used for leaning upon. Here, as elsewhere, customs must have varied. In certain texts, indeed, *sedilia* are spoken of, that the people might be seated. St. Benedict, who was not given to relaxation, admits monks to be seated during the Lessons, as this was a common practice.

The custom of prostration at the moment of the Elevation dates from the eleventh century. Before this time it was usual to stand upright ; and this too was the customary attitude for receiving the Eucharist in the hands, or for drinking the Precious Blood. From this Protestants have tried to argue against faith in the Real Presence, but their objection is really too easily answered ; and it is almost matter for astonishment that one writer has thought it necessary to devote a learned work to this question.[2]

Another custom, much discussed, and on which much has been written, is that of praying turned towards the

[1] Cf. DACL, article *Chaires*.

[2] Jean le Lorrain (d. 1710), *De l'ancienne coûtume de prier et d'adorer debout le jour du dimanche*, etc., 2 vols., Liège, 1700 ; Rouen, 1710. Cf. also our article *Liturgie, Dict. de théol. catholique*, col. 821 *seq*.

EXCURSUS

East. Christ is the Sun of Justice, and His light illumines the West, the region of darkness. The latter is thus the domain of the devil ; and it is to the West that men turn to curse him. Hence also the custom of *orientation* : that is, to build churches in such a way that the Priest while praying looks towards the East. But this practice often involved such difficulties that it was not always possible to be faithful to it. It was, however, generally applied in the construction of churches in the Middle Ages, from the fifth century onwards. Hence there were certain changes in the ceremonial. The Priest who, in the first centuries, celebrated before an altar shaped like a simple table, without gradines or retable (as is still the case in the Basilica of San Clemente at Rome), was obliged to face the East when the church was *orientated*, and thus, as to-day, turn his back to the people. Consequently when he addresses them in the words, *Dominus vobiscum*, he turns towards them, facing the altar again as he says : *Oremus*.

The *Ordo Romanus* (n. I) thus describes the attitude of the Pope when celebrating Pontifical Mass. The Pontiff stands upright facing the East at his throne, which is at the back of the apse ; turns towards the people to intone the *Gloria in Excelsis*, but turns again to face the East, remaining standing thus till the end of the chant. He then again turns towards the people to say : *Pax vobis* ; then back to the East when he says : *Oremus*, and the Collect for the day. After the Collect he seats himself. The Bishops and Priest present also seat themselves, as a gesture from the Pope invites them to do, but the congregation remains standing, as it does the whole time of the ceremony. It has been said that the Deacon caused all the faithful to kneel on Good Friday for the Prayer of the Faithful ; and this ceremony is yet observed.

In our churches at the present time these rules are
rather vague. Those usually observed by choirs of
Canons or Monks may be followed. It is thus customary
to stand upright at High Mass during the Introit, prayers,
Gospel, and Canon ; to sit during the reading of the
Epistle and other Lessons when there are any, as also
for the singing of the *Kyrie, Gloria in Excelsis, Credo,*
Gradual, and *Alleluia*, or Tracts and Proses ; to prostrate
during the Consecration ; and to bow for the blessing of
the celebrant.

2. *Processions, Stations, general ceremonies.*—All these
subjects have been treated by liturgiologists, often with
great learning. It can only be a question here of those
connected with the Mass, such as the Station, and the
defiling past at the Introit, the Offertory, and the Communion. The Procession of the Station is no longer made.
But in the time of St. Gregory and the following centuries
the Station began with a most solemn procession. The
suburban Bishops (the seven Bishops of Ostia, Porto,
Silva Candida, Albano, Tusculum, Sabina, and Praeneste)
and other Bishops present in Rome, the Priests of the
25 *tituli* (Rectors of the principal churches in that city),
the Monks, and lastly the people divided into groups
according to the seven regions (Quarters) of Rome, an
ensign-bearer at the head of each group carrying a silver
Cross on which were three candles—all these early
awaited the Pope (who came from the Lateran with his
cortège) in the church which had been chosen as the
starting-point. The Pope arrived on horseback. His
following was composed of all the acolytes of the region
where the function was being held. After the acolytes
came the *Defensores* of each region : these were a kind
of lay functionary charged with the administration of
the ecclesiastical patrimony. Acolytes and *Defensores*
were on foot. The seven Deacons of the seven regions,

with their regional sub-Deacons followed next, all on
horseback. Two squires were to the right and left of the
Pope, and in front of him an acolyte bearing the *ampulla*
of the Holy Chrism. Behind the Pope came the *Vice-
Dominus* and other dignitaries of his household. The
sub-Deacon who was to read the Epistle carried the
Epistolarium, while the Arch-Deacon bore the *Evangeliarium*, usually a luxuriously bound manuscript the
cover of which was encrusted with precious stones, and
which was carefully enclosed in its case.

When this almost royal procession, recalling in more
than one detail the ceremonial of the Emperors and
Consuls, had reached the church where the Bishops and
people were waiting for it, they all set out together for
the church at which the Station had been fixed, and
where Mass was to be celebrated. The whole ceremonial
for the reception of the Pope in this church is minutely
foreseen and described.[1]

The procession of the Pope and clergy for the beginning
of Mass is not less solemn. In the sacristy or *secretarium*
of the Basilica, which was vast enough to serve as a
council hall, the Pope was vested with the liturgical
garments, linen tunic, amice, dalmatic, chasuble, *pallium*.
At a given signal, accompanied by the Deacons, by the
sub-Deacon bearing the *thymiamaterium* in which incense
was burning, and by the seven serving acolytes with
their seven lighted candlesticks, he advanced up the
great nave (for at that period the *secretarium* was at the
atrium, or entrance of the Basilica, except at St. Peter's)
while the *schola* sang the psalm of the Introit. The
Pope saluted the *Sancta* (the *fermentum*, or Host conse-

---

[1] This description has been made in a most interesting way by
Mgr. Batiffol (p. 67 *seq.*) from the *Ordo Romanus*, I. This *Ordo*
had been edited and explained previously, even more in detail,
by E. G. F. Atchley, *Ordo Romanus*, I, Book VI of *Liturgiology*
(1 vol., 8vo, London, 1905).

crated at a previous Mass), prayed before the altar, then kissed the book of the Gospels, placed on the altar itself, and so moved to his throne, where he remained standing. He made a sign to the *schola* to stop the singing of the psalm, and to begin the *Gloria Patri* which ends the Introit.

The order followed at Rome for the Offertory and Communion has been already described (p. 60) ; that of precedence was most strictly observed : Bishops first, the ministers to the last rank of the clergy, Princes, nobles, the faithful, first the men, then the women. It was the Golden Age of the liturgy in Rome from the sixth-ninth centuries ; both clergy and faithful gave admirable examples of behaviour, order, dignity, and a simplicity which did not exclude a certain pomp.

3. *Gestures of officiant and ministers during the Mass.* —In describing in the various chapters of this book the Mass at Rome, Milan, in Gaul, Spain, and Africa, we have already pointed out the chief gestures prescribed for the celebrant, especially at the Consecration, the Fraction, and the Communion ; we have also spoken of censing, of the Kiss of Peace, and of some other rites of the same kind. We then said that all these acts and gestures were generally intended to express, in the eyes of the congregation, an act corresponding to the spoken word ; an act which emphasised it, and threw it into new relief. This idea has been explained at length[1] and with perhaps too much complaisance by Dom Claude de Vert in a work whose scholarship is more curious than solid. To him, the word infers the gesture. But, as we have already remarked, it is usually just the contrary which happens. In the ancient Roman liturgy, for example, a great many gestures were made without any

[1] Dom Claude de Vert, *Explication simple, littérale et historique des cérémonies de l'Église*, 4 vols. (Paris, 1720).

words at all. It was only later, in the course of the Middle Ages, that a prayer was composed to explain an act, such as *Oramus te* ; or for certain Offertory prayers : *Offerimus tibi* ; or again for the Communion : *Panem cælestem accipiam, Quod ore sumpsimus, Corpus Domini nostri Jesu Christi custodiat animam meam,* etc.

It must also be noticed that in the liturgy there are gestures which have not a merely simple, mimetic meaning. Certain unctions, the laying-on of hands, certain signs of the Cross, or blessings are supernaturally efficacious, and produce what they signify. For all these reasons, and without going back to different points which have already been sufficiently explained, we must here give a little supplementary information as to certain gestures of the Mass, the sense of which is by no means always understood.

The celebrant and his ministers were thus standing upright during Mass, except during the Lessons and the chants. This is still the custom ; at Solemn High Masses celebrant and ministers are seated during the reading of the Epistle and other Lessons, as well as during the singing of *Kyrie, Gloria in Excelsis, Credo,* Gradual, and other chants.

At certain moments the celebrant spreads out his hands to pray, reminding us of the attitude of the *Orantes* : this is done during the prayers of the Mass, the Preface, Canon, and *Pater.* At other times he bows himself, as at the *Confiteor,* the *Oramus te, Domine,* the *Suscipe sancte Pater* and *Suscipe sancta Trinitas,* at the words of the Canon *Te igitur* and *Supplices te,* as well as at the *Munda cor meum.*

The rubric prescribes that he shall raise his eyes to Heaven at the *Veni Sanctificator,* and at the Consecration of the bread and wine ; that he shall strike his breast at the *Mea culpâ* of the *Confiteor,* at the *Agnus Dei,* the

Domine, non sum dignus, and at the *Nobis quoque peccatoribus.*

Before the prayers he kisses the altar, turns towards the people, extends his hands and salutes them with *Dominus vobiscum,* from the middle of the altar ; at the *Oremus* he salutes the Cross and again extends his hands. He genuflects at the Elevation, at the *Homo factus est* of the Credo, and of the Last Gospel ; also, in Solemn Masses he does this each time he leaves the altar to seat himself, as well as when he returns.

The imposition of hands occurs only once during Mass, at the *Hanc igitur* ; this gesture, indeed, dates only from the fifteenth century, and is merely intended to design the oblation. This may appear rather singular when we know the importance of this act in the Catholic liturgy.[1] But it must be remembered that signs of the Cross, which often replace the imposition of hands, are frequent during the Sacrifice of the Mass, and we may now study their meaning.

The sign of the Cross during Mass is a subject which has long gained the attention of liturgiologists. It is presented here under different forms. The usual way of making the ordinary sign of the Cross is for the Priest to trace it upon himself by carrying his right hand from the forehead to the breast, and then from the left shoulder to the right ; it has thus been made since the ninth century, as, at the same time, the sign of our Redemption, and of a doxology to the Trinity, with the words : In the Name of the Father and of the Son and of the Holy Ghost, Amen.

Before this epoch (ninth century) it was more especially the sign of Christ, and answers to the *In Nomine Christi* so frequently recommended by St. Paul. The sign was then traced on the forehead, the lips, and the

[1] Cf. *Imposition des mains,* in DACL.

breast. Under this form it is still used before the Gospel.

The sign of the Cross is, with the imposition of hands, the most venerable and expressive act of Christian worship. Innumerable works, treatises, and articles have been written on this subject. We can only refer here to the articles *Croix* and *Crucifix* in DACL, where a Bibliography of the matter will be found.

The number, place, and form of these signs of the Cross in Mass has varied according to time and place. The Missal of St. Pius V adopted the greater part of those indicated in the most recent MSS. of that period, or in books printed at that time. But these are by no means equally ancient, or of the same importance.

Some are mimetic signs which are specially aimed at emphasising the text, as in *Hæc dona, hæc munera, hæc sancta sacrificia*. Others have the meaning of a blessing, like those which accompany the words *benedictam, adscriptam, ratam, ut nobis corpus et sanguis*, etc. As much, and *a fortiori*, must be said of the sign of the Cross at *Benedixit* upon the Host and chalice, at the Consecration, for this reproduces the gesture of Our Lord in blessing the bread and wine.

But what of those signs of the Cross made upon the consecrated elements ? A blessing upon the Body and Blood of Our Lord would seem superfluous, at the very least, and yet the signs occur many times, as at *Hostiam puram, Hostiam sanctam*, etc. There are as many as five, and specially again at the *Per quem* and *Per ipsum*, and at the *Pax Domini* and Communion. We may say at once that usually these signs are not indicated in the ancient Sacramentaries, nor in the *Ordo I*, while a certain variety is observed even in the other Sacramentaries. Thus, they are not considered essential, and often are merely figurative, the word having been the author of the gesture, according to the theory so dear to De Vert.[1]

At the *Per ipsum* the Priest, holding the Host in his right hand, traces three signs of the Cross over the chalice, two between the chalice and his breast, before elevating the Host and the chalice at the final doxology of the Canon.

During the embolism of the Pater, at *Da propitius pacem*, he makes the sign of the Cross with the paten, which he kisses.[2] At the end of Mass the Priest, turned towards the people, makes with his right hand a great sign of the Cross, which is the sign of blessing. A Prelate makes this sign once to his left, once in the centre, once to his right.[3]

The kissing of the altar is another act which frequently takes place in Mass. In the seventh century this gesture was far less common, but was surrounded with a greater solemnity. Thus at the beginning of the Office of Good Friday, as has been mentioned, the Pontiff, after the conclusion of Nones, left his throne to go and kiss the altar, returning afterwards to his place. This rite at the beginning of Mass was already a characteristic of the Papal Mass in the seventh-eighth centuries. It is still preserved to-day, with the *Oramus te, Domine*, which gives the reason for it—*Sanctorum quorum reliquiæ hic sunt*. The altar is a sacred stone, containing the relics of Saints ; it is the *mensa* which recalls the table of the Last Supper, or again, the stone of Golgotha. It is unnecessary to compare this act with that of the Romans,

[1] On this point see especially Brinktrine, quoted in the Bibliography, who has studied this subject deeply.

[2] On the gesture of the sub-Deacon who gives the paten to the Deacon at the end of the Pater, and on this sign of the Cross, cf. p. 82.

[3] On this blessing at the end of Mass, and on the prayer *Super populum*, cf. p. 87.

who kissed their pagan altars, in order to understand the act of veneration accomplished by the Priest at this moment.

To-day the Priest kisses the altar each time he comes to it, as well as before the *Dominus vobiscum* of the prayers.

We have already sufficiently explained the blessing of the people by the Priest at the end of the Roman Mass, as well as that blessing which in the other Latin rites preceded the Communion (p. 88).

BIBLIOGRAPHY

The articles *Baiser de Paix, Croix, Crucifix, Imposition des mains*, in DACL.

Our article *Liturgie*, in *Dict. de théol. cath.*, col. 821 *seq. La Prière des Chrétiens* (Paris, 1929),,p. 133 *seq.*

DE VERT, *Explication des cérémonies de l'Église* (Paris, 1713).

LEBRUN, *Explication des Prières et des cérémonies de la Messe* (Paris, 1726).

BRINKTRINE, *Die Heilige Messe, Der Altarkuss*, p. 56 *seq.* For the signs of the Cross, *Exkurs.* I, *Die Kreuzzeichen im Kanon*, p. 250 *seq.*, and BATIFFOL, *loc. cit.*, pp. 239, 251, 267.

DOLGER, *Zu den Zeremonien der Mess liturgie*, II, *Der Altarkuss, antike u. christent.* II, pp. 190-221 (1930).

See also our *Monumenta Ecclesiæ Liturgica* (table).

IV. THE BOOKS OF THE MASS

This subject having already been treated in another book (*Books of the Latin Liturgy*, see p. 28 *et seq.*), we may be allowed to sum it up shortly here. It may be believed that in the beginning no book was used for Mass. The Consecration of the bread and wine was made after the formula used by Christ Himself, handed down by St. Paul and the synoptic Gospels. The prayers of preparation or thanksgiving were left to the improvisation of the celebrant, who did this on a fixed theme, from which it was not allowed to depart ; for the most ancient formulas studied reproduce always the same thought.

In the aliturgical synaxis which became the Pre-Mass (cf. Chapter I) the Old and New Testament were read, and psalms were sung. Thus the Bible proved sufficient. But very soon the formulas mentioned were put into writing, and we have an example of this in the *Didache*, which dates, perhaps, from the year 100, while the *Anaphora* of Hippolytus dates from the first quarter of the third century. In the fourth and fifth centuries liturgical literature was in full flower, especially in the East. St. Hilary, St. Ambrose, St. Paulinus of Nola, Voconius, Musaeus, and many others are quoted amongst the authors who composed hymns, prayers, and Prefaces, or who chose Lessons drawn from the Old and New Testaments to be read at Mass or during the Offices.[1] In other books the parts that were to be sung were collected. From this time, especially during the period immediately following—from the sixth-ninth centuries— as the taste for these compositions developed, we have books specially devoted to the various liturgical functions : one for the readings from the Testaments, generally called the Lectionary, or book of lectures ; this, when intended for the Mass alone, was called *Epistolarium* (book of Epistles, or sometimes of Prophecy, or the Apostolic book). There was also the *Evangeliarium*, containing nothing but readings from the Gospels.

The chants of the Introit, Gradual, Tract, *Alleluia*, Offertory, and Communion were collected in a book called the *Cantatorium*, or book of chants. This was also sometimes styled *Liber Gradualis*, since the Gradual was the most important and most ancient of these chants.

[1] *Books of the Latin Liturgy* (Sands, 3s. 6d.), p. 24 *seq.*

EXCURSUS

The Priest used tablets (*plaquettes*, *Libelli*) in which he found the prayers and Prefaces with the Canon of the Mass ; he also had *Diptychs* : all these, collected together, were called *Sacramentaries*. This is the most ancient type of Missal, in use from the sixth-ninth centuries ; it contained only those parts recited at Mass by the celebrant. When the custom of Low Masses was introduced and multiplied, and the Priest was obliged to accomplish by himself all those functions which, in High Masses, fell to the lot of the Deacon, sub-Deacon, lectors, and cantors, it was necessary to add the Epistle, Gospel, Gradual, and other chants to the Sacramentary, which thus changed its name and its nature, and was henceforth called *Plenary Missal*, or simply *Missal*. The most ancient of these go back to the tenth century, or perhaps a little earlier. They went on multiplying through the eleventh century, and very soon after they eliminated and replaced the Sacramentary almost completely.

These liturgical books, some of which were illuminated and bound in the most luxurious manner, have always attracted the attention of artists, liturgiologists, and archæologists ; but at the present time it may be said that they are sought after and studied more than ever, so that erudite men have set themselves to describe them carefully (see Bibliography). The price of some of them represents a fortune. It is necessary to add that this subject is very far from being exhausted, and that in many ancient libraries precious manuscripts and early printed books still exist which deserve to be studied with care.

Prayer Books (*Paroissiens*).[1]—The history and biblio-

---

[1] The word cannot be translated literally. *A Paroissien* is a kind of abridged Missal, which includes the office of Benediction, several Litanies, morning and night prayers, etc. Vespers of Sunday (and sometimes Compline) are also included. (*Note by translator.*)

graphy of these books is yet to be written. That of the Books of Hours, which has tempted certain scholars, may serve as an introduction to it (cf. *Books of the Latin Liturgy*, pp. 128 *seq.* and 151 *seq.*). In that the history of the different Catholic devotions may be studied, according to period and country. Still more recently, in his *Sentiment religieux en France*, the Abbé Bremond has shown how much may be drawn from these little books. In them the Mass naturally has its place, whether the Latin text is given, with a translation, or whether we find merely explanations and commentaries, as was the usual practice at a certain period, when translation into the vulgar tongue was looked on with very little favour, if not actually condemned.

To-day the liturgical movement has driven the faithful more and more towards requiring the complete text of the Latin Mass, with its translation. Thus certain prayer-books are indeed real Missals for their use.

BIBLIOGRAPHY

LÉOPOLD DELISLE, *Mémoire sur d'anciens sacramentaires* (Paris, 1886). He has also written dissertations on the Psalters and other liturgical books (see catalogue in DACL, *Delisle*).

A. EBNER, *Quellen u. Forschungen zur Gesch. des Missale Romanum in Mittelalter* (Freibourg-im-Breisgau, 1896).

V. LEROQUAIS, *Les Sacramentaires et les missels manuscrits des bibliothèques publiques de la France*, 3 vols. (Paris, 1924). Cf. also other works on the same subject, *Books of the Latin Liturgy*, pp. 151, 156, and our article *Missel* in DACL.

V. DIFFERENT KINDS OF MASSES

The Papal Mass and the Stational Mass.—These have been described in Chapter IV. The latter was called

Stational because there was a Station on that day. Except a few points already mentioned, they were the same as the following :

Pontifical Mass.—It has been already stated that if we wish to understand the sequence of the ceremonies at Mass, and really enter into the spirit of them, we should be present at a Pontifical Mass, which, more than any other, has faithfully preserved that ceremonial described in Chapter IV. It is, in fact, the Papal Mass, and, with but few differences, that which is celebrated by Bishops and certain Prelates. It is described at length in the Ceremonial of Bishops.

Solemn, or High Mass.—All the ceremonies which are the privilege of Bishops, such as crosier and mitre, throne, the number of the ministers (assistant Priest, Deacons of honour, bearers of the insignia, etc.), are omitted ; but the Introit, Gradual, *Kyrie*, Lessons, etc., are sung as in Pontifical Masses, and by the same ministers. These comprehend, after the Deacon and sub-Deacon, a *Ceremoniarius*, acolytes, and a thurifer.

Sung Mass, or Missa Cantata.—Here there are neither Deacon nor sub-Deacon, the ministers being reduced to one or two servers ; but the same parts are sung as at High Mass. This Mass is sometimes called in French, *messe cardinalice.*

Conventual Mass is said in Chapters of Canons, in Collegiate churches, and monasteries. It may be either sung or said, with or without ministers.

Missa lecta, a Mass which is not sung, is often wrongly styled Low, or private, Mass, for the rubrics prescribe certain parts to be said aloud. At this Mass the Priest, with one, or sometimes two, servers, accomplishes the various ceremonies of Mass, but nothing is sung.

The history of Low Mass has given rise to certain errors ; its evolution is less well known than that of

Pontifical Mass. But there can be no doubt that in very ancient days—let us say about the third century, but most probably before that epoch—there were (beyond the Eucharistic synaxis celebrated by the Bishop, surrounded by his clergy and the faithful), both in cemeteries and in private houses, private Masses said, from which all the ceremonies had been shorn. The story of Hesperus, cured after a Mass had been said in his house, is well known ; Mgr. Batiffol relates it according to St. Augustine.[1] There are other examples of private Masses said in domestic oratories, the existence of which is proved from the fifth century.

About this time, too (sixth century), churches began to be built with several altars or chapels, a fact which evidently indicates private Masses. The Sacramentaries or Missals drawn up from the seventh-tenth centuries might have served either for a Pontifical or a private Mass. There must have been also, about this time, and even before it, *Libelli*, or leaflets composed of several Masses for the use of the Priest. Of these we have spoken in the *Books of the Latin Liturgy*, mentioning as one of the types of this *Libellus* that of the *Masses of Mone*.[2]

Missa solitaria.—In certain dioceses and missions the Priest has obtained permission to say Mass without a server, making the responses himself, in view of the practical impossibility of finding anyone to serve Mass.

Votive Masses.—As its name indicates, this Mass is said in virtue of a Vow (*votum*), or, in a wide sense, for a special intention. It is thus distinguished from the Mass of the day, the character of which is fixed by the calendar. There are certain days in the year, simple Ferials, or

[1] *Op. cit.*, p. 44. Cf. also Fortescue, *Votive Mass*, in *Catholic Encyclopædia*.
[2] See also our article *Missel* in DACL.

those on which the Mass is assigned to a Saint with a simple rite or a semi-double ; and on these the Priest can usually celebrate a Votive Mass. In the Missal a whole division, following the Common of Saints, is devoted to Votive Masses. Some are in honour of Our Lady, or other Saints ; others again for different circumstances, or devotions, as in time of war, or of peace ; of famine or epidemic, etc. They are thus devotional Masses which, unlike the Mass for the day, are not attached to the calendar, nor to the Office said on that day, which itself is in relation to the Mass.

Some of these Votive Masses are very ancient, and their texts deserve study. Some may already be found in the Leonine and Gelasian Sacramentaries. The Mozarabic *Liber Ordinum* contains a considerable number. A Missal attributed to Alcuin has Votive Masses for every day in the week, in honour of the Holy Angels, of the Eucharist, of Our Lady, etc. Franz, in the book we mention, has made a most learned study of them.

Here is the list of Votive Masses in our Missal :

> *De Sancta Trinitate,*
> *De Angelis,*
> *De SS. Petro et Paulo,*
> *De Spiritu Sancto,*
> *De S.S. Eucharistiæ Sacramento,*
> *De Cruce,*
> *De Passione,*
> *De Sancta Maria,*
> *Pro eligendo Pontifice,*
> *In anniversario electionis Episcopi,*
> *Ad tollendum schisma,*
> *Pro quacumque necessitate,*
> *Pro remissione peccatorum,*
> *Ad postulandam gratiam bene moriendi,*

239

THE MASS OF THE WESTERN RITES

Contra paganos,
In tempore belli,
Pro pace,
Pro vitenda mortalitate,
Pro infirmis,
Pro peregrinis,
Pro sponso et sponsa.

Missa sicca, or Dry Mass.—This is rarely in use to-day. Whether an abuse, or simply from singularity, it was fairly widespread in the Middle Ages. It was a Mass without Offertory, Consecration, or Communion ; and thus in reality not a Mass at all. Since there was neither Sacrifice nor Sacrament, it was merely a rite (sacramental, if we wish to call it so) which reproduced the ceremonies of the Mass, with the exception of the parts mentioned. It was regarded as a substitute for Mass. Thus, for marriages or deaths celebrated in the afternoon, a Dry Mass was said. As many Dry Masses as it was wished to say from private devotion could be celebrated on the same day ; they were also said for those who wished to have as many Masses on the same day as possible. Bona very justly protests against this custom, which seems to him an abuse. As a private devotion, the *Missa Sicca* is still in use among the Carthusians.

Mass of the Presanctified.—A very different thing is the dignity of this Mass, of which we have already spoken. In the Greek rite it is much used during Lent. Properly speaking, it is not a Mass, since the Sacrifice is absent. But Holy Communion is given at it, and it was really instituted to satisfy the piety of those who wished to communicate.

Some other kinds of Mass.—The *Missa Nautica* and *Missa Venatoria* are also Dry Masses ; since by reason of the fear of tempests, or for other causes, the essential parts are suppressed.

BIBLIOGRAPHY

The Stational and Pontifical Mass is described in Chapter IV ; see the authors mentioned in the Bibliography of that chapter.

On the ceremonies of the Pontifical Mass, see also :

ADRIAN FORTESCUE, *The Ceremonies of the Roman Rite* (London, 1918). Cf. also HAEGY, *Cérémonial* (edn. 1902), and L. HEBERT, *Leçons de Liturgie* (1921).

On Votive Masses the most scholarly work is that of AD. FRANZ, *Die Messe in Deutschen Mittelalter* (Freibourg-im-Breisgau, 1902), pp. 115-292. For the rules concerning these Masses, see HEBERT, *loc. cit.*, Vol. II, p. 118.

FORTESCUE, in his work *The Mass*, and in his articles to be found in the *Catholic Encyclopædia*, gives some information as to these Masses.